THE MENTAL ENVIRONMENT

Also by Bob Gebelein:

RE-EDUCATING MYSELF: An Introduction to a New Civilization (1985)

"The 'civilization,' to me, is what was programmed into my head as a representative product of the American upper middle class... In showing how I have changed my life into something better, I am showing how that culture can be changed into something better." — *Re-Educating Myself*, page 16

"The philosophy in your book is wonderful. Congratulations!"
— *Michael Murphy, Esalen Institute*

"This book (as it advertises) does indeed explain methods by which an individual can break free of his cultural programming..." — *The Bulletin of the National Alliance for Spiritual Growth*

"If you are forging your way on whatever frontiers of being, I heartily recommend this story by another explorer."
— *The Philosopher's Stone, The Stelle Group*

"As a philosophy student at [my university], I've felt trapped in disputes over trivial questions. So far, I've found *Re-Educating Myself* to be a refreshing exploration of the central questions of life. It is also an inspiring, honest account of one person's quest for personal maturity." — *name withheld by request*

"I think it's the best book I ever read." — *Debbie Kahn*

THE MENTAL ENVIRONMENT

(Mostly about Mind Pollution)

Bob Gebelein

Omdega Press
Provincetown, Massachusetts

Address inquiries to: Omdega Press, P.O. Box 1546, Provincetown, MA 02657

Publisher's Cataloging-in-Publication
(Provided by Quality Books, Inc.)

Gebelein, Bob.
   The mental environment : (mostly about mind pollution) / Bob Gebelein.
   p. cm.
   Includes bibliographical references and index.
   LCCN 2007928710
   ISBN-13: 978-0-9614611-1-9 (hardcover)
   ISBN-10: 0-9614611-1-X (hardcover)
   ISBN-13: 978-0-9614611-2-6 (pbk.)
   ISBN-10: 0-9614611-2-8 (pbk.)

   1. Thought and thinking. 2. Social influence.
I. Title.

BF441.G43 2007   153.4
                        QBI07-600157

Manufactured in the United States of America

Cover photo by Peggy Kerr

In memory of Ailene Wright and Jean Cantin

CONTENTS

PART I

INTRODUCTION

1. THE MENTAL ENVIRONMENT

Clean air. Clean water. Clear head.

We exist within a physical environment, and also within a mental environment. Except for the most solitary among us, we are immersed in a sea of other people's thoughts, ideas, theories, perceptions, worldviews, information, misinformation, hypnotic suggestions, fiction, prejudices, judgments, manipulations, ridicule, and horror movies. Some of this mental input may be beneficial, as when a child is taught reading, writing, arithmetic, basic skills, and accurate knowledge. But in with that basic knowledge are already cultural prejudices, fiction, manipulations, and judgments that may not be accurate.

Like the physical environment, the mental environment has also been polluted. When we talk about "the environment," we are usually talking about destruction and pollution. We didn't talk much about "the environment" until pollution became an issue. And so when I talk about "the mental environment," I am mostly talking about mind pollution.

Why don't I just call this book "Mind Pollution," then? Because I want to talk about other things than pollution, although right now pollution seems to be the main issue, blocking the way to mental and spiritual growth. Yes, there are uplifting elements leading us to knowledge and spiritual enlightenment if we are astute enough to

3

find them, but these avenues of human advancement have been so corrupted and polluted that it is more likely we will be led in the opposite direction in the name of knowledge or spiritual enlightenment. The words "truth" and "love" have been totally exploited by those who seek power over us. Just as we need to clean the sewage and trash and rubber tires out of our rivers before they can run clean again, so we need to clear the pollution out of our heads before we can be expected to think clearly again, and make real progress towards knowledge and spiritual enlightenment.

And what is "mind pollution?" Mind pollution is any thought, idea, fiction, hypnotic suggestion, judgment, etc. — any mental input — that makes one's view of reality less accurate. "Accuracy" is the subject I am dealing with here — how to make one's worldview as accurate as possible and free of the polluting elements in the mental environment — or, to start with, just to recognize those polluting elements.

I am using the word "accuracy" instead of "truth," for three reasons: First of all, "truth" is many times confused with absolute or ultimate truth, and I am not claiming to know the absolute or ultimate truth. Second, the word "truth" has many times been exploited to represent lies. "Pravda" means "Truth." Third, the word "truth" has been massacred in post-drug-movement America, as in "your truth" and "my truth," meaning one's perception of the reality instead of the quality of accuracy of that perception of the reality.

I get around all that with the word "accuracy." Accuracy is a quality, not an absolute state of being. There are degrees of accuracy, as for example accuracy to a certain number of decimal places. I don't have to argue with the philosophers that a viewpoint is absolutely accurate, but only that one viewpoint is more accurate or less accurate than another. And best of all, the word "accuracy" has not yet been corrupted by the mind-polluters.

This is not the definitive work on the mental environment, but only what I happen to know about it. I just want to introduce you to the fact that there is a mental environment and pollution of that environment, and describe some of the means of pollution that I am aware of — just to let you know that the subject exists, so that you can be thinking about it.

I am not writing so much about the obvious and deliberate inaccuracies created by advertising, the media, and political propaganda. These inaccuracies are external to most people. Democrats don't believe Republicans' propaganda, and Republicans don't believe Democrats' propaganda. They already have internal belief systems that cause them to accept some propaganda and reject other propaganda. I am writing about inaccuracies in these internal belief systems, especially in some of our most fundamental belief systems — the religious, the academic, and the New Age — and the social forces that create these inaccuracies.

The main source of mind pollution is social manipulation. If you belong to our tribe, you have to believe as we believe, and think as we think, not because it is accurate, but because we will ridicule you, ostracize you, and kill you if you don't. If you belong to our religion, you have to believe as we believe, not because it is accurate, but because we will despise you, shun you, and threaten you with the fires of Hell if you don't.

Ah, but we are more advanced than that today. We live in a free country. We have legal laws that guarantee us certain freedoms to think and believe and speak and act without government persecution. Actually no government, unless clairvoyant, can restrict one's freedom to think or believe as one wants. But our government also gives us the right to express our thoughts and beliefs, and act on them, within certain limits.

But in spite of all these legal guarantees of freedom, we don't really live in a free country. We have a whole other set of laws, the social laws, that govern our behavior within social groups. These laws are unwritten and often unspoken. If you belong to any social group, you must behave according to its norms and express opinions, attitudes, and beliefs that agree with those of the group, and also share their prejudices against members of other social groups.

These social laws are enforced by what are called "normative" pressures — that is, pressures to conform to group norms. These normative pressures have nothing to do with accuracy. They are only forces.

Would you rather believe that the sun travels around the earth, or be burned at the stake? We don't do that any more, but the modern equivalent is just as effective. If you are an academic person and you choose to believe in aliens, for example, you may quickly learn that academic freedom does not exist, as you are first cautioned by your comrades, then ridiculed, then scorned, as you lose first your status and then your job, and then your nice house, and you are forced to live in a trailer, and your children are ridiculed at school, and so on.

The enforcement of social laws, like the social laws themselves, isn't always articulated, or even thought. People will give you "looks." They will think of you as "one of those." They will pass you over for promotion or tenure because ... well, "It goes without saying."

Do you want to feel good, or do you want your thinking to be accurate? If somebody tells you you are the greatest person in the world, it certainly makes you feel good, but it has only about one chance in six billion of being accurate.

And so, if you conform to the norms of the social group, people will make you feel good by telling you you are the greatest, and if you deviate, they will make you feel bad by telling you you are "weird" and "strange" and ridiculing you and withdrawing love and hating you. None of this has anything to do with the accuracy of their belief system. It is purely emotional. And we know, thanks to Freud, that the emotions are far more powerful than the intellect. The emotions are the "motive" force, and they can force the intellect to rationalize whatever they want it to believe.

Is everybody "brainwashed" by their social group? To some degree, yes. People who have studied the brainwashing done by the Chinese Communists to American prisoners of war in the Korean War have noted that there are certain similarities to the normal socialization process of growing up in California or Kansas (Winn, 1983, page 5). Maybe the normal process isn't as harsh, but the same elements are present: pleasure and giving of love for conformity, and pain and withdrawal of love for deviance or non-compliance. And anybody who has ever been in the eighth grade knows that that process includes torture.

So why not just go along with your social group and feel good? First of all, the things they are pressuring you into believing may not be accurate, if that bothers you. Second, they may march you off to war, or mass suicide, or to some place that will ultimately make you feel <u>not</u> good. But worst of all, you might wake up some morning and find that you don't have a <u>self</u>, and that really is the loneliest feeling of all. And conversely, the people who have studied brainwashing report that those with a well-developed self are the most resistant to brainwashing.

We live in a free country, but you can't just be what you want to be or think what you want to think, even on the most personal level. Ultimately we all have to face the peer-group pressures — the tyranny of those people we think of as our "friends." You have to get permission from your social group to read this book, and if you don't, you will have to lie to them about it.

PART II

THE MIND

2. THAT WHICH KNOWS

In 1967, after visiting the spiritual teacher at the ashram, I had the following dream:

A spiritual teacher was lecturing me on the laws of the universe. On one side there was a landscape where she pointed out the physical laws, quite clearly, just as I understood them: sex and reproduction, kill to eat, kill to survive — the laws of the jungle, precise and unchangeable and absolutely binding. These were the FIRST level laws. Then we passed over an area of clouds, and on the other side was another clear landscape, where she pointed out the spiritual laws, equally precise, unchangeable, and absolutely binding, and not always compatible with the physical laws. These, she said, were the THIRD level laws.

The message that there were spiritual laws as precise and as binding as the physical laws was a fairly powerful message, and if the dream hadn't specifically mentioned a "first" and "third" level, I wouldn't even have asked myself what was the second level. But what was the second level?

The second level was the area of clouds in the middle. These were the clouds I had seen while meditating at the ashram, the clouds that prevented me from having a clear view of the spiritual. These were the clouds of my own mind. The whiteness could also be seen as the blank page of my mind upon which I constructed my image of the universe and resolved the apparent inconsistencies of the physical and spiritual laws coming at me from both sides. I recognized the second level as the area of the mental, and I recognized that the mental was my particular area of study.

Although there was more to the dream that invited me to explore the spiritual, and the spiritual teacher was encouraging me to explore the spiritual, and the spirit of the times was to explore the spiritual, this dream, just by showing me clouds, helped me to realize that my area of exploration was the mental. I had been exploring my own mental processes for more than a dozen years, and I had made some discoveries — a few discoveries that the culture wasn't aware of.

My dreams had showed me the approximate location of the ashram, close enough so that the spiritual teacher had let me know the exact location when I told her about the dream. The spiritual teacher tried to dissuade me from dream analysis. She said I might reach my spiritual destiny in fifty incarnations with dream analysis, but that I could reach it in one incarnation with meditation. But it was the dreams that had led me to the ashram in the first place, and I decided to stick with the method that had been my source of education in the past. In 1972, a life reading told me what I wanted to hear, that my purpose in this incarnation was to study "the earth thinking," and so here I am.

My exploration of the mental is described in detail in my first book, *Re-Educating Myself* (Gebelein, 1985), but I am going to review some of the main events later on. Also, because most people haven't read *Re-Educating Myself,* and the ideas in it have not yet become part of the culture, I will be repeating many of the things I already said in that book (as you may have already noticed).

In the dream, the area of the mental is not really noticeable, just as in real life. Most people look outside themselves at the physical or the spiritual. How many people, in studying some aspect of the universe, have paid any attention to that thing which is doing the looking, that faculty with which they are studying the universe — the mind? Whatever area of study they may be focused on, be it physical or spiritual, there is a thing doing the focusing, and the accuracy of the particular study is totally dependent on the thing doing the focusing. And whatever knowledge a person has is totally dependent on the accuracy of the thing doing the knowing — the mind.

When I first set out in search of "the truth," my first objective was to make my own mind reliable, because how else would I have an accurate view of the universe unless I made accurate that instrument doing the viewing? The method I chose to make my mind reliable was psychotherapy.

(I am using the word "psychotherapy" as a general term to cover psychoanalysis as invented by Freud and all its more modern variations — talk therapy as opposed to drug therapy, and depth psychology fixing the childhood misunderstandings as opposed to just the quick fix of current problems. Yes, the drug therapy and the quick fix have their usefulness, but I am not talking about them when I say "psychotherapy.")

I saw psychotherapy as education, and as a necessary part of my education. I am wondering how many people who have set themselves up as "experts," with MD or PhD degrees, or have set themselves up as spiritual gurus, with "powers," have made the same effort to make their own mental processes accurate? Have they considered that their influence on the culture may not be the positive thing they envision, if their mental processes aren't accurate? What does anybody really know, if that which knows isn't accurate?

Given that the human mind is unreliable, we have this method, called "science," that helps us to achieve more accurate results. But this isn't the only possible approach to accuracy. Since the beginning of the twentieth century, we have also had this other method, which I am calling "psychotherapy:" Given that the human mind is unreliable, make it reliable.

The two approaches are not contradictory; they are complementary. Used together they will give us more accurate results than either alone. As I describe some of the "unscientific methods" that have been accepted as "science," perhaps this will become more obvious.

It seems that I have the area of the mental pretty much to myself. I don't see anybody else studying the mind. The psychologists, following the lead of John B. Watson in 1913, abandoned the mental and began studying physical behavior, observable with the physical senses, in order to be more "scientific," and more recently have placed their hopes in the study of the physical functions of the brain. And since the Drug Movement of the sixties, the New Age people have bypassed the mental in favor of the spiritual.

In 1970, I remember, a guy I knew who had become a "Jesus Freak" dismissed my philosophy as a "mind trip." The trouble with that is that if Satan comes to you, he will come disguised as Jesus, and you will have to know the difference, and that would be a "mind trip."

Actually "spiritual" development is really mental development — the understanding of spiritual laws, reconciling them with physical laws and one's physical drives, programming oneself for behavior on a higher spiritual level, opening up higher sense perceptions, and so forth.

Intellectuals and anti-intellectuals alike think of "mental" as meaning "intellectual." The mind, as I see it, is much more than that. In addition to intellect, which is memory plus reason, there is perception, emotion, creativity, intuition, will, dreams, motivation, and curiosity. There is a subconscious component, some of which can be made conscious in the process of psychological growth, uncovering more mental attributes and abilities. When I say "the mind" or "mental," I mean the total of all these things.

I'll have more to say later about the mind, as I see it. But first I want to say a little about the man who steered us away from the study of the mind, John B. Watson.

3. JOHN B. WATSON, SCIENTIST

" ... there is the misconception going the rounds that there is such a thing as the mental ... "
—- John B. Watson (1925, page 243)

I have studied the mind by exploring my own mind. My evidence to support my view of the mind comes mostly from observing my own mental processes, and especially from observing and interpreting my own dreams. The psychologists, the people with the credentials, don't do that any more. So I feel obliged, first of all, to show that their choice of what to study does not invalidate my choice of what to study, and in a later chapter I'll explain the process that makes dreams and dream-interpretations valid as evidence.

The obvious way to study the mind is through direct observation of one's own mental processes. The early psychologists used this method, which they called "introspection." Because a normal person can observe only his/her own mind, they trained their "subjects" to observe and report their mental processes — except that different psychologists trained their subjects in different ways, according to different theories. First of all, the different theories created confusion. Then, on top of that, the subjects could be inaccurate in describing their internal mental observations, or could be actually lying, and there was no way that one person's internal perceptions could be checked or verified by another person. The result was chaos in the field of psychology.

To extricate psychology from this chaos, John B. Watson proposed, in his famous paper, "Psychology as the Behaviorist Views It," in 1913, that psychology, instead of studying the mind, should study physical human behavior observable with the physical senses. In his concluding remarks, he said:

> ... What we need to do is to start work upon psychology, making *behavior*, not *consciousness*, the objective point of our attack. Certainly there are enough problems in the control of behavior to keep us all working many lifetimes without ever allowing us time to think of consciousness *an sich*. ...
> (Watson, 1913, pages 175-6)

This is perfectly and totally reasonable: Let's see how far we can get studying physical behavior, with no reference to that elusive thing known as "mind." He even emphasized that it was invalid to make inferences about the mind on the basis of observed behavior. But please note that in doing this he was abandoning the study of "mind," at least for the foreseeable future.

It would also have been totally reasonable if "Behaviorism" had become a branch of "Psychology," and other psychologists had continued to study mental processes, but virtually the whole field of psychology followed Watson. (I hate it when somebody uses the word "virtually." I translate it as "not really.") Here I mean I don't really know who followed Watson and to what degree. They certainly didn't all call themselves "Behaviorists." But the rules of evidence changed. The observation of mental phenomena through "introspection" went out of fashion and lost status, to the point where it was no longer considered "evidence" by many, and to the point where many people even maintained that observations of things in the mind had no referent — that nothing real was being perceived. Maybe there are people still observing the mind, but they certainly aren't the dominant force in psychology.

Psychologists of the mid-20th-century were careful to describe their observations of mental processes as "theories." Actually they were theories, insofar as the psychologists were trying to represent what was going on in the minds of their subjects.

My observations are different. They are still "observations," because I am observing directly what is going on in my own mind. But this kind of evidence has gone out of favor, in favor of the perception of physical phenomena with the physical senses.

I think I am saying essentially the same thing as historian-of-psychology Duane P. Schultz wrote in 1969:

> ... No psychologist today calls himself a behaviorist — it is no longer necessary to do so. To the extent that American experimental psychology is today objective, empirical, reductionistic, and (to some degree) environmentalistic, the spirit, if not the letter, of Watsonian behaviorism lives on. ...
> (Schultz, 1969, page 236)

John B. Watson and his followers were loyal to a method, and that method was science. Science had achieved enormous success with the study of physical phenomena, where results could be demonstrated, verified, and proved to other people, because those other people could observe the same physical phenomena. The enormous success of science led to enormous status, where it was more important to be able to be called "scientific" than to be making accurate discoveries where it might be questioned whether the methods employed were really "scientific." And from the enormous status of science came the status-snobbery of people of the physical sciences looking down their noses at people doing psychology, and saying that they weren't really doing "science."

In the vocabulary of the times, the perception of things with the physical senses that could be observed by more than one person was called "objective," and the perception of internal states that could be observed by only one person was called "subjective." What was "objective" was "scientific," and what was "subjective" was not. All introspection was "subjective," and therefore the study of the mind using introspection was not considered "scientific." Since the only way to observe the mind was through introspection, there was no way to study the mind "scientifically."

Faced with this problem, John B. Watson and his followers abandoned the mental in order to do what they saw as "science" — to study something which their method was capable of studying with an anticipated high degree of success and high status, like the already-established physical sciences. In other words, they were loyal to the method at the expense of the subject matter.

But please note that Watson, in deciding to adopt the rules of evidence of physical science, was only making a choice, and the masses of people who followed him were only following that choice, and in no way has that choice, even by such huge numbers of people, invalidated the study of the mind by direct observation.

Going from the reasonable to the unreasonable, Watson later argued, in his book *Behaviorism*, that the mind didn't even exist, as is shown in this chapter heading:

X
TALKING AND THINKING
*Which, When Rightly Understood, Go Far In
Breaking Down the Fiction That There Is
Any Such Thing As 'Mental' Life*
(Watson, 1925, page 180)

His argument for this rests heavily on his theory that thinking is subvocal talking:

> The behaviorist advances the view that *what the psychologists have hitherto called thought is in short nothing but talking to ourselves. ...*
> (Watson, 1925, page 191)

Note that he is dealing here only with "thinking," or conscious thought processes. What about perception, memory, dreams, creativity, intuition, will, emotions, motivation? And what about the subconscious? He hasn't shown that these things don't exist. He just doesn't mention them, keeping us focused on "thinking."

I would agree that in most cases thinking is subvocal talking. I even do subvocal singing, complete with the musical notes. But the "nothing but" is hard to prove. To do this, you have to show that every instance of thinking is subvocal talking. Conversely, only one instance of thinking that is not subvocal talking is necessary to disprove it.

And what kind of evidence does he present to show that all thinking is subvocal talking?

> ... The evidence for this view is admittedly largely theoretical ...
> (Watson, 1925, page 191)

And what kind of evidence is theoretical evidence?

I know that I do nonvocal thinking and also experience mental processes which aren't "thinking," and I knew I would be able to come up with examples to refute the "nothing but," but for a while Watson's assertion acted as a hypnotic suggestion, blocking my own thought processes. The only thing that came to mind right away was that I am FURIOUS when anybody tries to tell me we think only in words, because it is so difficult for me to express my thoughts in words.

It took the experience with the extension ladder to break me out of the hypnotic trance. I was trying to explain to my friend that when the ladder was properly locked in place, the steps of the two sections would be in the same plane. I was using the words "equal" and "parallel" and "level," but none of them said what I wanted to say. I was then holding out my hands, first one six inches higher than the other, and then both in the same horizontal plane, trying to explain what I was trying to say. I know of no one word in English to say that when the ladder is locked in a stable position, the top surfaces of the steps in the extension section are in the same plane as the top surfaces of the steps they are locked in place with, respectively, in the base section. And even these convoluted words may not represent accurately the very simple PICTURE in my mind's eye of how the ladder is supposed to work.

On the subject of "my mind's eye," I remember a face — a picture, not words. I remember a place the same way, or the intersection where I turn off the road. I remember tastes, I remember smells, I hear the instruments that are playing in a band — all without words.

As I write this, I am about to go to the doctor's office, trying to remember the pain, to decide whether to call it a "pain" or an "ache."

A dream is like a movie — words and sounds and sights, plus feelings. One of the reasons I dream in symbols is because the dream is trying to tell me something for which the culture has no words.

I remember the job interview where I was trying to describe a computer program I had written:

"How many overlays did it have?" asked the interviewer.

"What's an overlay?" was my reply.

When he explained what an overlay was, I then knew that the program had 7 overlays. How could I construct overlays if I didn't know the word for it? The same program also had "user hooks" and a "meta-language," long before I knew the words for those things.

A co-worker once asked me how I designed computer programs. I looked deep into my mind to see what was going on, and the best words I could come up with to describe the process were "primitive art." I see pictures and patterns of how things should go and flow. I then translate these pictures and patterns into a logical succession of events, into mathematics and flow charts, and ultimately into computer code. The particular computer language is unimportant. The words definitely come last.

> ... How do we ever get new verbal creations such as a poem or a brilliant essay? *The answer is that we get them by manipulating words,* shifting them about until a new pattern is hit upon. ...
> (Watson, 1925, page 198)

This sounds like the attempts people have made to get computers to write poetry by combining random words in likely patterns — with interesting but bizarre and meaningless results. A real poem comes from the depths, and all but the most gifted grope for words to express the feelings.

Did I say "feelings?" Where are feelings in Watson's theory?

If the mind doesn't exist, then there is no such thing as scientific thinking; there is only scientific talking.

Even with only "theoretical evidence," and even though the theory is so easy to disprove, Watson's theory of subvocal talking may have given rise to beliefs that are widely held in academic circles:
1. We think only in words.
2. There is no such thing as creativity. It is all just a synthesis of known elements. (If we only think, and not create, and if we think only in words, then creativity has to be just a recombination or rearrangement of words, as Watson stated in the quote above.)
3. There is no such thing as intuition. (If we think only in words, then we don't think in pictures or patterns.)
4. Self-education is impossible — a delusion, a myth. (If we think only in words, and words of course come from the culture, then there is no thinking beyond or outside of or independently of the culture.)
I think some academic people need to examine the foundations of some of their beliefs.

While the psychologists were having problems with introspection and rejecting it in favor of something more "scientific," Sigmund Freud and his followers were learning something from introspection, and even learning something about the nature of its inaccuracies.
Introspective methods were used successfully by Sigmund Freud in developing a huge new body of knowledge, namely:
1. There exist subconscious processes motivating people, sometimes in conflict with their conscious motives.
2. These conflicts are caused by unresolved childhood traumatic experiences.
3. Dreams are not just meaningless nonsense. Dreams are a clue to these subconscious elements, "the royal road to a knowledge of the unconscious," as he put it.
4. People employ "defense mechanisms" to avoid seeing their subconscious motivations and their true selves. Anna Freud

identified a dozen or so of these "defense mechanisms," including "repression," "projection," "displacement," "rationalization," "sublimation," and "denial," described in any textbook (Alloy et al, 1999, page 96).

5. Freud developed the method of "psychoanalysis," using dreams and free association, in a confidential and non-judgmental setting, to get rid of these conflicts by slowly and patiently bringing them out into conscious awareness and dealing with them there.

These central ideas and methods of Freud's have all been proved many times over by thousands or millions of people, including myself, who have enjoyed the positive results of his methods.

And yet Freud has been dismissed in recent times by members of the academic establishment, who are saying that Freud did "bad science." Yes, I know that Freud made mistakes, but beyond that I can't really take this criticism seriously, because I know from first-hand experience that Freud's discoveries were enormous and his methods work

Carl Jung, Freud's number one pupil, carried Freud's tradition further and corrected many of Freud's errors: No, psychological problems don't all have to do with sex. No, dreams are not "wish fulfillment," but rather a correction to, or compensation for, the conscious attitude. No, the subconscious is not just a place where we bury our unwanted thoughts and feelings, but also a source of ideas and inspiration and spiritual knowledge. When I first read Jung, I thought he had not yet broken free of the religious beliefs of the pre-scientific era, but actually he was moving ahead into a new era, an era where people can believe in the spiritual not on the basis of "faith" or somebody's authority, but on the basis of EVIDENCE. His discovery of "original experience," whereby one is able to see God for oneself, is potentially his most valuable contribution to the culture (but not yet recognized).

I personally have benefited from Jung's refinements to Freud's discoveries and methods, and have verified in my own experience the things I have mentioned above, and more. Most of Jung's evidence came from dreams, and I was able to find the evidence in my own dreams to support what he was saying. The many people who have successfully completed Jungian analysis have also verified the accuracy of Jung's ideas.

I once mentioned the name of Carl Jung to a scientist I knew, and he said, "Carl Jung was a mystic." I couldn't imagine what he was talking about. A mystic is a person who attempts to bypass the intellect and the evidence of the physical senses — just the opposite of science — in trying to perceive or experience a deeper reality. To call Jung a "mystic" is a gross misrepresentation. I thought my friend was using the second definition of "mystic," the derogatory definition, meaning "illogical" or "irrational." But since then I have seen the word "mystical" applied to Carl Jung in a textbook:

> ... One of the most mystical and metaphysical of psychological theorists, Jung has had greater acceptance in Europe than in America. The popularity of his works, however, appears to be growing in America, especially among persons interested in mysticism and nonempirical aspects of psychology.
> (Lazerson, ed., 1975, page 423)

I know that Carl Jung was mostly rejected by the academic community in the beginning, and that he has gradually gained acceptance over the years. But why call him "mystical?" They don't explain what they mean by this. And why do they say "nonempirical?" Jung's discoveries were very much based on evidence, although, as with Freud, much of this evidence came from internal perceptions, and mostly from dreams. Carl Jung discovered a spiritual reality because that's what people were presenting to him in their dream material.

But, as I see it, an academic community that was trying to break away from the spiritual to a purely physical view of the universe had to find a way to say "not one of us," and the word they found was "mystical."

In my 1996 dictionary, and not in the older dictionaries, there is the following definition of "mysticism:"

> mysticism ... 2: the belief that direct knowledge of God, spiritual truth, or ultimate reality can be attained through subjective experience (as intuition or insight)
> (Merriam-Webster, 1996)

This pretty much describes what I have already said was Carl Jung's greatest discovery. It looks as if this definition appeared in recent years just to justify the academic opinion of Jung. They might as well have defined "mystic" as "whatever Carl Jung was." The academic people define the words, and based upon their usage those definitions appear in the dictionary.

Carl Jung was a "mystic" because academic people say he was, and because academic people say he was, whatever he was becomes a dictionary definition of "mystic," and therefore it becomes true by definition. That's what status can do for you.

So Carl Jung is here bundled in with people who reject reason and the evidence of the senses, and spend most of their time meditating. And his major discovery is set up to be dismissed as "mystical," and therefore "unscientific." How long will the culture live with this kind of inaccuracy?

I just happened to come across the following, from an interview with Jungian analyst Marie-Louise von Franz about her former relationship with physicist Wolfgang Pauli:

> vFr: Pauli was afraid of the content of his dreams. It frightened him to draw conclusions from what his dreams said. They said, for instance, that he should stand up for Jungian psychology in public. And that he feared like hell. Which I understand. He moved in the higher circles in physics. They were very mocking and cynical and also jealous of him. If he had stood up for dreams and irrational things, there would have been a hellish laughter. ...
> (van Erkelens, 2002, pages 146-7)

We all know there would have been a hellish laughter. But "hellish laughter" doesn't have anything to do with science. "Hellish laughter" is part of the bullying that children learn to do in the schoolyard.

The quote from John B. Watson at the beginning of this chapter is embedded in an even more sweeping statement:

As long as there is the misconception going the rounds that there is such a thing as the mental, I suppose there will be mental diseases, mental symptoms and mental cures. ...
(Watson, 1925, page 243)

With the one word "misconception" he sweeps away the mind, and with it all the discoveries that Freud and his followers made about the mind.

In another statement he describes "Psycho-Analysis" as "Based largely upon religion, introspective psychology, and Voodooism" (Watson, 1925, page 18). "Religion" is his own fiction, which I will get to later. "Introspective psychology" is true. "Voodooism" is simply a smear word, in this context. This man who was so intent on being "scientific" is here discrediting himself with his own smear tactics. But because of his high academic status, people have read this book and have been influenced by it.

Psychotherapy exists today because it works. Thousands if not millions of people have benefited from it. And most of what psychotherapy is today owes its credit to Freud, with minor credits to Jung and many others. And the methods used by Freud were mainly introspective, studying his own mind and reports of clients about their own minds. So introspection has, in fact, produced something valuable and positive and accurate, something that can be called "knowledge."

Freud and his followers also addressed the problem that introspection was unreliable, just assuming as a "given" that people's reports of themselves were distorted, and never taking their clients' statements at face value. They also identified the source of the distortion (childhood traumatic experiences), and identified characteristic ways in which people distort the truth about themselves (defense mechanisms).

But the tradition of Freud keeps being replaced, more and more, by the tradition of Watson. The need to be "scientific," or to limit "science" to the study of physical phenomena, and the huge status of physical science, have kept people away from the study of the mind, and have seriously slowed down or even reversed progress in our knowledge of the mind that Freud started.

When the scientists discovered rapid eye movements, and REM sleep, I didn't know what they were so excited about. But of course it was a way of observing with the physical senses that a person was dreaming — well, no, not really. The person still has to observe the dream with his/her inner perceptions in order to know that he/she is dreaming. By the strict rules of physical science, all the scientist knows with the physical senses is that when people are awakened from REM sleep, they REPORT having dreams.

And then instead of studying the dream content, these physical scientists study the words in the report of the dream. They count how many violent words, how many pleasant words, how many sexual words, and so on. And then they try to draw conclusions from that. It is as if one were to take a great novel, say *The Grapes of Wrath*, and count the words in it. Some understanding might be gained, but a much greater understanding would be gained by simply reading the novel.

The study of the physical brain right now seems to be the great hope for the future. The instrumentation they are using, and the discoveries they are making about brain chemistry and the functions of every segment of the brain, and the success they have had in developing mind-altering drugs, are all enormously and genuinely impressive. This is still in the tradition of Watson: There is still a great deal being learned, and to be learned, by the study of physical processes.

But, like Watson, the scientists of today can't help going over the line into extra-scientific thinking — that is, thinking beyond the scope or range of validity of science — and claiming that their discoveries have disproved Freud or made Freud obsolete. Yes, the discoveries are remarkable. Yes, the equipment is remarkable. I would imagine that one would need high scientific status just to be able to get the funding to use this equipment. And then it is up to us poor common folk to discern just to what extent they are able to draw accurate conclusions from the observations they are able to make with this expensive equipment — or have they gone one or two or three steps further in "winging it" with conclusions that are unjustified but that they can probably get away with because of their high high scientific status.

Even if we set aside for now the question of an immortal "psyche," the brain and the mind are different things. The brain is the instrument and the mind is the output from that instrument. It is as if we were trying to study music by studying the atoms and molecules and shape and vibrations of the instrument, but not hearing the music. There is no substitute for the actual perception of the output of the instrument.

When the brain-scientists can play me back a recording of my dream, with not only the sights and sounds, but also the thoughts and feelings, then I will concede that they are truly studying the mind by studying the functioning of the physical brain.

4. UNTANGLING THE MESS

John B. Watson and his followers, by switching over to the study of physical behavior, avoided the problem of how to study the mind scientifically, and not only left us with that problem but also created other problems as a result. I don't think anybody seriously believes that the mind does not exist, but certainly many people believe that observations of the mind made with one's internal perceptions are not "evidence." "Introspectionism" has lost status, and the accurate and valuable discoveries made by Freud and Jung using introspective methods have been declared less than "scientific" and ridiculed by many. If we can get past the problems that Watson and his followers have created, maybe we can address the problem that they avoided in the first place — how to study the mind accurately.

At this point in my writing, I experienced what I thought was a "writer's block" for seven months, until I realized that I was trying to solve a problem that the psychologists had failed to solve in the entire twentieth century — not only how to study the mind, but how to disentangle that study from the total cultural snarl surrounding it. I was never caught up in the snarl. I just went along in the tradition of Freud and Jung, innocently observing the workings of my own mind. But now I feel I must solve this problem just to give my own introspective explorations the credibility they deserve.

The problem is a cultural tangle of status-considerations fed by science-fantasy and the confusion of English words. But actually the whole problem can be expressed in terms of one variable, and that variable is accuracy — not fine distinctions of accuracy that require high intelligence or precise mathematical equations to discern, but the most gross comparisons of what is accurate, not accurate, more accurate, or less accurate.

THE STATUS OF SCIENCE

Accuracy is a major component of knowledge. Things aren't "known" unless they are represented accurately. Science has been successful because it has been proven to be an accurate method for obtaining knowledge. Accuracy is the key to knowledge, and accuracy is the criterion by which science is judged. The basic criterion for judging science or any other approach to knowledge is not whether it can be called "scientific," or even whether it is truly "scientific" in the strictest sense, but whether it is accurate.

As science has been successful in providing us with accurate knowledge, its reputation has grown. As its reputation has grown, the status of science and scientists in society has grown.

The reputation of science is not the same thing as science. Science is what science does, by the scientific method. The reputation of science, on the other hand, is how science is thought of. The reputation of science exerts a social force, independent of what science is.

The status of science is not the same thing as science, either. "Status" means one's rank in the social hierarchy — who is respected, who is taken seriously, who is listened to, whose word is taken over another's in court, who is allowed to dominate, and who pecks who in the social pecking order. "Status" should not be confused with "stature." The word "status" refers only to one's position or rank in society, and not to ability or merit.

Status is achieved by some kind of merit, unless one is born into a high position. But once achieved, status operates according to laws of its own, independent of any merit that may have led there. Yes, there are methods of social domination and manipulation employed by persons of status, but first just the fact of status exerts a social force. Persons of status are listened to, believed, and followed, more than persons of no particular status. What persons of status say is more likely to be accepted as "knowledge" by the culture, whether it is accurate or not. And conversely, persons of no status are more likely to be ignored, dismissed, or ridiculed, independently of the merit of what they are saying.

C1.5 The higher the rank of the member within the group, the more central he will be in the group's interaction and the more influential he will be.

The corner boys as well as members of formal organizations observe channels; that is, the same suggestion that will be rejected or ignored if made by a low-status member may be acted upon if made by a high-status member. Many earlier experiments have been devoted to showing that subjects perceive and judge content differently according to their assumptions about the character of the source [Bales, 1959, p. 299, referring to Whyte, 1943].

(Berelson & Steiner, 1964, page 341, citing Bales, Robert F., "Small Group Theory and Research," in Robert K. Merton et al., eds., *Sociology Today: Problems and Prospects*, Basic Books, 1959, pp. 293-305, and Whyte, William Foote, *Street Corner Society*, U. of Chicago Press, 1943.)

Of course in citing all these people above, I am drawing on these same forces of status.

The status of science, like the reputation of science, also exerts a social force, independent of what science is. These forces don't affect the accuracy of the scientific method itself, but they create a major bias in the interactions between science and the culture at large, drawing people towards anything that can be CALLED "science" or "scientific." Thus we have Computer Science and Political Science and Social Science and Christian Science and Creation Science, drawing upon the reputation and status of science.

In reply, in defense of their social position, some persons of established science are busy trying to argue what can legitimately be called "science," or not, and what is "pseudoscience." This argument is usually based on some narrow definition of "science," a definition that would exclude a great deal of legitimate scientific work. If you look up "Philosophy of Science" in the *Encyclopedia Britannica*, you will find that the definition of "science" goes on for pages and pages. It is not so easy to demonstrate, for example, that phrenology or Christian Science or Jungian analysis are not science. And what is the point? The real argument is whether an approach to knowledge is accurate or not, and this argument bypasses all the complication of trying to define what is "science."

The whole point of arguing what is "scientific" is status. This argument is usually pursued by persons of science, from a position of status (where they can expect no rebuttal), to assert that status, and to exclude those others who haven't attained that same status. It is the pecking of the pecking order. It has very little, if anything, to do with science, the method.

There is also a social bias against anything that is not science, drawing people and resources away from anything that cannot be studied according to the exact methods of already-established science. The first rule of established science is that observations must be made with the physical senses. Obviously this excludes observations of the mind made with one's internal perceptions.

So Watson was right. If he wanted to do "science," as it was defined, he should not be studying the mind, but should be studying something that could be observed with the physical senses. But then he went on to make the claim that the mind doesn't exist. Many other scientists on many other subjects have tried to make the same kind of a claim: If something can't be observed with the physical senses, then it doesn't exist.

This can be taken as some kind of psychological denial. The most favorable interpretation I can make of this is that scientists are dedicated to their profession, and are limiting their thought processes to those accepted by their profession. They are saying, in effect, "We will act and think AS THOUGH the mind did not exist, or anything else that cannot be observed with the physical senses." If you want to live within the rules of a "science" which accepts only the evidence of the physical senses, this attitude may be useful. But I see it as "Putting the blinders on." (If you don't remember horse-drawn wagons, "blinders" were put on the sides of the horse's head so that the horse could see only straight ahead, and not to the sides.) For those of us who want to see a more complete universe, this attitude is restricting, to say the least, and introduces enormous inaccuracies in one's view of the universe — inaccuracies which then must be defended by introducing even more inaccuracies.

It would be more accurate to say that present-day science has its limitations — that the study of anything that can't be observed with the physical senses is beyond the scope of present-day science, and that scientists are not presently qualified to study the mind.

Of course, to say that science has "limitations" and that scientists are "not qualified" is blasphemy, in view of the status-considerations. Physical scientists are treated as God in our culture. They are considered to be able to know everything.

This is what I mean when I say "science-fantasy" — inaccurate beliefs elevating established physical science into a position of omniscience. The fantasy that with present-day physical science we will be able to know everything is actually steering us away from being able to know everything, by deceiving us into thinking that no other approaches to knowledge are necessary.

The status of physical science, by drawing people and resources away from the study of things like the mind which can't be observed with the physical senses, has created huge gaps in the culture, huge blank areas not covered by any official "knowledge." Maybe status does not affect the accuracy of science per se, but the bias created by that status affects knowledge in general, giving us an incomplete picture of reality.

The word "science" is used to mean the scientific method for obtaining knowledge, and the word "science" also means the social group of people, the "scientists," who practice the scientific method. The two definitions get confused, and it is necessary to distinguish the two. Not all opinions of scientists have been arrived at by the scientific method. Group dynamics, as in any other social group, determine to some degree what scientists think, what scientists believe, and what scientists say.

The status of scientists within the culture and also the status of individual scientists within the social group are major factors influencing "scientific" thinking. I am sure that anybody who is within the social group "science" recognizes that there is a pecking order, and that that pecking orders influences not only what scientists think and say, but also what they decide to study by the scientific method, and also (most important) what scientific projects receive funding.

The status of an idea or theory held by the social group "science" can create a bias. For example, *African Genesis* tells the story about how the discoveries about human origins by certain African scientists were so far out of line with the established theories of the day that the evidence was ignored and the process of science was blocked. It took a dramatist to dramatize those discoveries and bring them to the attention of the world (Ardrey, 1961).

Also things like telepathy and precognition are dismissed as coincidence, because scientists are convinced that such things are not theoretically possible: The probability of coincidence, no matter how slight, is large compared to a probability of zero that such things really exist.

Status also works as a motivation for hoaxes. If one were to gain great status by showing something that would greatly revolutionize existing "knowledge," then there is an incentive for fraud.

In the case of *African Genesis*, the status of a theory also blocked communication. Communication is an important part, a necessary part, of the scientific method, because a key to the scientific method is replication, and replication requires communication. If people refuse to replicate, then science is defeated. So a very important part of science is influenced by group dynamics.

I am wondering how science has managed to be so successful with all this "politics" of group dynamics going on. I think the answer is that the primary values of the social group are focused on the scientific method, and that the persons with the highest status in the social group are those with the strictest allegiance to the scientific method. As a result, group dynamics, for the most part, seem to serve the needs of science, the method.

Last but not least, with status come the methods of status, methods of social domination and manipulation which I call the "unscientific methods." I would like to say that "few" scientists employ these methods, but my honest belief is that the vast majority, as members of a social group, use these methods. Certainly "hellish laughter" requires some kind of a consensus. I think all scientists should be on the lookout to see if they are using these methods. It is interesting to note that some of those same physical scientists who insist on such strict adherence to the proven methods of physical science use these unscientific methods to argue their position.

One of these unscientific methods is "labeling," also known as "name-calling." If the label on the bottle says "poison," one is not tempted to drink it. If Carl Jung is labeled a "mystic," one would be more likely to go to him to do meditation, not psychoanalysis. Obviously labeling is inaccurate, and usually derogatory. A true scholar would investigate further, to see if the label was accurate.

A related method is definition-switching. A "mystic" by one definition is not the same as a "mystic" by another definition. A "communist" by one definition is not the same as a "communist" by another definition. Definitions can be switched in order to create inaccuracies and discredit people. Just the fact that English words have multiple definitions is a major source of confusion, as I describe in the next section, "Words Define the Culture," and in a later chapter with "evolution-1" and "evolution-2." Yes, definitions are being switched, perhaps deliberately, perhaps subconsciously, introducing inaccuracies, but mostly I think this is just a problem inherent in the language.

Another unscientific method is argument-by-ridicule. The "hellish laughter" is real. I once mentioned the name of Edgar Cayce to a scientist I knew, and his response was "Ha, ha, ha. That's so funny!" And ten people at the table laughed with him.

There was no discussion of evidence or documented facts or scientific studies that made Edgar Cayce so funny. He was just an object of ridicule within the scientific community. He could not be explained within their belief structure, and therefore their psychology had to get rid of him, and this was the method that had been socially agreed upon.

Ridicule is a way that human beings have of pecking those of lower status to keep them in their place, putting them down and keeping them down. It has nothing to do with science or accuracy.

A third unscientific method is the authoritarian pronouncement: "There are no such things (UFOs, Bigfoot, spiritual beings)." In order to make such a statement scientifically, one would have to have a complete knowledge of the entire universe, because only one instance of the thing would disprove the statement. Another example of the authoritarian pronouncement would be the statement by Watson that thinking is "nothing but" subvocal talking. Again, the "nothing but" is logically very hard to prove.

Another variation of the authoritarian pronouncement is "You didn't see what you saw."

The answer to that is "You weren't there."

I mean, how could they possibly know what you didn't see unless they were there to witness the same non-event? From a position of total ignorance, they are trying to get people to believe them on their authority, on the basis of their status. Scientists have replaced the priesthood as the voice of authority in our culture, for those who want to submit to that kind of social domination.

If lawyers use illegal methods, they can lose their license to practice. Similarly, if scientists use unscientific methods, they should lose their accreditation as "scientist." Until Government puts such a law into effect, it's up to us common folk to recognize the difference between scientific and unscientific methods.

To differentiate between science and the unscientific methods, I would ask the questions: Where is your evidence? What scientific studies support this?

Scientists are knowledgeable in a particular field of study, and get their PhDs by becoming expert in a very narrow segment of that field. They qualify as "expert" only in that very narrow segment, and outside of the broader field I would question whether their opinion should carry any weight at all — except that they are listened to because of their social status as PhDs and scientists. Physical scientists criticizing the work of psychology are operating well out of their area of expertise. I suppose, because they are scientists, they are more qualified to say what is "science" than poets, priests, or rock stars. But that is all. You can bet that their opinions aren't based on scientific studies, and even if they are, they are largely uninformed.

I have read about experiments by physicists trying to disprove astrology (CSICOP, 1996). I would like to see studies testing the accuracy of astrology, but by people knowledgeable in astrology. I don't think that physicists have the necessary knowledge of astrology to perform accurate studies in that field. I am wondering whether physicists would accept experiments in physics performed by astrologers?

Instead of saying "bad science," it would be more accurate to say that the methods of physical science aren't exactly applicable to the study of the mind, in that the mind is not perceived with the physical senses. Freud and others have done the best they could, given the nature of the subject matter. If the physical scientists had explained how they might have done better under the circumstances, we might elevate their comments to the level of "criticism," but since they haven't, I see their status-snobbery only as "noise" — dogs barking and birds singing.

Yes, this noise is distracting, but why do psychologists have to pay any attention to it? Why can't they just continue their work in psychology and ignore what physicists and biologists are saying about them?

The answer is that physical scientists dominate scientific societies, and therefore determine what is defined as "science," and what gets published in scientific journals, and what receives funding as "science." Yes, you can study the mind independently of all that, but without pay, without recognition, without being published, and without any status — without any of those benefits that membership in the scientific community will give you. In other words, the status-snobbery affects status. It is not scientific, but it can make honest scientific work invisible to the culture. And just the threat of "hellish laughter" can keep scientists of status from speaking out.

People talk about the "hard sciences" and the "soft sciences." The major "hard sciences" are physics, chemistry, and biology. The "soft sciences" include psychology and sociology, and also (I would say) subjects like economics and political science. The hard sciences deal with phenomena that can be observed with the physical senses. The soft sciences deal to some degree with what people are thinking.

The "hard" sciences are established. Their methods have been worked out, and their methods have been proven to work. The "soft" sciences are not yet fully developed. Their methods are still being worked out. Economic theories don't always work. Psychotherapy doesn't always work. So the "hard" sciences are like people who have "arrived" socially. They have that social status that the "soft" sciences are still struggling for, and some of them take advantage of that social position to peck those who have not yet "arrived" — just as in America those who have "arrived" socially have sometimes been brutally unkind to those who have not. But that has nothing to do with science.

Actually it is easier to observe a ball rolling down an inclined plane than to observe human thought processes. The "hard" sciences are actually the "easy" sciences. Their subject matter is more easily observable and provable, and their theoretical underpinnings have been worked out for hundreds or thousands of years. The foundations of physics date back to ancient Greece. In contrast, the sciences dealing with the human mind are relatively new, and still have difficult problems to be worked out. Psychotherapy a hundred years after Freud might be compared to medicine a hundred years after Hippocrates.

Yes, the "hard" sciences are currently more accurate than the "soft" sciences, but that is not a reflection of the quality of the scientific work being performed, but only of the difficulty of the subject matter and the fact that these studies are relatively new.

The high status of physical science has led some people to the absurd conclusion that if something can't be studied precisely by the established methods of physical science, then it doesn't exist. Well, it might as well not exist if "science" is equated with "accuracy," and nothing outside the range of established science can be known with accuracy. But that negative has not been established. The positive has been established, that the methods of physical science give accurate results, but it has not been established that methods outside of the precise methods of physical science do not or will not give accurate results.

It is more accurate to say that the mind exists than that it doesn't exist. And, given that the mind exists, it is more accurate to study the mind than to not study the mind. The question is not whether to study the mind, but how to study the mind. While the psychologists are spending their many lifetimes not studying the mind, maybe we can be figuring out how to study it. We will have to start without the status of physical science and earn that status gradually with proven results. We will have to start with no money and no status and no recognition. Our observations will be labeled "useless." Our findings will be ignored or dismissed.

WORDS DEFINE THE CULTURE

I have gone ahead and studied my own mind, using my own internal perceptions, in the tradition of Freud and Jung, for my own information and clarity, oblivious to the fact that the introspective approach has lost favor with those who call themselves "scientists." I don't call myself a "scientist." I think of myself as an "explorer" of my own mind and my own mental processes. But I have some background in science, and I have applied the scientific methods of observation and proof to my explorations. Also my psychiatrist trained me to be an observer of my own mental processes, as I shall explain later. I see no reason why the methods of science can't be adapted to the study of the mind.

First of all, science has had problems with words. Where science is normally very precise, and scientific language is very precise, scientists have had problems at the most fundamental level with ordinary English words, which aren't very precise.

Words are defined by a culture, and a culture is defined by its words. There are a few words in our culture that have been very misleading in defining the study of the mind.

The first of these words is "introspection.' Psychologists have talked about "introspection," and have rejected "introspection" as a means of studying the mind, because it has proven unreliable. "Introspection" is a vague word. It can mean one's perception of one's mental processes, but it can also mean other things, like one's internal contemplations, as in "To be or not to be ..." "Introspection" can include thinking, brooding, meditation, rationalization, and fantasizing, along with perception.

All this is confusing. I prefer to introduce the concept of "mental senses," to include only the means of seeing or perceiving what is in the mind. All we want, in order to observe our mental processes, are those internal perceptions. To start with, we need to recognize that there is such a thing as internal observations. Then, the first question would be, "What do you observe in your mind?" The second question, to differentiate between fact and fiction, would be "Did you create or invent it?" Certainly the most direct way, if not the only way, of studying the mind is by using these mental senses.

For centuries our culture has limited our thinking by defining the perceptions as "the five senses" and then using the expression "sixth sense" to mean something unusual, like psychic abilities. So immediately we are boxed in by words, because in between the five physical senses and the rare psychic abilities we have at least one other sense, a mental sense, by which we view the contents of our own minds. I am counting on you to supply the evidence from your own experience to verify that this is true for the "we" and not just for myself.

For example, if I am looking at the logical proposition, "If A is greater than B, and B is greater than C, then A is greater than C," I don't just compare the letters on the page, but I construct some images in my mind, and compare those images, and then say "I see." I am seeing not with my physical eyes, but with some internal mode of perception. Similarly when somebody explains something to me and I say "I see," I am seeing something with these mental senses.

When I recall anything from memory — a face, a place, a statistic, a line of verse, a melody — I am employing some kind of perception in order to see it or hear it again. When I feel any kind of emotion, not physical pain or pleasure, but any of those mental things like joy, sadness, excitement, fear, anger, horror, depression, or elation, these things are coming to me through a mental sense, not a physical sense. When I experience a dream — the sights, the sounds, the physical pain or pleasure, and the emotional feelings of the dream — I am using these mental senses, that is, those perceptions used by the mind to perceive the mind. Physical senses perceive physical phenomena, and mental senses perceive mental phenomena.

Is the mind only playing these things back through the normal means of physical perception? I don't know the answer to technical questions like that. All I know is that I have senses by which I perceive things in my own mind.

It is usually pretty obvious to me whether the thing I am perceiving in my mind is fact or fiction: Did I create this or not? I see three categories of things I am observing in my mind: fact, fiction, and dreams. "Fact" includes memories I have of real events that I have witnessed, be they mental or physical or spiritual. "Fiction" includes those things I know I created in my mind, like the "mind's-eye" mapping of the logical proposition. "Dreams" means the actual perception of dreams, as I am experiencing them. Dreams are not the same as fiction, because they are created by a different mental process, outside of my conscious control. The memory of a dream, after I wake up, I include as "fact," because it is the memory of an internal event. People who meditate might add another category of what they experience during meditation.

Anything can be called a "fact" once it becomes a memory. And are Mickey Mouse and Santa Claus "factual?" I can see people arguing things like this endlessly. I don't want to get into a philosophical tangle on this. The main question is, "Did I make this up?"

And what about emotions? I really don't know. It seems that emotions are a component of all three categories, just as they are a part of experiencing physical reality.

It is possible to confuse fact, fiction, and dreams, as my psychiatrist pointed out to me. On one occasion, I was walking down the street and saw an angry man, and this made me feel angry.

My psychiatrist said, "You didn't know that that man was angry. But you did know that you were angry. Therefore you were projecting your feelings of anger on that innocent man."

I couldn't really argue with that, and it is certainly worth thinking about, whenever you "sense" what another person is thinking or feeling.

On another occasion, I had a magnificent dream, which I wrote down for my psychiatrist, and it went on for pages and pages. He took one look at it and said, "You didn't dream all this. A dream only lasts for 5 to 20 seconds. You made up most of this."

That made me furious, because taking the time to write down the dream had made me an hour late for work. It required considerable description of details, because it took place in some strange country where I had never been before, and there was a house I had never seen before, and the people assembled at the dinner table were from different aspects of my life — people who would never be together in real life. And those 3 snapshots were worth 3000 words. So I defend my accuracy in reporting the dream, but only after having given it some thought. It is possible, in remembering a dream, or writing down a dream, to make up things that weren't actually there. It is also possible that scientific investigators might ignore accurate reports because of theories that they hold to be true.

It is much less confusing to talk about "mental senses" observing various categories of mental phenomena than to talk vaguely about "introspection." And with more than a hundred years of experience with psychotherapy behind us, it should be possible to make these mental observations much more accurate than in Watson's day.

With these mental senses I can observe, in the scientific sense, my mental processes. The only problem is that normally this is a private view, as opposed to the public view of the physical senses. The only mind I can see is my own, and I am the only one who can see my mind. So there is not the "objectivity" of multiple viewers, keeping each other honest.

I say "normally" because clairvoyant people can observe, to some degree, other people's mental processes. Ideally, scientists studying the mind should be clairvoyant, so that there could be multiple viewers of the same mental process, thereby fulfilling the condition of "objectivity." Then, if the evidence of the mental senses were accepted, all the rules of established science would apply. But since present-day scientists are not clairvoyant, and most scientists don't even believe there is such a thing as clairvoyance, that's only a possibility for the "many lifetimes" in the future.

For the present, we are left with our "subjective" perceptions. "Subjective" is another word that has messed up our cultural thinking. Any internal observation is called "subjective." Implied in the word "subjective" is the assumption that such observations are biased and therefore inaccurate. But this assumption has not been arrived at scientifically. Where are the scientific studies to show that internal observations are any less accurate than external observations? I would say that the bias and inaccuracy created by scientists' universal rejection of anything that can be labeled "subjective" is far greater than the bias and inaccuracy created by "subjective" observations themselves.

The word "objective," on the other hand, has been used to describe observations made with the physical senses. The word "objective" carries with it the impression of absolute truth and total accuracy — the true nature of the object, independent of anyone's perception of it.

There is this aura of "objectivity" attached to scientific findings. Many times they are expressed in the impersonal mode, as "It has been determined ...," as if no fallible human being had ever been involved in the making of observations or the drawing of conclusions.

Actually, all observations are subjective. There is no observation without an observer. Whether observations are made of external events or internal events, those observations are made through the perceptions of an individual human being, subject to the bias inherent in those perceptions, and edited through the mind of an individual human being, subject to the mind-set inherent therein. What about instrumentation controlled by a computer? Human beings designed that instrumentation with some idea in mind of what they wanted to observe. And human beings are looking at the output of the instrumentation. There is no way of getting around the subjective element, as long as human beings are going to look at or interpret the data.

The quality of "objectivity," of having more than one person observing the same phenomenon, is actually a "collective subjective" perception. It does have the effect of averaging those subjective observations and their inherent inaccuracies, such that the mean of the observations is more likely to be nearer to the objective truth than any one observation — that is, if the observations are all truly independent. But scientists all belong to the same social group, and share the same beliefs, the same social norms, and the same needs to be accepted and respected by members of their social group, not to mention needs for jobs and promotion and publication. So scientists aren't really independent observers. I would predict that where there are multiple observers of the same event, the collective view would be biased towards the viewpoint of those who were most dominant or who had the highest status.

So much for "objectivity." This is another case of "science-fantasy." The aura of infallibility ingrained in the word "objective" breaks down. Yes, science has had an enormous amount of success with these collective observations, but they are not infallibly superior to anything that can be called "subjective."

Also Freud and Jung had some degree of success with "subjective" observations and reports of "subjective" observations. So there is no clear case that what has been called "objective" is all that much better than what is called "subjective," except in the aura which has been given to the words.

Throughout the twentieth century the word "objective" has acquired propaganda-value, like calling something "American." It is approved, good, and positive, and certainly one does not want to be called "Un-American." This kind of propaganda-value doesn't belong in scientific discussions, because it interferes with accuracy.

If we could get rid of the aura of "objectivity" and the stigma of "subjectivity," then scientists might actually do studies to determine whether external perceptions are more accurate than internal perceptions, and if so by how much. Of course the physical scientists, some of them, would want to maintain the bias to maintain their position of domination.

One more little thing: The real argument for "objectivity," the only argument that is actually valid, is that there are multiple observers observing the same event. But how many scientific experiments actually have multiple observers observing the same event? I don't know the answer to that, but I'm sure it isn't all. I don't recall ever reading, in any report of any scientific experiment, any accounting of how many observers witnessed each event. In other words, it isn't important to have multiple observers. That key aspect of "objectivity" just doesn't happen. Science works in a different way.

Scientists who study gorillas don't all study the same gorilla. They each study their own gorilla, and then they compare notes, to see if their findings agree. This is the process of "replication," and replication is what makes science a collective subjective, instead of just subjective, kind of observation.

Minds can be studied the same way, if multiple observers are not necessary. As I have replicated some of Freud's and Jung's findings, so other people should be able to replicate some of my personal explorations. If similar persons were to follow a similar process, they should arrive at similar results.

In physical science there is at least the possibility of multiple viewers. You can come and see my gorilla if you don't believe me. But with mental phenomena, I could be lying about my internal states, and you would never know the difference, unless you are clairvoyant. Smart criminals fool the psychiatrists all the time, first to convince them they are insane, to escape punishment, and then to convince them they are sane, to be released from the mental institution. In the famous hearings of Clarence Thomas vs. Anita Hill, we know that one of them was a very successful liar, but we may never know which one. Lying is successful because the evidence is not perceptible to others, only hearsay.

It is as if each one of us can explore a strange country where nobody else has ever been and nobody else can ever go. It is as if each one of these strange countries was an island, and boats haven't been invented, but we all get to talk to each other on our cell phones.

Replication won't always work with lies and delusions. People can lie and share the same set of lies with other people. I can always find people who will agree with me. If I am forceful enough, I can make them agree with me, through the power of hypnotic suggestions. Thus we have many conflicting belief systems, all claiming to know "the truth."

I see two ways of dealing with this: The first way, to make sure one is not deluded or lying to oneself, is to work at psychotherapy to make one's own internal perceptions as accurate as possible. The second way is replication for liars: Pick people at random and see how much you agree on.

With gorillas, each scientist is able to observe many gorillas, whereas with minds, each scientist (in the normal case) is able to observe only one mind. They might get around that problem by training observers, as I was trained by my psychiatrist to recognize certain mental distortions like fantasies, rationalization, projection, displacement, and ulterior motives in general. Titchener and others had the right idea in training their subjects, but I think now, more than a hundred years later and with Freudian methods, science should be able to do much better.

And so I am the trained observer, presenting my one view of my one mind, for whenever science might be ready to incorporate my explorations.

I said once in a psychology paper that I had precognitive dreams, and the professor commented in the margin, "Can you prove this?"

Actually, in my explorations of my own mind, my efforts had been totally concentrated on proving things to myself, not to anyone else. I had proved many times to myself that I had precognitive dreams, but I hadn't even thought about the problems of proving such a thing to somebody else.

And what is "proof," anyway? The ultimate proof is that one has seen something for oneself. If one has not seen the phenomenon for oneself, one has a right to remain skeptical, no matter how convincing the "proof." This reminds me of a story, or maybe I should call it a "legend:"

We used to sail our boats from Provincetown to Wellfleet, to race against the Wellfleet people. It was 11 miles to the headland, and then 3 miles farther along a narrow sand spit called Jeremy Point, and then 3 miles back along the inside of Jeremy Point to where the yacht club was located. Sometimes you could actually see the water on the other side of this narrow sand spit, and it was often a fantasy that if our boats could be miraculously transported to the other side, we could save 6 miles, which in a small sailboat took at least an hour.

And then I heard the story of how three men from Provincetown, three men that I respected and trusted, had found a small channel one day and waded their boat across — well, three men also with a sense of humor. Were they spinning a tall tale for our amusement, to play on our fantasies? I trusted them, but also I was wary of being taken in, and so I remained skeptical.

And then it happened that I was sailing my boat back from Wellfleet all by myself, on a Thursday, when there was hardly anybody around. And as I started down Wellfleet Harbor, it seemed that I could see a clear opening out into the bay. I sailed over to investigate, and sure enough, there was a swiftly moving stream out into the bay. I pulled up my centerboard and was swept out into the bay, saving myself almost 6 miles. So now I knew, but other people thought I had decided to become part of the spoof, perpetuating the legend.

So the answer is no, I can't prove to another person that I have precognitive dreams. You will have to experience it for yourself. Replication is the answer.

But then if enough people have experienced precognitive dreams, and you haven't, do you have to believe it? We could all be a liars' club, or deluded in the same way, or a religion. So if you have not experienced the things I have experienced, I don't expect you to believe them. I expect you to be skeptical.

But — one last shot at the unscientific methods — if one has experienced a phenomenon, one can say with certainty that it exists, but if one has not experienced the phenomenon, one can't say with certainty that it does not exist. Ignorance is not evidence. If one is blind, that does not prove that there is no such thing as sight. Instead of making authoritarian pronouncements based upon ignorance and blindness, it would be more accurate for those members of the scientific community to say simply, "I don't know."

5. MY EXPERIENCE, AS I REMEMBER IT

I just want to do a brief review of my key mental experiences, because this is the evidence that supports my view of the mind, and it also shows the perspective from which I am viewing the various cultural institutions. If you have read *Re-Educating Myself*, you won't miss much if you skip this chapter.

BEGINNINGS

When I was four years old, I had the conviction that I had always existed. I knew that I was just a little boy, and that I was only four years old, but it seemed that I was much more than that, and had existed much longer than that.

I was six when my little sister was born. I got the news while I was at play school, and as I walked home later, I pondered the question, "How can it be that a person exists who didn't exist before?" I remembered the date and time very carefully, Thursday, June 13, 1940, at 4:30 PM, as if it were very important evidence of some cosmic event.

So I was ready with my question the following fall, on my very first day of Sunday School. The teacher was explaining the life hereafter, and I raised my hand and asked "Where was I before?"

The teacher's answer was unconvincing. It didn't fit with my conviction. (Consequently, I was never a strong believer in the Christian religion, because I learned on the very first day of Sunday School that they didn't have all the answers.)

When I got home, I asked my grandmother the same question. My grandmother, Harriet Seaver, was no ordinary grandmother. She was a student of ancient and occult and mystical teachings, as well as being an artist and a law-school graduate, among other things. She explained that the Hindus believed that we lived many lives, one after another. That made much more sense to me, and was consistent with my conviction that I had always existed. So I believed in reincarnation from that day on. She also was careful to explain that it was a Hindu belief, and not a Christian belief, and that if I wanted to believe in reincarnation, I better keep it to myself.

The question of my existence, as in "Who am I, really?" intrigued me throughout my childhood. One day when I was nine, when I had been sent to my room for being a bad boy, after I became tired of the kicking and screaming, I took advantage of the solitude and sat down on the floor and began to contemplate the question of my existence.

Suddenly there appeared to me, in some inner sense, the image of a huge "self" stretching far out into the stars and far back in time, with some degree of importance — "the big I in the sky," as I have later described it. The image flashed on my consciousness for maybe a second or two, and then it was gone. I tried to make it come back by thinking very hard, but that was all. This image reinforced my conviction that there was more to me than just this one physical life.

When I was twelve, in the eighth grade, I was first introduced to science. I welcomed scientific thinking as a relief from the religious dogma and the judgments of "good" and "bad" that came with it. With science there was no "good" and "bad" — only "true" and "false." With science I didn't have to believe things on the authority of other people — I could make my own observations, and conduct experiments, and find out for myself. With science I didn't have to be afraid of the spooks in the night, because "Scientists know there are no such things." I quickly adopted the scientific way of thinking.

As a freshman at Harvard I was first given official permission to use my own mind, to think for myself. This was the single most important influence in my life, and I want to give Harvard credit for that. I learned later in life that not everybody who went to college had been given that same permission. With my newly granted freedom to think, I had a wonderful time, for the first time, exploring the power of my mind and entering into intellectual arguments with my roommates and other friends. But as for Harvard, I soon learned that freedom to think meant freedom to think as they thought, when my original ideas expressed in papers received comments like "immature" and "far-fetched." (One of these ideas will appear later in this book. I'll identify it when I get to it.)

In 1953, when I was 19 years old, the Soviets exploded their first hydrogen bomb. Suddenly the world changed. Suddenly this powerful adversary, committed to the destruction of the United States, also had the ultimate weapon. Suddenly the technology which had given us never-ending "progress" now threatened to annihilate civilization and humanity and most of life on earth. It was a case of massive systems failure. I asked myself, "How could this have happened?"

The atomic bomb was the result of an arms race that had been going on throughout history. The side with the better weapons won wars and determined the fate of humanity. The Nazis had also been working on an atomic bomb. The Nazis were the first to develop rockets and jet planes. Where would the world be if the Nazis had developed an atomic bomb first? We were fortunate that the United States had developed it, and not our enemies. But now we were in a position where the United States and the Soviet Union could destroy themselves as well as all of humanity with their military power (and later had the power to destroy humanity many times over, as the word "overkill" was coined).

I realized that the technology was not at fault. It was the desire to use the technology for destructive purposes, and the desire to develop technology for destructive purposes, that was at fault. It was the manly virtues of fighting and warfare that were at fault — virtues which had been instilled in every boy child since before history began, and had been instilled in every girl child, insofar as she learned to respect and admire and love the men who protected her. And, most important, I realized that those virtues of fighting and warfare had been instilled in ME. The solution that came to me was "We need a whole new way of thinking."

(Einstein said essentially the same thing in 1945, but I didn't agree with him at the time, because only the United States had an atomic bomb, and what was the danger? But Einstein saw the theoretical possibility, whereas I had to wait for the practical situation to develop, in order to see it.)

I started work on the solution by starting work on myself. I decided that I would try to live my life without ever doing warfare, if that was at all possible. And by "warfare" I mean anything that is deliberately destructive to another person, physical or mental.

In 1954, at age 20, I was thinking about what I wanted to be in my adult life. My father was a businessman. He had worked hard to earn money. He had brought me up to be a businessman. But that didn't interest me. I reasoned that with the same natural abilities as my father, and the advantage of a better social position that he had given me, it would be much easier for me to make money than it was for him. Making money didn't interest me because it wasn't challenging to me. I wanted to do something "worth my sweat."

There was also another problem. With all my advantages of money and social position, I wasn't happy. This was unheard-of in America. The American Dream was to work hard and be "successful," which meant making money. Implied in that dream of "success" was the idea that it would bring happiness. But for me, the American Dream had already come true, and yet I wasn't happy. Certainly money had bought me a degree of happiness, as opposed to living in poverty, but there was more to life than that. My goal was happiness, however it might be found.

I asked myself who was the happiest person I knew, and the answer was my great-aunt, Margaret Seaver, "Tada" to me. She had a calmness and a peace of mind that I admired. It seemed that her natural abilities weren't as great as those of my parents, but where my parents had achieved success by the standards of the culture using only a fraction of their natural abilities, she used more of her potential as a human being. It made sense to me that if I were to use 90% of my potential as a human being, instead of 30%, I would be living life to a much greater degree, and therefore should be happier. So I decided that the way to happiness, or at least the way that I would try, was to develop my human potential as much as possible.

If my parents had achieved success by the standards of the culture by using only a small part of their human potential, I realized that in developing my human potential I would have to go beyond the standards of the culture, and probably beyond the ability of the culture even to judge. Instead of being somebody admired or venerated, I might just become some kind of "fabulous freak."

(Well, the hippies have since appropriated the word "freak" to mean somebody who conformed to their group norms, so let's just say I imagined I would become "strange" or "weird" in the eyes of the culture.)

In April 1955, I studied "The Waste Land" by T.S. Eliot, ostensibly to write a paper on some academic subject. but really to answer a question of my own. "The Waste Land" had been presented to me in two separate English courses as THE example of twentieth century literature, and yet it was apparent madness. We weren't expected to understand it, and we were told "This won't be on the exam."

But I wanted to understand it. I wanted to understand why this was the most famous poem of the twentieth century, if it was apparent madness.

It was depressing. The more I studied it, the more depressed I became. I didn't know why it made me so depressed. I had to find a good movie now and then, to take my mind off it.

I could see the references to death and desolation. I could see in it snatches of twentieth-century life, and what I had to look forward to. I could see the people waiting at railroad stations for endless commutes to boring jobs with companies they didn't care about.

And then one day I saw why it was so depressing: "The Waste Land" was my world. I was living it — the artificiality, the lack of values, and my friend who was very rich and very much bored with everything.

An old civilization had crumbled, leaving twentieth-century Western people stumbling around among the broken images. Nietzsche had recognized it when he announced "God is dead." T.S. Eliot had portrayed it brilliantly and artistically in "The Waste Land." The poem was an instant smash hit in 1922. People talked about it in their seminars and soirees. And obviously they hadn't done anything about the problem it portrayed, because I was seeing the same Waste Land in 1955. I vowed that I would do something to solve the problem, now that I was aware of it.

The religious beliefs, which had once been the source of all our values, had collapsed, leaving twentieth-century Western humanity stumbling amid the rubble of broken images.

What we needed was a new civilization. We needed new values, new beliefs, new ideals, new goals, a new standard of living, a new way of thinking, and a new way of life, and "new civilization" was the best expression I could think of to mean all these things. A civilization was not just buildings and cities and large numbers of people. A civilization, I could see, was based on a set of ideas that determined how people thought, how they lived, and what they built. We needed a whole new set of fundamental ideas.

I turned to T.S. Eliot in "The Waste Land," because he had given me such good insights into the problem, to see if he had any solutions, but all he said was:

Shall I at least set my lands in order?

That wasn't the answer. My lands were in order. It was the world that was a mess. But the more I thought about it, the more I realized that it was the way to go. I didn't have the power to change the world, or even one other person, if they didn't want to be changed, but I did have the power to change myself. Gradually I came to realize that the civilization was something that had been programmed into my own head as a representative product of the

American upper middle class. As I changed the programming in my own head, I was becoming a new civilization.

And so, in 1955, at age 21, I turned my back on the culture and set out to design a new civilization. The culture was represented by the six million books in Widener Library at Harvard, and I symbolically turned my back on all those books and their contents. I wanted to figure it all out for myself, from the beginning.

The first question I asked myself was whether I could use logic. By "logic," I mean not only formal logic, but also all of mathematics, and the ability to reason. I decided that I had to use logic. If what was true could also be false, then I wouldn't be able to know anything.

Along with logic, I decided to accept, as a foundation for my civilization, anything that had been proven by science — not scientific theories, and not authoritative statements by prominent scientists, but only what had been proven, in my opinion, by the scientific method.

"In my opinion" is important here. I realized that my own mind was the ultimate authority to decide what to believe. And as for "authorities," it didn't matter who said it, whether it was Darwin, Freud, or Einstein.

I wanted to build my new civilization on truth, not lies, so I became dedicated to the truth. As people scoffed at my ambition to find the truth, I became more determined. As I formulated it, "I don't care what I believe, as long as it is true." I became as ruthless in my pursuit of truth as some people are in the pursuit of money. I didn't care who I hurt, especially myself, in my pursuit of truth.

I realized I would have to look for truths from among the "wrong" things, or those things that the culture considered wrong, because if I built my civilization from all the "right" things, I would end up with the same civilization all over again.

At one point I was contemplating suicide, not really seriously, but as an intellectual choice that had to be made. I decided that it would be a waste just to throw my life away. If I was willing to die, then I should be willing to die (or undergo any lesser humiliation) in pursuit of my goals. That would give me an enormous amount of power that I wouldn't otherwise have. I decided that I would find a new way of life, or die in the attempt. I became a fanatic on a suicide mission.

If I was dedicated to the truth, then I certainly had to get rid of the bias created by my religious beliefs. They weren't strong beliefs, but still I had this notion of a God and reincarnation. As a scientist, I had learned to believe on the basis of evidence. So why did I believe in this invisible God on the basis of hearsay of what people claimed to have experienced thousands of years ago? The Bible was not evidence; the Bible was legend. But then there was this superstitious fear that I should not offend God by questioning His existence. I imagined that whatever my father would do to me if I said I didn't believe in God, God would do to me many times worse. But I dared to allow myself the fullness of the thought, "God does not exist," and no thunderbolt came. I experienced a great feeling of relief. I was free. Either there was no God, or if there was, God had given me free will to think anything that I wanted to, even to deny the existence of God.

This was my proof of free will. Whether or not there was a God, I was free, on this earth, to experiment with life any way I chose — subject, of course, to natural laws, legal laws, and social laws. But there were no moral laws imposed on me by a jealous God, an angry God, a petty God, or a Puritan God. If there was a God, I adopted the Hebrew idea of JHVH — God the unpronounceable and therefore the unknowable, beyond my capacity to think or imagine.

I never became an atheist, but only an agnostic. I truly didn't know. As a scientist, I formulated the working hypothesis: "I'll believe in God when I see God."

I asked myself, "Who am I to be designing a new civilization? What are my qualifications?"

First of all, I felt uniquely qualified because I was the only one who seemed to recognize the need for a new civilization. The generation who first read "The Waste Land" had done nothing. People I talked to about it at Harvard just gave me blank stares. Somebody had to start somewhere and do something.

Beyond that, what were my abilities for this job? Of course there was no education within the existing civilization that would train a person to design a new civilization, so it boiled down to raw mental ability. Maybe I was the smartest kid in Taunton, Massachusetts, but at Harvard it seemed I was about average.

I wouldn't even be using my greatest talents. My greatest talents were in math and science. But with those abilities all I could see was creating more of the same — dishwashers, television sets, nuclear bombs. It just didn't interest me. The idea of creating a new civilization interested me, even though I realized I might not be very good at it.

I was pondering these questions when I applied for Navy Officer Candidate School (OCS) in the spring of 1956, my senior year. I took their physical and mental exams, and about a week later I received a phone call from Navy Headquarters in Boston:

"Can you come down here right away?"

"Sure."

When I arrived at the office, there were three Naval officers, just sitting around. The man behind the desk said, "We just wanted to see what you looked like. You got the highest score we have ever seen on the Mental Test."

This was in competition with students from Harvard and MIT and all the colleges in the Boston area. This was all I needed to convince me that I was the person to be designing a new civilization.

Of course the test was biased in my favor. In addition to the usual mathematical and verbal sections, there was a "mechanical" section, which tested one's knowledge of boats and the maintenance of boats. I had been involved with boats every summer of my life. I had had summer jobs working on boats, and I had worked in a boatyard. So of course I got a perfect score on that part of the test, and beat out people who were more intelligent than I was. But I didn't think about that at the time. I just took the encouragement that I wanted to hear, and went with it.

That wasn't the only thing I learned from Navy OCS. I passed the dreaded physical exam, which had been the downfall of many, even star athletes. I was qualified, they said, to do anything in the Navy, from flying jets to Naval Intelligence. But on the medical history questionnaire, I checked "Yes" to "Are you often depressed?" and "Do you have frequent or terrifying nightmares?" So they sent me to a psychiatrist for further evaluation. I read the psychiatrist's report. He said that I had a "mild chronic anxiety" condition, but that that would not interfere with my performance of duties as a Naval officer. (Friends of mine commented that a little bit of anxiety was just what the Navy wanted in a junior officer.) But the Navy used this as a reason to reject me when the class was oversubscribed.

Here was proof, in the real world, of a deficiency that I had. I had been turned down for a job for which I was otherwise very highly qualified, because of my psychological condition. I thought of this as a necessary part of my education that was missing. I had been educated intellectually, and now I needed to be educated psychologically. With that thought, I decided that I needed psychotherapy. But those were the days of Eisenhower's Universal Military Training, and I had to serve my time in the Army first.

There were other reasons why I felt I needed psychotherapy. My mind was like a wild horse, with a will of its own. Sometimes it caused me to succeed, and sometimes it caused me to fail, with no regard for what I consciously wanted to do. Also my love-life was disastrous. I just couldn't see myself in the role of husband and Daddy. I still wanted to be a child, playing games and shooting water-pistols.

In the Army I did a great deal of reading, mostly in psychology, and I tried to psychoanalyze myself. But as I absorbed more and more information, and thought about my problems more and more, I just kept going around in bigger and bigger circles. I realized I needed the help of another person to keep me going in a straight line.

While I was in the Army, I was contacting various universities, thinking I might go back to school and get a PhD in psychology. But a friend of mine, a psychology major, gave me a bit of wisdom. He said that most people who study psychology are really trying to find out what makes themselves tick. What they really should be doing is going to a psychiatrist. With that bit of wisdom, I chose psychotherapy over the PhD in psychology.

While I was in the Army, my grandmother fell and broke her hip, and was confined to a bed for nine months. Once the hip was mended, she was able to get up, but it seemed that she just didn't want to. I empathized with her. I compared her time confined in bed to my time confined in the Army. The only difference was that at 23 I had a whole life to look forward to, whereas at 83, what did she have to look forward to?

Still, I tried to write encouraging letters to her, and when I came home, I would make pancakes for her, which were about the only thing she would eat.

She had reached a state where she just lay in bed all day, and hardly spoke to anybody, and if she did, she just mumbled incoherently.

And then one weekend when I came home, she sat upright in a chair and carried on a discussion of philosophy with me for an hour and a half, as intelligent and profound and lucid a conversation as there ever was. And when it was all over, she said, "I'm surprised you know all these things already." I was surprised, too. We were discussing things I hadn't known before.

That was the last time I saw her alive. I felt that in that last conversation my grandmother had given me, by direct mental communication, her most valuable possession — her knowledge of philosophy.

As my grandmother's condition deteriorated, I was in empathy with her. Easter weekend I was very depressed. On Monday morning I had a hard time getting out of bed — I couldn't seem to move my legs. On Tuesday morning it was worse. I had to ask a buddy to pick up my feet and place them on the floor. At lunch time I was totally exhausted. I had a quick lunch and lay down on my bunk to take a nap, and had the following dream:

Sort of family gathering, dark hall, waiting for dinner — like Thanksgiving, except Friday after Easter. Many unidentified relatives, uncles, men, waiting to enter door.

My grandmother and Tada are sitting next to each other at the table in the dining room in Taunton. My grandmother mentioning old relatives, says she wants to go to Louisiana or visit Aunt Louisa.

Tada replies, "You know Aunt Louisa is - - - -," omitting mention of death. My grandmother gets up and leaves the table. Now she is a skinny little twelve-year-old, running very fast. She is going out the back entrance, stucco walls, like Uncle Ed's house. I get up and start to chase her, but she is out of sight already. My father from behind me calls, "Don't go on a marathon, Bob." Then I am on a city street with a crowd of people coming the other way, most of them under 30. I nearly collide with a thirtyish young man in a brown suit. Then I notice my grandmother coming out the cellar door which was the maids' quarters, saying, "The dinner is ready. Everything will be all right," (or something like that) at which point she returns to the table, looking thirtyish and dressed in Victorian costume of the early century — hair reddish brown, eyes blue, and slightly more plump.

Quick scene shift from dining room to front of house, saw young kid with man's face, dressed in black cowboy hat, red shirt, blue jeans, with six-guns. He had a Russian name, came from Wellfleet. I sensed him as a competitor.

I woke up from the dream totally refreshed, after having slept only about 15 minutes.

It was obvious to me that the dream was about my grandmother's death, with my father's voice behind me telling me not to try to follow her, but to get on with the business of life, as a young man in the world. But all I knew about dream-interpretation at the time was Freudian wish-fulfillment: I wished she would die? We all wished she would die? She, herself, wanted to die? None of this seemed to fit the dream. After struggling with it for a while, I had to get back to work.

When I walked into the office, my boss said, "There's a telegram for you at the Message Center, Bob."

The hair stood up on the back of my neck. My grandmother HAD died. The funeral service would be on Friday, the Friday after Easter. As it turned out, it was held in the dining room, an unlikely place, but the easiest place for the funeral director to set up the chairs. The dream had conveyed that message to me, faster than Western Union. I couldn't have received the news the night before, because she died at 9 AM. The earliest opportunity to have had the dream was during my lunch hour.

I go into the whole argument of "coincidence" in *Re-Educating Myself*, and I'm not going to repeat it here. Basically the "coincidence" argument is based on the false certainty that such things couldn't possibly happen, and therefore the slightest probability of coincidence is more likely than a probability of zero.

This message had been conveyed to me a distance of about 350 miles, from Taunton, Massachusetts to Frederick, Maryland, past the radio interference of New York, Philadelphia, Baltimore, and other cities of the Northeast Corridor. I thought of it at the time as like a radio message that my grandmother had transmitted at the time of her death, or my whole family was transmitting to me. But a radio message needs a certain wattage to be broadcast a certain number of miles in the daytime, and I am sure that my family, with all their mental effort, could not have generated that amount of wattage. This message defied all the laws of physics I had learned at Harvard. It was my first real evidence of a non-physical reality.

PSYCHOTHERAPY

I was planning to go to New York after I got out of the Army, to share an apartment with a friend, and find a good psychiatrist. Before any of that happened, I had the following dream:

I was arriving in New York at Grand Central Station. The psychiatrist was there to meet me. He was shorter than I was, with graying hair. He held out his hand to shake my hand. When I shook his hand, he held me in an iron grip and threw me down on one of the stone benches and began unscrewing my navel with a screwdriver, causing me enormous pain.

When I met the psychiatrist, in reality, he was a man considerably shorter than myself, with graying hair, and his greeting was always to hold out his hand to shake my hand. When I told him about the dream, and said I thought it was prophetic, he said I was probably dreaming about my father. I didn't press the issue, since it didn't affect my treatment in any way. But for me, this was one more instance of a phenomenon my Harvard education couldn't explain — a dream of the future.

One day shortly after I began therapy, I was sitting at home alone, trying to find my real self. And suddenly I realized that my real self, the self I identified with, was my four-year-old self. My psychological growth had been arrested at age four. My life since then had been an act, trying to play the twelve-year-old, the eighteen-year-old, and the twenty-four-year-old, making up the kind of lines that I thought my contemporaries would say, and then reciting them. The farther I was removed from four years old, the more uncomfortable it became. So of course I was very uncomfortable at age 24, looking for a job as a grown man in New York City, and trying to have relationships with grown women.

My friends wanted to know what kind of "method" my psychiatrist was using. I didn't particularly care. When I asked him, he said, "Let's just call it 'treatment.'" That was OK with me. My understanding was that he didn't want to distract from the treatment by getting into an intellectual discussion of what the method was. This is just one of the many ways people have of avoiding therapy.

Basically I lay on a couch and talked to the ceiling for 50 minutes. He sat behind my head. He participated actively in the discussion, sometimes arguing his point strenuously.

He had me write down my dreams, and hand them in to him, like some kind of homework, and we discussed them. If I hadn't brought him a dream in a while, he would complain. So he played a very active role in this "treatment."

Lying on a couch may be thought of as outdated, but for me it was very important — first of all in revealing things about myself that I really didn't want to be saying TO another person. (I remember one day thinking, "Do I want him to hear this?" and then realizing that I didn't care whether he heard it, but I didn't really want to admit it to MYSELF. That was when I was well on my way to a cure.)

But also, for me, looking at another person is a major distraction. I can't concentrate on my own thoughts looking another person in the eye. It is as if that person's mental process is interfering with mine. In order to see my deepest thoughts and express my deepest thoughts, I have to look away.

My psychiatrist trained me to be an observer of myself, both physical actions and mental processes. In the early sessions, he would ask me to tell him everything I had done that day, and everything I had thought, in detail. This drill went on for a long time, and the disciplines continued throughout therapy. The specifics were important, as opposed to generalizations. For example, if I didn't like somebody, then exactly what did that somebody do and say, and exactly what was my response, physical, mental, and emotional? Proving my case to him was like proving something in court. I really had to have the evidence.

I know that all the defense mechanisms are real, because I used all of them, and my psychiatrist pointed them out to me as I was using them. He made me see that my intelligence was actually a hindrance to therapy, in a way, because it enabled me to invent more clever rationalizations and avoidance tactics.

Not everybody succeeds at psychotherapy. For that, I give major credit to my psychiatrist, who was very good and had a reputation for success. But also I brought some things to the process, mainly that I had already experienced the process of looking inward when I studied "The Waste Land."

Studying "The Waste Land" was the most difficult thing I had ever done at the time — difficult because in order to understand the poem and understand why it made me so depressed, I had to be able to see myself. I had been trained to look outward at external things, but not inward at myself. It was as difficult as trying to focus on the tip of my nose. I finally succeeded by imagining my mind as looking down from "on high" at myself, as a person struggling with the problems of life "down there." This isn't out-of-body travel. This is just being able to remove the mind, for a moment, from identification with the self, to be able to look at that self with some perspective.

Also I brought to therapy a talent for solving problems. The case histories I had read always seemed to emphasize how the brilliant analyst had solved the problem. But that isn't how psychotherapy works. In order to succeed at psychotherapy, the client has to solve the problem. The client has all the information, buried somewhere. The client has the entanglement in his/her head that has to be unraveled. All the therapist can do is apply certain general rules of behavior to guide the client. Even if the therapist does see the brilliant solution, if the therapist tries to communicate it before the client is ready to accept it, the client's defenses will reject it. I think one of the reasons that psychotherapy sometimes fails is because the therapist is trying to take credit for solving the problem, and the client resents it.

I spent hours at home pondering the problems, unraveling, unraveling. Sometimes I would come home from a session and spend hours sitting in the dark before I even felt like eating dinner.

I also brought to therapy an attitude: I always looked for the ulterior motive in whatever I did or wanted to do. I always looked for the fault in myself, no matter how glaring the fault in the other person.

My friends told me, "Everything is part of the treatment." That was a valuable insight. Every interaction with the therapist is part of the treatment, whether the therapist is giving you bad advice, or you are angry at the therapist for something, or whatever. Even the bill is part of the treatment. If you have to pay two days' salary out of your week's wages, you take it more seriously than if somebody else was paying for it.

People also told me, "You have to trust the psychiatrist." I don't know what they meant by that. Maybe they just meant I had to be able to tell him everything. But beyond that, I never trusted the psychiatrist. He had too much power over me — power to destroy my mind as well as to fix it.

Sometimes I think he gave me wrong advice deliberately. One time when I had a serious date with a girlfriend, he became the voice of the Establishment, telling me that if I was a mature person I would take her out to the movies, and open the car door for her, and so forth. So I did all that stuff, and neither of us had a very good time. I realized that this just wasn't my style — not the person I really was, and not the person she enjoyed being with. This was a very strong lesson to me, and it helped me discover who I really was, in the face of this "voice of authority." When I asserted my real self and my real feelings, he backed down from his authoritarian position. Everything is part of the treatment.

I was under the impression, from reading Freud's and others' accounts of case histories, that psychological problems were caused by one crippling traumatic experience. But actually in my case there were several traumatic experiences. I would say they were all within the normal range of what children experience at an early age. When people asked me "Why did you have to go to a psychiatrist?" I would answer "Because I grew up in the United States."

I'm not going to talk about my specific traumatic experiences here. I am just going to give you some broad generalities.

First of all, the experience doesn't have to be obviously traumatic to an adult observer. The way the child perceives it or misunderstands it can also make it traumatic.

Working mothers beware: Children who are dumped off at day care can get the idea that they aren't wanted or loved by their mothers. You need to let them know they are loved, and try to make them understand, as well as possible, why you can't be with them all the day.

Not all parents are psychologically adults. As I discovered my "real self" at age four, other adults have had their psychological growth arrested at some age of childhood. When the child reaches that age, and discovers that he/she is outgrowing a parent, that is traumatic. I would say that it is almost a certainty that the child's psychological growth will be arrested at that same age.

Even some things that are thought to be beneficial for the child can be traumatic, as, for example, attempts to teach the child morality. The child is told that he/she should share his/her toys. The child doesn't want to, or doesn't feel like it, and from this gets the feeling that his/her real self is "bad" or somehow inadequate. This is another reason why children abandon their real selves in favor of an artificial self.

Children are criticized or punished just for being children. Given time, if allowed to grow naturally, they will grow into adults.

In therapy, I opened up mental abilities I never knew I had. I had never thought of myself as a "creative" person, but I needed creativity on my first computer project. This was a huge project, enormously difficult, calling for original solutions in an area I had never dealt with before. I remember having long dreams at night where I was the computer, iterating and iterating, trying to reach a solution. The demands of my job helped very much to open up my creativity.

Before therapy, I wasn't able to write an original song. It just seemed, mathematically, that there weren't that many combinations of 7 notes, and that they all must have been covered already. But as I developed my creative ability in therapy, I was able to write original songs, many of them. I had become "a creative person."

Another mental ability that emerged in therapy was intuition. I was in the middle of a strenuous argument one day with my psychiatrist when suddenly I "saw" what he was trying to say. It all flashed on my mind, instantly, like a picture before my eyes. He was still arguing strenuously, and I was saying, "Wait! Stop! I see! I see!"

This ability to see the picture or pattern that fit all the particulars helped me later on in interpreting my own dreams.

A third mental attribute that emerged from my subconscious in psychotherapy was my will. The reason my mind had seemed like a wild horse with a will of its own was because my real will was buried in the subconscious. What I consciously thought I wanted, or should want, was not my real will. And when my real will emerged from my subconscious I could see that it was quite different from what people had told me I should want. When this will buried in the subconscious caused me to fail, it was like the French in World War II sinking their own ships so that the Nazis couldn't have them. My real will was keeping me from using my energies for the wrong purposes.

In addition to making me more conscious, or more aware, therapy also developed my ability to differentiate, or know the difference. People who are underdeveloped psychologically tend to think in broad generalities, as in racial stereotypes. As one becomes better able to differentiate, these broad generalities are replaced with a more accurate understanding.

Every month when I received the bill from my psychiatrist, I asked myself, "What have I gained THIS MONTH (not last month or last year) that is worth this much money?" And each month there were levels of improvement I had reached that were worth many times the money.

After three and a half years, the psychiatrist told me I was OK — I could stop treatment any time I wanted to. But I still felt dependent on him and stayed on for another year, until my company moved me to California. I did feel OK, and more like an adult, but I wasn't entirely satisfied. There still seemed to be something missing.

In California I had a stressful experience with a woman who called me a "wimp." I wanted to see the psychiatrist, but since he wasn't available, I sat myself down in a comfortable chair and asked myself what the psychiatrist would have said. And I found that I had learned enough about the disciplines and the kinds of things to look for, so that I could play psychiatrist for myself and resolve these difficult situations.

And so, once launched in a positive direction by a competent therapist, my psychotherapy continued on its own as long as I was motivated to actively pursue it. A couple of methods available to me were dream analysis and something I call "scribbling."

"Scribbling" I learned in a management course I took in the Army, as a brainstorming technique. You just write down as fast as you can whatever comes to mind, without caring about grammar, spelling, punctuation, or literary style, and with the understanding that nobody else is ever going to read it. This may or may not be what is now called "journaling."

"Scribbling" was useful to me in the Army, where I had nobody to tell my troubles to. I didn't feel that it was fair to dump my misery on my Army buddies, who had the same troubles I did, or to burden somebody outside, like a girlfriend, so I just dumped my problems onto a piece of paper. One morning, I remember, I just started off writing "Shit Shit Shit Shit ..." until I got tired of writing the word "Shit," and beneath the shit something more profound emerged.

The word "Shit" is appropriate, because scribbling is like a mind-dump that keeps the thoughts flowing and prevents mental constipation. Just thinking the thoughts isn't enough. It is the act of writing them down on paper that gets them out and lets one move on to something else. I have used scribbling to help me design complex software systems, resolve confusion, relieve stress, and help me get to sleep at night, as well as to work on my psychological development.

Many times psychotherapy was frightening, painful, or humiliating. Many times I had to move into the face of fear. Many times I had to remind myself that if I was willing to die, I should be able to face any lesser pain or humiliation. And each time that I was able to resolve something painful, I removed that much pain from my system, and moved that much closer to happiness.

WITHDRAWAL

In 1964, I dropped out of computer programming and returned to Provincetown, which had been my family summer home, ostensibly to write my philosophy, but actually I was building a philosophy, independent of what I had read in books. In the solitude of Cape Cod winters, I discovered what Toynbee called "withdrawal" (Toynbee, 1957, Vol. 1, page 256). Freed from the constant chatter of cultural ideas, I could literally hear myself think. My mind was able to see things for itself. My own original thoughts began to emerge. They seemed weird at first, but then they became more familiar.

Thoreau experienced withdrawal on the shores of Walden Pond. Isaac Newton experienced withdrawal when he lived on a family farm for a year or so, to escape The Plague in London. It was there that he observed the falling apple and formulated the Law of Gravity.

I recognize the mental environment, the environment of other people's thoughts, because I have experienced this separation from it.

DREAM ANALYSIS

In December 1966, with the help of my nine-pound dictionary, I read *The Basic Writings of C.G. Jung.* I asked myself what evidence did Jung have to support his ideas about archetypes and other things. And it seemed that his evidence was from dreams. So I set out to study my dreams, in search of archetypes.

But the dreams had another purpose in mind. They were picking up where the psychiatrist had left off, with my psychological growth.

I had a dream that portrayed me as being psychologically ten years old. It also showed me that psychological-age-ten was normal for the culture. At the same time, in real life, there were some ten-year-old boys that wanted to play with me. That was very convincing.

This was all a surprise to me. I had thought, when I finished therapy, and the psychiatrist told me it was OK to quit, that I had become psychologically an adult. At least I felt comfortable as an adult. But the psychiatrist, in pronouncing me "OK," only meant I was normal for the culture, as opposed to being subnormal. What the dreams were now telling me was that the normal person in the culture was not psychologically an adult, but was psychologically ten years old.

Suddenly this is not just about me, but about the whole culture. And it isn't very flattering. Knowing something, as I do, about psychological defenses, I wouldn't expect this is the kind of thing that most people would want to believe. So I would expect this discovery of mine to be invisible to most people. But one of the most gifted people I have ever known immediately recognized her real self as her eleven-year-old self. And I know that there are other gifted people like her who will recognize that the "self" they identify with is a childhood "self."

The other way of looking at it, which is more flattering, is to say that the normal adult has managed to succeed in life using only a fraction of their potential as a human being, namely the level of psychological development they had at age ten, or thereabouts. One's level of psychological development becomes a measure of

how much of one's potential one is using, and if one isn't totally
satisfied with one's life, then here is hope for improvement.

And so it was with me. I felt that I had never lived up to my
potential in my relationships with women. I immediately recognized
that psychological-age-ten was still not yet the psychological age of
puberty, which I imagined was psychological-age-14. If I could
reach the psychological age of puberty, I hoped, my relationships
with women would improve. This then became my goal, and I was
motivated to work hard at it.

*I dreamed that the first three letters of "superman" were
"S-E-X."*

Well, obviously they aren't, and after wrestling a while with S =
sex, U = uterus, P = penis, I realized of course that S-E-X referred to
reaching this psychological age of puberty.

The man who thinks he is a man but is really still psychologically
a child imagines that he must become "superman" to realize his
potential as a man. Really all he has to do is become a man,
psychologically. This drive to become "superman" explains many of
the excesses in the world.

I spent that winter, except for a two-week break at Christmas,
totally immersed in analyzing my own dreams, 24 hours a day, 7
days a week. In my sleeping hours I would dream, and in my waking
hours I would analyze.

I asked myself what would happen if my interpretations of my
own dreams were wrong? Would I drift off into some never-never
land where I was far removed from the reality? Would I make
myself crazy?

The dreams themselves answered these questions. After a series
of dreams with male erotic images, I was thinking that I was really a
homosexual. I was adjusting myself mentally to life as a
homosexual, which of course was no problem in Provincetown.
Then I had the following dream:

A beautiful woman is lying on a couch naked, absolutely drooling with desire for me. As I start towards her, suddenly I am in a car full of boys — teenagers or homosexuals — driving around town and having a wonderful time. But all I want to do is get out of that car and back to that woman. Finally, with a supreme lunge, I get out of the car — and wake up.

It was such a powerful dream that for a week afterward I was trying to get back into that dream and back to that woman. There has never been any question in my mind, ever since, as to my sexual orientation. There has never been any anxiety, either, about what would happen if my interpretations of my dreams were wrong.

Carl Jung described dreams as a correction to, or compensation for, the conscious attitude. Taken one step further, if the interpretation of a dream becomes part of the conscious attitude, then the dreams can correct or compensate for that, too. It is a self-steering process, like the self-steering mechanisms on ocean-going yachts, exerting the forces necessary to keep them on course: If my interpretation of a dream is wrong, future dreams will correct me. And the farther off course I am, the more powerful will be the correction.

I presented a paper on "The Self-Steering Process" at the annual conference of the Association for the Study of Dreams (ASD) in 1991, and other dreamworkers reported having experienced the phenomenon in their own work. So I can claim some universality for the process.

The question arose, how does this help when one person is interpreting another person's dream? And the answer was that the correction then was in the dreams of the person doing the interpreting.

If the dreams can bring you back on "course," then what is this "course," and who is charting it? I just thought of it as the subconscious mind, which has far greater wisdom than the conscious. But a Catholic priest I was talking to at the dream conference raised the question of whether this voice of truth that is correcting me and charting my course might be God. This, I think, is the view put forth by Swedenborg a couple of centuries ago. Well, it might be God, and it might not be. I really don't know. All I know is that the process operates.

I had thought of myself as intelligent before this dream winter, but this mind that was giving me an education from my dreams was many times more intelligent and wiser than my conscious mind. And if I didn't understand the message the first time, this mind would break it down into simpler and simpler little pieces, until it was simple enough for my conscious mind to understand it.

The question has been asked, "Who psychoanalyzed Freud?" With the self-steering process, I didn't have to worry about answering that question for myself. Here was a natural process, just waiting to happen — a deeper resource, just waiting to be tapped. All I had to do was take advantage of it.

As for Freud, he spent a couple of years analyzing his own dreams. I am surprised that he never discovered the self-steering process. Or maybe some scholar will discover that he did.

On March 11, 2004, in between the writing and the typing of this chapter, I learned that Carl Jung knew about the self-steering process and presented it in a paper in 1931. This doesn't change anything I have already said, but only adds Jung's support to it:

> ... An obscure dream, taken in isolation, can hardly ever be interpreted with any certainty. ... A relative degree of certainty is reached only in the interpretation of a series of dreams, where the later dreams correct the mistakes we have made in handling those that went before. Also, the basic ideas and themes can be recognized much better in a dream-series, and I therefore urge my patients to keep a careful record of their dreams and of the interpretations given. ... At a later stage I get them to work out the interpretation as well. In this way the patient learns how to deal correctly with his unconscious without the doctor's help.
>
> (Jung, 1983, pages 178-9)
> (quoted by Bogart, 2004, page 38)

Why do we dream in symbols? One of the reasons, I discovered, is because there are no words in the language to describe what the dream is trying to say. For example, for me there was the "moose principle." The moose didn't attack me, and yet the moose didn't get out of the way for me, either, when I was coming up the trail. The moose was an image of masculinity that was being taught to me, strength without aggression, an image that the culture didn't have. Hunters think of the moose as stupid, because it will just stand there and let itself be shot. But as a symbol of courage and strength without aggression, it was perfect.

The dreams had to teach me through symbols what love was, because the word "love" had been so corrupted by our culture. "Love" was something you fell in. "Love" was something everybody knew was good, so they all claimed to love. "Love" was a word people used to manipulate me, as in "I love you (therefore, implied, you are obligated to love me)." And I had learned, in an early childhood traumatic experience, that love was weakness and hate was power.

The symbol for love in my dreams was light, and darkness symbolized the absence of love. But it wasn't as simple as that. I had a great many dreams illustrating the power of love, interspersed with many other things I had to learn, starting with the combat lessons. As was appropriate for a ten-year-old boy, I was in the wilderness with wild animals, like lions and bears and wolves, that threatened to kill me, and usually did. And then there was the white wolf, that could kill me if he wanted to, but seemed to want to be my friend.

Then there was a dream where I was in the jungle in total darkness and a lion brushed against my leg. And instead of panicking, I said "Oh you poor thing, all alone in the dark." And immediately the sun came out. I was learning to love, and the love that I was being taught was something that has been called "compassion."

For something that has been characterized as a simple clearing-out of one's memories, my dreams presented many marvelous theatrical productions. The best of them are described in *Re-Educating Myself*, which gives a more complete representation of the many facets covered by my dream education. But this one dream, which is my favorite, illustrates the power of love:

In a modern building with glass doors, like a post office or bank. The manager is giving a lecture on violence, gives a trivial example, then one slightly larger, then looks out and says "Here they come!" as Pancho Villa and his 400 outlaws ride into town. There are four of us to defend the place — the manager, a child, myself, and an old cop with a crutch, asleep.

The bandit chief comes in, pointing his gun at me, giving me orders. I pull out a pack of cigarettes as I am trying to decide what to do. He says to the manager, "I'll have a 'querenda,'" meaning a cigarette. The cop, now awake in his chair, also asks for a cigarette. I toss one to the cop, and the bandit, lunging to intercept it, throws his gun across the room, so that now I am closer to the gun than he is. I start for the gun, and he starts out the door. I stop — the gun is now unnecessary. He and his outlaw band ride out of town. We are safe.

Not knowing Spanish, I thought "querenda" meant "cigarette." But then I recalled that in Latin, "querenda" meant "Having been asked." Here was the tiniest gesture of love — having been asked if you wanted a cigarette. The outlaw leader with all his power couldn't get that tiniest bit of love — and love is something we all want. So in his frustration and desperation he is throwing away his gun — his power — in an effort to get that tiniest bit of love.

I experienced many of Carl Jung's archetypes, sometimes with a personal twist that was more important to me than the archetype. For example, the "great mother" became my own great-aunt, Tada. But my main interest in my dream education was reaching the psychological age of puberty. After I had learned enough of the combat lessons and the various other lessons, and learned that "love" meant "compassion," and learned enough of the power of love to know that love was more powerful than hate, I was ready for the initiation:

It was my first day in the Coast Guard. The waters had risen, burying man, woman, and child under 120 feet of water. It was my job to go out in a very small dinghy and mark the spot, so that other people could rescue them. There were huge 14-foot sharks in the water, and it was almost certain death to go out in such a tiny boat. There were larger boats, but I hadn't earned the right to use them. I was to be married that afternoon to the beautiful young woman I had met in the supermarket the day before. I didn't want to die, when suddenly I had so much to live for. Two older Coast Guard men stood patiently holding the boat for me, waiting for me to make my decision. As I stepped into the boat, I woke up with a jolt.

I was never so glad to be alive as when I woke up from that dream. I walked across to the ocean, to where the dream had taken place, and the water seemed bluer, and the sun seemed sunnier, than ever before.

The number 14 represented psychological-age-14. This was the test, to see if I had reached the psychological age of puberty — to see if I was willing to sacrifice my life for the sake of man, woman, and child — not for the glory of being the hero and rescuing them, but only to mark the spot, so that others could rescue them.

The psychological age of puberty was a major transition point in my life — a point where "human nature" itself changed, where the dominant self-interest or drive for self-preservation of the child gave way to an equally natural drive or desire to give and share with others, including the willingness to sacrifice my life for others, a point where the meaning of "love" changed from "passion," as in "I love sex," to "compassion," as in "I love humanity."

It makes sense, in terms of survival of the species, that the child should be interested predominantly in his/her own preservation, but that as the child reaches puberty and is able to have children of his/her own, that drive should be modified to include the willingness to sacrifice oneself for the sake of the survival of one's children.

Nobody else that I know of has identified this transition point, but I believe it is universal, either as a point already reached, or as a potential. The vast majority of people haven't reached it, and those who have reached it naturally I think just take it for granted and wonder why everybody isn't like them.

The psychological age of puberty gave me the answer to my search for a new civilization. The American system of having people compete in their own self-interest works because it matches the level of psychological development of the normal person. More altruistic systems like socialism fail because most people aren't psychologically motivated to live at that level of giving and sharing. If a majority of people were to reach the psychological age of puberty, we would see an end to the greed and warfare that now threaten to destroy us. The world would be changed profoundly. We would have a new civilization far surpassing anything we have ever seen.

As the dreams were showing me the meaning of "love" and bringing me closer to the psychological age of puberty, they were also introducing me to the spiritual:

Resurrecting the wreck of a great ship, with 5 out of 7 masts still intact — steering it out into the harbor, half sunk, it travels erratically in a big "S." Anchoring by the fish weirs, on the wrong side of the harbor. Somebody is announcing, as in a weather report, "Wind shifting around to west, through south." I am thinking "north" as a cold, clear breeze comes from the south.

Sailing around Race Point (coming IN, not OUT), we have just passed through a strait between high mountains, sheer cliffs. The sea is deep, calm, peaceful, blue-green. Looking back, in a niche in the rocks, is a great statue — huge white horse and man dismounted. Few have seen it, because few pass this way.

Now sailing the ship over country roads, watching out that the masts don't hit electric lines, avoiding them ...

The large "S" was signaling "soul" or "spirit." The opposites — things in reverse, like the weirs on the wrong side of the harbor, and the north wind coming from the south, and sailing out of the harbor in a direction that would take us in — all were characteristic of a spiritual dream, as I learned over time, as if signaling that this is the opposite of physical reality, a different aspect of the universe. Also this ship that travels equally well over land and sea is obviously not anything physical. And as we sail through the straits into another ocean, again, we are passing into another aspect of reality.

The large white horse was where the Race Point Coast Guard Station stands, a large white building. Instead of the usual military hero on a white horse, whose job was killing people, here was the Coast Guard, whose job was saving people.

As I began to accept that there was a spiritual reality, I had the following dream:

In a darkish room somewhere, unidentified. Tada comes in and sits down, at something like a dressing table. I realize she is dead and confront her with "You are dead." I am afraid, and cross myself. She crosses herself. She looks different, very old.

A young man comes in, towering over me as I sit on the bed. He looks like me. He is dead, too. Then he becomes old. He goes past me, towards Tada.

Then blackness, and a total sensation comes over me. I am going to have an original experience. I am going to see God. The sensation is one of great joy, not fear. I see clouds, like a very heavy fog bank, not dark but light, as if a light many times more powerful than the sun is trying to break through the fog. Dimly, in front of the clouds, I see a small gold cross.

Neither Tada nor I were Catholic. She never went to church, except for weddings and funerals and to join the family at Easter. But, as Carl Jung had explained, the symbols, rituals, and dogma of the Catholic Church helped to protect people from the dangers of original experience.

Also Jung had warned us that looking directly at the face of God could be overwhelming (Jung, 1959, pages 292-3). So I was protected from looking directly at God by very heavy clouds. But the Light was there, behind the clouds, unmistakably, because there was no light in my known universe that was anywhere near that powerful.

The small gold cross in front of the clouds was there to indicate that, while God was much too potent a force to deal with directly, as a human being I could deal with Christ, as God's representative: "He makes intercession for us."

This dream answered my challenge, "I will believe in God when I see God." I had seen God, or at least as much of God as it was safe for me to see. Light in my dreams had been a symbol of love, and so this supreme Light represented a supreme Love, as compassion, and this supreme Love was the supreme power of the universe. I was brought back to "God is Love," which I had seen on the wall of the Christian Science Church, except that now I had seen the evidence for myself.

Can I use dreams as evidence of anything? On the surface, it seems that dreams are fantasy, illusion, wish-fulfillment, and at best theatrical productions, like the movies. They are seen as just the opposite of "reality," and therefore the opposite of anything anybody would call "evidence." I can see myself trying to present dreams as evidence in court: "Inadmissible!"

But there is no question that with skillful interpretation dreams can yield valuable information, insights, and even wisdom. My psychiatrist used dreams as insights into the problems I was having. My winter of dream analysis gave me a complete education, that rivaled my Harvard education or my four years of psychotherapy. The dream process uncovered and resolved a traumatic experience that my psychiatrist had missed. It also continued my psychological growth up to the psychological age of puberty. Given that the dream process had steered me accurately in these two instances, there was no reason that it would change and steer me wrong, in presenting to me a spiritual reality.

But the main thing that guarantees the reliability of the dream process, the trump card over everything, is the self-steering process: If my interpretation of a dream is wrong, it will be corrected. How can anything possibly be any more reliable than that?

And so I can trust the accuracy of these things my dreams have taught me, because my interpretations have never been corrected, beyond just minor enhancements.

Dream: *I am hanging by my hands from a college lecture-room chair-arm (the kind with the writing surface), which is sticking outside the top-story window of a large modern building, not tall, but massive, about 4 or 5 stories in height. The chair-arm breaks, sending me plunging down. It is a soft landing. I land in mud. But then all I can find is a spine, and I know the injury has been fatal.*

The education I received at Harvard, the indoctrination into a purely physical universe, has died. Yes, I still accept the biological discoveries (the spine), but I don't assume, as I once did, that they covered the whole human being. There was much more to life than the purely physical.

My first clue that I hadn't learned the whole truth at Harvard was when I discovered *The Prophet*, by Kahlil Gibran, in 1965. Here was a book that had been an instant smash hit in 1923, a year after "The Waste Land," and had gone through many printings and sold millions of copies, and my Harvard education had never even let me know that it existed. I began to see that there were very large gaps in what I had learned at Harvard, that their version of what they considered "knowledge" had been very severely edited.

My dreams had helped me to solve not only all my personal problems that I was aware of, but also all the cultural problems I had seen when I set out to design a new civilization. On the personal side, along with having resolved a serious traumatic experience and having reached the psychological age of puberty and having seen the evidence of God, I had also found the thing that was missing when I had left psychotherapy: It was the spiritual component. Pinocchio was no longer a wooden puppet; he was now a real boy, with a spirit, a soul.

On the cultural side, if a majority of the people were to reach the psychological age of puberty, then the governments created by that majority would not be motivated to use nuclear weapons, and the threat of nuclear annihilation would go away. A few terrorists might get their hands on such weapons, but that would not destroy the civilized world.

Of course this solution is still a long way off. People first have to recognize that there is such a thing as the psychological age of puberty, and then recognize that they haven't reached it yet, and then work hard to reach it. But at least I have found a solution, and I have done my part in attaining it.

On the second problem, the American Dream come true, I had solved the problem of my personal happiness, and also I had discovered a new goal to work towards — developing one's potential as a human being. I had not only defined the goal, but also had made a major discovery of what the potential was, in reaching the psychological age of puberty.

As for "The Waste Land," the rubble of broken images of old religious beliefs and values destroyed by scientific materialism, I had discovered, first hand, the source of religious beliefs. I had seen, first hand, that God was not dead but very much alive. I didn't have to believe, on faith, in legends told thousands of years ago, but I could believe in a spiritual reality on the basis of evidence. Other people, of course, have also experienced a huge revival in spiritual beliefs, as they have found their own evidence in their own ways.

BEYOND PSYCHOLOGY

Once I had resolved the problems of my childhood, then, I wondered, what would I dream about? I was having some really strange dreams, that didn't make any sense, until finally this dream gave me a clue:

Movie camera car, taking pictures, coming to a railroad crossing, almost colliding with huge locomotive coming on tracks at an oblique angle. Car doesn't stop, just keeps going at a constant speed, approaching intersection as light turns yellow, red, then instantly green as camera car goes through. I remember having seen this before, look in rearview mirror of camera car and see my '48 Olds following behind. I am trying to get a better look to see if it is really me.

My '48 Olds represents the past. So if I am looking in the rearview mirror and seeing the past, then of course what I am seeing through the windshield is the future. This camera car which travels at a constant speed represents the passage of time. The camera represents my ability to see ahead of me in time as well as behind me in time, not forever, but some limited range, as a camera would see.

This explained some of my confusing dreams. As I reviewed them, I could see that many of them were about future events.

I dreamed that a friend came to see me, a friend I had not seen in about a year. He showed up the next day. I told him about the dream. He said it could have been caused by telepathy — that he was planning the trip, and he knew he would see me, and I could have picked up his thoughts. I couldn't argue with that. But in December of the following year, when I was living on Beacon Hill in Boston, I had the following dream/experience:

Dream: *It is a very cold morning as I start off to work. My car is parked against the left-hand curb, facing downhill. Thus the door swung open downhill, and I left it open as I got in to start the car. I turned the key and nothing happened — it wouldn't start.*

The dream was at about 7 AM, and at about 8 AM I started off to work. It was a very cold morning. My car was parked against the left-hand curb, facing downhill. Thus the door swung open downhill, and I left it open as I got in to start the car. I put the key in the ignition, and at that point remembered the dream. I had never had any trouble starting the car in the five years I had owned it, so I had total confidence that it would start. I turned the key and nothing happened — it wouldn't start.

There was a subtle problem in the starter wiring, which was to cause me a great deal of trouble and expense. I made 5 trips to 3 different garages before an expert mechanic finally was able to fix the problem.

First of all, let's get rid of the "coincidence" argument: The car had started perfectly for 5 years and 9 months, or about 2000 days, and the dream had prophesied exactly the first time it failed to start. That's one chance in 2000 of coincidence.

And then, to get rid of the "telepathy" argument, here was a machine that had a malfunction that nobody knew about, until the dream revealed it to me.

I had seen evidence of a spiritual reality, but I knew very little about it. I had studied physics to learn about the physical reality, and psychology to learn about the mental reality. Now I needed some kind of education to help me to understand the spiritual reality. Just as I was pondering this, an old girlfriend came to town and handed me a copy of *There Is a River: The Story of Edgar Cayce*, by Thomas Sugrue.

Briefly, for those who don't know, Edgar Cayce (pronounced "Casey"), American psychic, 1877-1945, was able to go into a trance state, and in that trance state was able to answer questions about things that he did not consciously know. These trance sessions were called "readings," and present at these readings were always a "conductor," who asked the questions, and a stenographer, who recorded everything that was said. The stenographer, of course, was very important, because now we have a permanent record of all these readings.

Most of these readings were medical diagnoses and suggestions for treatment. He always worked with a licensed medical doctor, who made the actual prescriptions, so that he wouldn't be practicing medicine without a license. They followed up, or tried to, on all treatments, to see whether they were effective. That information was documented, too. And in more than 90% of the cases, his treatments were proven to be effective. The other 10% weren't all proven to be ineffective, as some people didn't follow the treatments, and some didn't report back. This rate of success is even more remarkable because a great many of these were cases where conventional medicine had failed.

After Cayce had been doing these medical readings for a while, a man named Arthur Lammers came and asked for a horoscope in a reading. Without having been prompted, Cayce volunteered the information that this was the third incarnation on earth for Lammers. This was the first of about 2500 "life readings" that Cayce gave, describing people's previous incarnations and how they influenced their present lives.

For me, this was the proof of reincarnation. Here was an unknown mental process that produced verified accurate results in more than 90% of 9000 medical readings. So this process had a verified error rate of less than 10%. Then what was the probability that the process was wrong in all 2500 life readings, which could not be verified, that asserted that reincarnation was a fact? Note that this is not the probability of any one particular life reading being accurate, but the probability that there is such a thing as reincarnation, an assertion stated or implied in every life reading, and never denied. The probability of Cayce having been wrong about reincarnation in every one of 2500 life readings is a number so small that it is meaningless. The probability of reincarnation being a fact, based on this evidence, is as close to certainty as you can get.

Was there any bias operating here, that would have biased Cayce towards a belief in reincarnation? First of all, no suggestion of "reincarnation" had been given to him in the initial life reading. He had been asked for a "horoscope," and he spontaneously came out with the information on reincarnation.

But, most important, Edgar Cayce was a devout Christian, who read the Bible once for every year of his life. There was nothing about reincarnation in his Christian beliefs. To him, it was something they believed in in India. So he had a hard time reconciling reincarnation with his own conscious beliefs. First he saw nothing in the Bible against reincarnation, and then he found passages which even hinted at the possibility of reincarnation:

John 8:58 ... Before Abraham was, I am.

John 9:2 ... Who did sin, this man, or his parents, that he was born blind?

The fact that Edgar Cayce was biased initially away from reincarnation made the fact of reincarnation, as revealed by him, even more convincing.

Other sources have also reinforced my belief in reincarnation. *Twenty Cases Suggestive of Reincarnation* by Ian Stevenson is a fine research study of reincarnation. Also the Dalai Lama is chosen as the reincarnation of the previous Dalai Lama, by having to identify objects that belonged to the previous Dalai Lama. Also people have been regressed, by hypnosis, back past the year of their birth and into previous incarnations. In all these sources of information, there is a possibility of error, but the overwhelming probability, as I see it, is that reincarnation exists.

Along with reincarnation comes the Law of Karma. This is the other half of the Golden Rule, "Do unto others as you would have them do unto you," because whatever you do unto others will be done unto you — maybe not in this incarnation, but in some incarnation. "Those who live by the sword shall die by the sword," again, maybe not in this lifetime but in some lifetime. Every soul is responsible for its actions here on earth and is subject to some kind of cosmic accountability. All this is explained in great detail in *Edgar Cayce on Reincarnation* (Langley, 1967) and *Many Mansions* (Cerminara, 1950).

Reincarnation and karma explained many things to me. They explained why all people are not created equal — because of bad karma from previous lifetimes or skills developed in previous lifetimes and carried over into this one. They explained why I was born with a great mathematical talent and no literary talent. They explained why I was so different from my parents — because there are two lines of heredity, the physical line and the line of soul development, and in that second line I had very different purposes in this lifetime.

Also Edgar Cayce introduced to me the idea of the Akashic Records. There is a record, somewhere, in some aspect of the universe (non-physical, of course), of every action of every soul that has ever existed. These records can be tapped by anybody who has the necessary abilities. (And Edgar Cayce used to say, "Whatever I can do, you can learn to do.") Cayce saw these Akashic Records in his readings as "God's Book of Remembrances." He experienced them in his readings as huge books in a huge library. He would then go to just the right volume and just the right page to find what he was looking for.

The Law of Karma, for me, was a theory to be tested. The Akashic Records were part of a consistent structure presented by Cayce, but beyond my ability to test in this lifetime. One thing that made Edgar Cayce believable to me was that the information he presented was consistent with things I knew about psychology and the culture didn't. If he had been a fake, he would have built his elaborate fiction on things the culture knew at the time.

Other information from the Edgar Cayce readings was that there had been a continent of Atlantis, which was inundated about 10,000 years ago, that they had a technology more advanced than ours, with flying machines, that their technology had caused their destruction, that they had done genetic experimentation and created monstrosities such as the centaurs and minotaurs in mythology, and that their technology was carried to ancient Egypt, where it was used to build the Pyramids, including the use of levitation to lift the stones into place. I thought about that. We just assume that the ancient Egyptians were primitive, using primitive methods. I have seen artists' drawings of thousands of slaves dragging the huge stones up huge ramps. But that is fiction. We really don't know. None of the things Edgar Cayce was saying were inconsistent with what I already knew, and all of them helped to explain things that were previously mysteries to me, like the "Lost Cities" of Fawcett (1953), or Stonehenge, or the stones on Easter Island. Also there was a large wall found off Bimini in 1968.

His prophecies for "earth changes" at the end of the twentieth century were wrong, but there he kept saying that the future depended very much on the free will of human beings, either individually or collectively.

In the summer of 1967, the Drug Revolution was in full swing. They had been at Haight-Ashbury while I was having my dream winter, and now they had taken over the world. People were coming at me with "If you haven't done drugs, what do you know?" I realized that I had to experience drugs in order to know anything about drugs.

I didn't want to take LSD. I had had a dream which warned me of the dangers of opening myself up psychologically too far too fast:

I am descending a stairway down into the blackness. I know there is something lurking there, and I am ready to face it. I challenge the darkness: "I am not afraid. What can you show me?" A face flashes at me, pretty bad, but I am still there, still challenging. Another face appears, really awful this time, in a subtle way. This face is so awful that I am dreaming that it has made half of my mind insane.

Now I am dreaming that I have woken up and I am sitting on the edge of my bed. One eye is blind, as one side of my mind has become insane. I have several more dreams to resolve the experience and build back the half of my mind that has been destroyed.

The message here was clear: Don't push it; you can make yourself crazy. As it turned out, that ugly face that made my mind half insane was a bad aspect of myself that I was able to deal with and resolve only two weeks later. But at the time of the dream, my mind was just not ready to handle it.

Taking LSD I felt would be opening me up instantly and uncontrollably to all of the inner spooks that might still be lurking there. That was out of the question, because I didn't want to risk destroying my mind completely. So I decided to try marijuana.

Within a couple of weeks of smoking marijuana for the first time, I had the following dream:

I am having a pleasant dream which is interrupted as I am woken up by an old lady coming up the stairs to my apartment. As I open the door to greet her, she is so weak, nothing but a bag of bones, that I have to grab her arms in order to hold her up. She has a black sweater on. She says "You have your black glasses on, Ernie." As I look into her eyes, I see a deep and terrifying blackness.

The old woman was a nice lady I had known and liked, who had died when I was 7, in 1941. "Ernie" was my father's name. She thought I was Ernie, because in 1967 I looked very much like what my father looked like in 1941. I had had dreams of Tada and my grandmother, knowing they were dead, and they had always made me uncomfortable. But this one really spooked me out, as I looked into the eyes of this dead person, into an infinite depth of blackness.

This was not like a symbol that I created coming into my dream. This was another entity coming into my dream, as indicated by the interruption of the pleasant dream, and I didn't like it. During the six months or so that I smoked marijuana, I had several dreams of the dead coming into my dreams. Starting with this nice lady that I liked when I was seven, they became more sinister, with gangster-like voices and voices out of a horror movie. In one dream the phone was ringing and the dead were on the line, and the phone kept ringing and the voice kept talking, even after I hung up the phone. So I put the phone in a desk drawer, just to muffle the sound.

Finally I had a dream, and I forget the details, that told me "Marijuana is poison." I never smoked marijuana again, and I went around Provincetown for the next five years preaching "Marijuana is poison." The only thing that accomplished was to make me socially undesirable.

Getting back to the summer of 1967, I think it was the marijuana that had opened up a small amount of clairvoyance in me. I could see all the games people were playing, and the mental attitudes, and I didn't like it. I think this is a real test of whether a person is really clairvoyant, or just faking it — whether they have experienced the unpleasantness of being able to see all the inner ugliness in people. That's why I backed off from clairvoyance, and consciously made an effort to block it off.

Also, I believe under the effect of the marijuana, I was having beautiful "spiritual" dreams, night after night, that were sweeping me away. I was losing control of my own mind, and afraid that I was losing my sanity.

It was at that point that I met the spiritual teacher, and at least tried meditation. But I decided that I would have plenty of time to meditate on the spiritual plane, in between incarnations. During this time on earth I have incarnated into a body in order to interact with the earthly environment and learn the lessons it has to offer. Whatever time I spend in a non-thinking meditative state I feel is time subtracted from this valuable time on earth, experiencing the earth environment.

I decided I had to get back to computer programming, just to prove I was sane. It didn't take very long — one phone call, and one interview, and I had a good job with a very good company, and one day on the job was all it took. On the first day of work, after having spent about two hours studying the 250-page set of specifications of the project I was to be working on, I announced "There is a major flaw in your system." Nine months later I was proven right, when people started using the system, and I got to rewrite it my way. My logical mind was working better than ever.

But there were residues of the mental upheaval I had been through. First of all, I was the mental equivalent of uncoordinated from having gained four years worth of psychological growth in three months during my dream winter. And since I had removed myself from the normal psychological range, I felt that there was no place for me in this world. I saw everybody living their competitive lives, and saw no place for my new-found altruism. I had read that it was possible for people to will themselves to die, and I was afraid that I would will myself to die, seeing that I was so out of place in this world. When the dead people started coming into my dreams, I was even more afraid, as if they were coming to get me, or as in the

game of "Ghost," where if you talked to a ghost you became a ghost.
On top of that, the long-term effects of the marijuana lasted about a
year, and heightened my emotional state.

I was afraid to go to sleep at night, afraid that if I lost
consciousness I would die, and I used to say the little children's
prayer:

> Now I lay me down to sleep.
> I pray the Lord my soul to keep.
> And if I die before I wake,
> I pray the Lord my soul to take.

So I found a good psychiatrist, highly recommended by two
different sources. And I told him that I was suffering from fear,
because dead people were coming into my dreams. He didn't believe
that there was such a thing as spirits from the dead, and was trying to
tell me I had a deep-seated problem. I knew I didn't have a deep-
seated problem, because I had already successfully completed
psychotherapy and followed that with dream analysis. And so the
argument went back and forth until I asked myself, "Why am I
paying this guy $30 an hour (top dollar in 1968) to give HIM an
education?" I realized I was beyond the belief structure of people in
the field of psychology. I was on my own to solve this problem. The
same weekend when I made the decision not to go back to him, I had
this dream:

*A beautiful silver-haired woman was coming into my apartment
in Cambridge. She had with her a great many followers who were
telling me what a great honor it was that she was paying me this
visit. They didn't come in through the door; they sort of all came in
through the walls at the same time. I thought the woman must have
been a friend of my grandmother and Tada, from Cambridge. She
spoke fine and beautiful words of spiritual meaning, but as she
spoke, she began to tarnish, first just little flecks, and finally she was
all brown and misshapen and ugly. I screamed "Get the hell out of
here!" And they were all gone, instantly. I went around, looking
everywhere, in the kitchen and behind the toilet, screaming over and*

over again, "Get the hell out of here!" But there was no sign of them anywhere. They had vanished.

When I woke up, it was 7 AM on a beautiful sunny Sunday morning. I had solved my problem. All it took was an assertion of my will to get rid of the spooks. You can't shoot them, and you can't keep them out with walls and locks, but you can say, "I don't want you here," and they leave. (Or at least that was my first-approximation to a solution.)

The clairvoyance made the city overwhelming. Thoreau said "The mass of men lead lives of quiet desperation." (*Walden*, page 7) I could feel the agony of millions of souls crying out mentally for help. I had to get out every weekend to Provincetown, just to restore my energies. But that wasn't enough. I got the Hong Kong flu, and decided I had to get out of the city for good, and back to Provincetown.

On Easter morning, 1969, I decided I finally had something worth writing about. For a month I began assembling my material, and began to see what an enormous amount of material I had and what an enormous task lay ahead of me. One day I was just totally exhausted and depressed trying to deal with it all. I just flopped down on the bed. I didn't much care if I lived or died. I didn't bother to say the little prayer.

Immediately I lost consciousness. Immediately I shot up, up, up from my basement apartment through some kind of a tube, at an enormous rate of speed for an enormous distance, until I was in the presence of a blinding Light. I knew enough not to look directly at the Light, so I held my right arm up to shield my eyes from the Light. Off to the left, or at the right hand of God, stood the figure of Christ. He said, very simply, "Get back to work."

And back down I went, down, down, down, as fast as I had come up. Then it was as if I was on a sleeping car, on a train, slowing down as it was coming into a city. I thought I had died and was being reincarnated, and I thought to myself, "This time I'm not going to start smoking."

I was delighted to wake up and find myself in the same bed. It was dark outside, where it had been light when I flopped down. Two or three hours had passed, where to me it had seemed like less than five minutes.

I was never again afraid that I would will myself to die. I felt that Christ had given me assurance that the Powers That Be would never let me do anything that foolish. Also I felt that this was what dying was like, and I have never again been afraid to die. But most important, I felt that I had been given some sanction to do my work, that I was on "God's Payroll."

Not long after that, one beautiful day, I took a beautiful walk on the dunes, and came back into town thinking beautiful thoughts. I saw a beautiful woman with a friend of mine, and of course I was curious to make her acquaintance.

"You are very disturbed," she said.

"I am not disturbed. How can you say I am disturbed?"

"I just know," she said. "You are very disturbed."

And the more I argued, the more disturbed I became. And when we were finished, the sky had clouded over, and it wasn't a beautiful day any more.

She was trying to tell me I needed her "help," and I could see that she had serious psychological problems herself. So if I was the least on God's Payroll, then here was the least on Satan's Payroll, come to bug me. I had proved to myself the existence of God. Now I had reason to believe in the existence of Satan, or a force of Evil in the world.

It took me nine months to organize my material and six months to write the book (the first time). It was rejected by four publishers and a youth culture that rejected logic, science, truth, reality, psychotherapy, and anybody over 30.

In the winter of 1971, I was teaching dream analysis at the Free University of Provincetown. I was saying I would like to put an ad in the Free U. Newsletter, "Organizational meeting to start a new civilization." One of my students said, "Why do that? Somebody has done it already." And he handed me a copy of *The Ultimate Frontier*, by Eklal Kueshana, the fundamental text and organizational philosophy of The Stelle Group. I thought it would be much easier to organize a new civilization where somebody already had a core philosophy to build upon. So I took the book home and read it.

"Eklal Kueshana" is the pen name of Richard Kieninger, working in collaboration with his teachers. These teachers are members of the Brotherhoods, organizations of Masters and Adepts dedicated to the advancement of humanity. This book is not "channeled," as one major bookseller advertised. These Brotherhoods are very much here on earth, but they keep their identity secret to avoid political and religious persecution. One of the requirements for membership in the Brotherhoods is a controlled clairvoyance, so they can identify each other without needing any passwords or secret handshakes.

Like Edgar Cayce, they prophesied cataclysms at the end of the twentieth century, but unlike Cayce, they were very definite about it. Richard Kieninger had incarnated specifically to lead a group which would develop the means to survive these cataclysms and preserve the technology of the present culture. That part, of course, didn't work out as prophesied, but there is a great deal in this book and the other writings of Richard Kieninger that I have found very plausible and have assimilated into my own philosophy.

First of all, it is presented not as Gospel to be believed, but information to be tested. That is how I take it all — as a working hypothesis, and as stuff that makes more sense than stuff I was previously asked to believe.

To them, reincarnation and karma are facts. They even differentiate three kinds of karma — physical karma, emotional karma, and economic karma.

Very briefly, as I remember it, the teaching is that our purpose in being incarnated here on earth is to learn everything there is to learn about the first four planes of existence (whatever that is). When one does that, one becomes a Master. There are an equal number of male and female Masters. One can develop in that direction by practicing the Twelve Great Virtues. I recognized these as virtues which I had been trying to live up to all my life. My understanding of them is as follows:

SINCERITY is total honesty with myself and with others.

KINDNESS means never to hurt another person. I have had trouble reconciling sincerity and kindness, and have decided that sincerity is kindness, even if it is unpleasant. Of course it can be expressed in the kindest possible way.

PRECISION means to strive for the highest degree of accuracy, both in understanding things and expressing myself.

EFFICIENCY means not to waste my time on earth, but to use it efficiently, to the best of my abilities.

HUMILITY means knowing exactly where I stand. It does not mean false humility, or self-deprecation. For example, Muhammad Ali, when he said "I'm the greatest," was expressing humility.

COURAGE doesn't mean lack of fear. It means pursuing my objectives in the face of fear.

TOLERANCE means recognizing that if I were that other person in that particular situation, I would be doing exactly the same thing.

FORBEARANCE is the same as tolerance, in those cases where I am actually injured by another person. It means forgiveness, and no desire for retaliation.

DEVOTION means dedication to a task or a purpose.

CHARITY means giving to others in need, but only if they ask for it.

PATIENCE is the willingness to wait for the outworking of natural processes, as in psychological growth.

DISCERNMENT is differentiation, or knowing the difference, taken to the highest level.

I judged the Brotherhoods very much by the genuineness of the "virtues" they presented, as opposed to other teachings presenting "virtues" that I didn't happen to agree with, like obedience, chastity, and vegetarianism. The philosophy of the Brotherhoods stressed free will, freedom of sexual expression, and a diet containing plenty of meat, to sustain one's mental energy level, especially to resist the intrusion of spirit entities.

The most important thing I learned from Richard Kieninger and his teachers was about the Black Mentalists. If you can read auras, they said, you can see their influence directly. Otherwise this is theory to be considered, as I have, over the years, to see if anything fits.

Allegedly there are souls whose karma is so bad that they could never incarnate. If they did, they would self-destruct immediately. Since they are doomed, they are determined to take everybody else down with them. They manipulate people on earth by way of telepathic hypnotic suggestion. If you are never on their wavelength — hate, greed, vengeance — and never seek out their influence via such things as Ouija Board, Tarot, or mediumism, you are fairly safe. Also the Holy Spirit (Masters and Adepts) protect us from interference by them. No Black Mentalist has anywhere near the power of a human Master. Still, their influence on this earth is visible as the color black at the very highest level of our culture — the black robes of the clergy, the black tuxedos, and the black limousines.

I had an inkling that there was such a force in the universe, because I had had a couple of dreams with intensely black, evil, and frightening forces operating. Also, the more I think about it, the more things are explained by such a force operating.

Richard taught us the Protective Prayer to protect us from these influences. Basically, it is "Dear Christ, Please protect me." You don't pray to just anybody, and you don't pray for "help" or "guidance," because these evil spirit entities would be glad to pick up on it and guide you — to your doom. You pray specifically to "Christ," and only for "protection." (People complained to Richard that this was religious intolerance, and so he added Moses and Mohammed and Buddha. They are all members of the Holy Spirit who protect us. The main point is not to pray indiscriminately to just any spirit entities — they aren't all dedicated to our best interests.)

The Protective Prayer has worked wonderfully for me. There have been times when I have been two levels deep in a spooky dream, and an act of will just isn't working for me. And if I can remember the Protective Prayer, I come bubbling right up to the surface.

Through all of this, I kept working on my psychological growth. In 1972, thanks to many hours of scribbling, I reached the psychological age of adulthood, or psychological age 18. There were only three people I knew in my youth who reached this level naturally. I grew a beard to celebrate my manhood. I have been very comfortable as an adult ever since, and I have not been motivated to work on my psychological growth since then.

6. THE MIND, AS I SEE IT

> Gisors looked at him:
> "What do you mean by 'intelligence'?"
> "In general?"
> "Yes."
> Ferral reflected:
> "The possession of the means of coercing things or men."
> Gisors smiled imperceptibly. Each time he asked this question the other person, no matter who he was, would answer by producing the image of his desire. . .
> (Andre Malraux, *Man's Fate*, page 239)

Or, as I remembered it almost fifty years after reading the book, people when asked to define "intelligence" tend to describe themselves.

Psychologists define "intelligence," officially, as "Whatever is measured by an intelligence test." This makes some people furious, but it allows psychologists to make meaningful scientific studies, such as correlating scores on intelligence tests with grades in school, etc. They could make the same meaningful studies by saying "IQ is measured on an IQ test," and leaving the definition of "intelligence" open until their knowledge is more complete.

Who designs intelligence tests, and what kinds of questions do they decide to ask? The Navy test I took was definitely biased in favor of one's knowledge of boats and the maintenance of boats. But they didn't call it an "intelligence" test. They called it a "mental" test.

From the other perspective, my boss Flyer at the boatyard was telling me I was doing a pretty good job, remarkable for somebody who was going to Harvard. He said, "Most of them people at Harvard are educated fools, all full of theory, can't do nothin' practical." Other people were also surprised that I could do practical things, like change a tire, when they found out that I went to Harvard.

African Americans have long complained that "intelligence" tests are biased towards white people. To offset that bias, Adrian Dove designed "The Dove Counterbalance Intelligence Test." Here are a few questions from that test:

> Jazz pianist Ahmad Jamal took an Arabic name after becoming really famous. Previously he had some fame with what he called his "slave name." What was his previous name?
> (a) Willie Lee Jackson (b) LeRoi Jones (c) Wilbur McDougal
> (d) Fritz Jones (e) Andy Johnson
>
> In "C. C. Rider," what does "C. C." stand for?
> (a) Civil Service (b) Church Council
> (c) County Circuit, preacher of an old-time rambler
> (d) Country Club (e) "Cheating Charley" (the "Boxcar Gunsel")
>
> A "Handkerchief Head" is
> (a) A cool cat (b) A porter (c) An "Uncle Tom"
> (d) A hoddi (e) A "preacher"
>
> (Lazerson, 1975, page 386)

Then there are "street smarts," which are the mental skills enabling one to survive, better or worse, in an urban jungle.

And there is "emotional intelligence," which is a mix of intelligence and emotional maturity and the ability to manipulate people.

Just as there is disagreement on what intelligence is and how to measure it, so there is disagreement on every aspect of the human mentality. The best I can do is cast my vote for my own particular point of view.

First of all, I think everybody would agree that there is such a thing as intellect, although we don't all agree on how to evaluate it. "Intellect," to me, means the same thing as "intelligence." Intellect, as I learned long ago, is memory plus reasoning ability. I was able to succeed in school with intellect alone, with a small amount of creativity in writing papers and solving math problems. Most of schoolwork is just memorizing things, with math and science also requiring some reasoning ability.

I think I could also have succeeded in adult life on intellect alone, if I had just satisfied the job requirements. My most creative and inventive projects were things that management did not reasonably expect an employee to be able to do, most of them done on my own initiative. (My first computer project that required creativity had already been called "impossible" by people more experienced.)

In my personal life I also got by, before psychotherapy, on intellect alone, with a minimum amount of creativity required to compose the standard lines that I would then recite, as an actor. There was no emotion or will involved in what I said or did. I did what was expected of me, or at least tried.

And so I think it is possible to go through life on intellect alone — learning job skills, using one's reasoning ability, and following the rules. Therefore it is quite reasonable to believe that other mental abilities like creativity or intuition or free will don't exist. I define an "intellectual" as a person who functions on intellect alone — memory plus reasoning ability. This is ideal for success in the academic world, where one's job is to learn the culture of the past and pass it on to others. And because there are so many intellectuals in the academic world, their particular point of view is passed along to millions of students, and thus carries with it the status of academia.

So I have to pay attention when the intellectuals argue that creativity and intuition and free will don't exist, because these people have status and write books and influence people. And I am certainly tolerant of their point of view, if they haven't experienced these things. The way to know whether something exists is to experience it. But the reverse is not true. It is not logically accurate to say, "I have not experienced these things; therefore they do not exist." These people are simply uninformed, and their opinion should be taken as such. The fact that I have experienced creativity and intuition and free will overrides any intellectual argument to the contrary.

The counterculture, reacting to the cultural overemphasis on the intellect, rejected the intellect in favor of a more "intuitive" approach. This isn't a smart thing to do, either, because the intellect is the most important human mental function. Without intellect, we wouldn't be able to put on our clothes in the morning, or find food, or find our way home at night. But we aren't using our full mental potential until we open up and learn to use the many other human mental functions, and coordinate them with the intellect.

I developed creativity and intuition and the will in psychotherapy. That means, first of all, that not everybody has these functions, or is able to use them. It is pretty obvious that these functions are suppressed by the educational system, if not by the whole environment of the child growing up. Creativity is squashed in favor of memorizing things, intuition is squashed in favor of reason, and the will is squashed in favor of obedience to authority. These functions have to be brought back from the subconscious, and the way to do that, of course, is through psychotherapy.

If I have observed certain life forms by sailing to Galapagos, then it is reasonable to say that if other people want to observe these same life forms, they should also sail to Galapagos. Similarly, if I have uncovered certain mental attributes through psychotherapy, then other people can experience these same mental attributes by going through psychotherapy. If they don't do that, or don't succeed at it, then they are simply uninformed, as I have said before.

That's really the only way I can answer the intellectual argument that "creativity" is really only a "synthesis" of known elements. I have to avoid the intellectual argument, because I can't say intellectually that it is not so — except that in the synthesis there is some value added, some new thing which is not just the sum of the ingredients.

When I was a kid, I used to visit the Belle of Taunton soap factory which was on my way home from school. One day they gave me the ingredients to make soap, and I took them home and mixed them with water, and voila! No soap, just a mess. So much for synthesis.

As for intuition, my dictionary seems to know more about it than the psychology books:

> Intuition ... 2c: the power or faculty of attaining to direct knowledge or cognition without evident rational thought and inference
> (Merriam-Webster, 1996)

This pretty much describes my experience with intuition.

Richard Kieninger's definition agrees with this and then takes it further:

> Intuition falls into two categories. The first covers the receiving of information by thought transference, which includes telepathic communication ... The second category includes the ability to combine facts instantly into a correct conclusion without consciously using rational processes. Intuition allows ready insight into people and situations, and it is often manifested as immediate cognition or apprehension of a matter previously unknown and unconsidered.
> (Kieninger, 1978)

Telepathy is another whole ingredient of a larger definition of "intuition" that I am not talking about here. I am only talking about the second category, the sudden flash of understanding, where suddenly I "see" something fairly complex that I haven't known before.

The psychology books, on the other hand, describe "intuition" as some pre-logical childrens' way of thinking that is not always accurate.

Lazerson (1975, page 181) has a section heading, "Intuitive Thought and Its Limitations," and then goes on to describe pre-operational intelligence in children, and its limitations. Bernstein et al (1997, pages 395, 398) says "During the second half of the preoperational stage, according to Piaget, four- to seven-year-olds begin to make intuitive guesses about the world." The text then goes on to describe the inaccuracies in this preoperational thinking. These were the only references to "intuition" that I could find in either textbook.

These textbooks make no mention of the "intuition" that I experienced. My experience with intuition, once I discovered it, was that it was probably never wrong, but I never really trusted it, and always had to check it out logically. Maybe the reason I never trusted it was because it had been unreliable when I was a child, as the textbooks were saying.

I think of intuition as the analog function of the mind, like an analog computer, where the intellect is like a digital computer, with memory plus reasoning ability. An analog computer is a hard-wired electrical circuit which models (is "analogous" to) some kind of a complex network, like a natural gas distribution system, traffic flow, or whatever. A current coming in at one end represents the flow of gas or traffic, and then the distribution of that flow can immediately be read for any point in the network. The analog computer is useful for complex network problems that are too complicated to be solved by ordinary mathematics.

And such is life — a complex network of interactions of an individual with one's environment — and so the analog function comes in handy.

As for the hard wiring, I do know that whenever there is a sudden upheaval of my belief system, my mind goes churning away, resolving everything. Is that just rationalizing, or is some re-hard-wiring going on as well?

On the subject of the will, intellectuals for centuries have been trying to argue that there is no such thing as free will, with an argument that goes like this: If God knows everything, past and future, then God knows everything that you are going to do, and therefore you have no free will. The fallacy here is that just because God knows what you are going to do doesn't mean that God is making you do it. The arrogance here is people pretending to know how much God knows. Maybe God doesn't know how it's all going to turn out.

More recently, B.F. Skinner has tried to deny the existence of free will by theorizing that our lives are totally determined by heredity and environment. Of course, being a behaviorist, he doesn't include in his definition of "environment" the mental environment, which includes a free will. Or it might be said that our free will is part of our heredity. Either way, it is too bad that the behaviorists ignore the free will, because the free will is an important factor that makes experiments with human beings unpredictable.

The cognitive psychologists start with the analogy of the mind as a computer. If you see only intellect, this is a pretty good analogy, because memory and reasoning ability are the central attributes of a digital computer. But as you add other mental attributes, some fit the computer analogy and some don't. You can add intuition, and say that this computer has an analog function as well as the digital. But a computer has no creative ability. And it has no will. It only follows orders. It does exactly what it has been programmed to do, unless there is a malfunction somewhere.

Another aspect of the human mentality that computers don't have is emotions — joy, sorrow, anger, fear, and mental pain and pleasure as opposed to physical pain and pleasure. "Emotions" are the same thing as "feelings."

Emotions are mental. It may seem like a "gut" reaction, but it is processed through the mind. For example, if I meet a bear in the woods, that is scary. But if I am at the same distance from that same bear in a zoo, it is not scary. My mind has to judge the situation before telling me to experience fear.

The classical philosophers since the time of the ancient Greeks have seen the ability to reason as the highest human mental faculty, and rightfully so, because we use our reasoning ability to verify all our knowledge, from all sources. These same philosophers dreaded the thought that the emotions might be more powerful than the intellect. But, as Freud discovered, our ability to reason is not our most powerful mental faculty. It gets batted around and twisted and distorted and enslaved by powerful emotional forces emanating from the subconscious, and will come up with whatever rationalizations those forces require of it. And until these powerful forces are brought into the consciousness and become part of the "self," one can't be sure that one's reasoning is either reliable or accurate.

When I was at Harvard, my radical intellectual friends used to define "philosophy" as "a complex rationalization of the universe." All of Western philosophy needs to be rewritten, or at least re-examined, in view of Freud's discoveries. "The pursuit of wisdom" involves more than just the intellect. It involves opening up all of one's mental powers through psychotherapy.

And what about love? Is love an emotion? Is love derived from the physical drives? I have read accounts of altruism among animals, where animals have sacrificed themselves so that others could survive, for the survival of the species. Physical scientists are always trying to explain everything in terms of physical evolution and physical survival. But I have observed differently. I have observed that there is at least one other dimension in the universe, and that dimension or dimensions can be called "spiritual." And the supreme power emanating from those spiritual dimensions is a Force that can be called "Love," which was represented symbolically in my dreams as a supreme Light, the most powerful source of light in the universe. This supreme power of Love was close enough to the representation "God is Love" that I used to see on the wall of the Christian Science Church, so that I could say "This is God." But I have only caught a glimpse of God, and only one aspect of God. Also in the Christian Science credo were "God is Mind," "God is Principle," and others I don't remember. God, to me, is still the Hebrew "JHVH," the unpronounceable, and therefore the unthinkable and unknowable. All I want to say here is that I have had a glimpse of a spiritual dimension, and the supreme power influencing us from that dimension is love. This "love" I have already defined as compassion, as caring for one's fellow creatures.

I have explained the transition point at the psychological age of puberty, where "human nature" switches over from self-interest to compassion, in terms of survival. Yes, it helps to protect one's young. But it doesn't have to be that way, for the sake of survival. Species like alligators eat their young and still manage to survive. And why was I having all those spiritual dreams leading up to the psychological age of puberty? There seems to be more to it than just physical survival.

I think the physical scientists are complicating things (as well as being wrong) by trying to explain everything in terms of physical laws. It reminds me of the time when the Church enforced the belief that the sun travels around the earth, and the complications and convolutions that astronomers went through to explain planetary motion in terms of that theory. It would be so much easier at least to postulate that there might be such a thing as spiritual dimensions in the universe, and that the forces of love emanating from those dimensions might explain such things as altruism, compassion, and caring in the universe.

Also, if life on earth were purely a matter of physical survival, where did we get such ideas as mercy, kindness, justice, and human rights?

Emotions are the "motive" forces, the "motors" that supply the power. My psychiatrist was always asking me, "What are your feelings?" The lesson of psychotherapy is to try to get these motive forces moving you in the direction you consciously want to go, instead of working against you. Therefore the process has been called "emotional growth," leading to "emotional maturity."

But "emotional" to most people means some kind of outward expression of emotions, some kind of outbursts — screaming, yelling, crying, stomping. And "maturity," to many people, means "old age." So if I talk about "emotional maturity," some people might think I was talking about some kind of emotional outbursts in old age.

So instead of talking about "emotional maturity," I am talking about "psychological development." This is deliberately vague, but in being vague it is more accurate than something that seems to mean something and really doesn't.

In addition to emotions, there are also "drives," like hunger and thirst and sex, that are basically physical. There is also this word "motivation," which covers all these "motive" forces — the physical drives, the emotions, and the will. It covers long-term goals as well as short-term goals. And then psychological development is measured in terms of physical behavior, although it isn't that. It is the mental state producing the physical behavior. Rather than use a word like "emotional" that doesn't really cover it, I would rather be vague.

PSYCHOLOGICAL PROGRAMMING

Let's get back to the computer model and talk about "programming." We are born into this world with raw, undifferentiated emotion. As we develop, this emotion is separated into pain and pleasure, and the not-so-pleasant feelings into pain, fear, and anger. I assume that the mind is doing this separating, this differentiating. Maybe the physical circuitry has to develop first. Psychologists have thoroughly documented human physical growth — at what age a human being can expect to crawl, to walk, to run, to talk — and to some degree human mental growth, like the ability to reason or to see things from another person's point of view.

A baby deer is born and immediately gets up and starts following its mother around. For all I know, it also immediately thinks like an adult deer. Some creatures have enormously complex built-in instinctual systems. After a summer of education, this baby deer is ready to function as an adult. A human baby, on the other hand, spends years learning to function physically and mentally as an adult. Baby deer are pre-programmed. Baby humans have to program themselves.

The job of programming is to create mental circuitry through which the raw energy of the drives and emotions (fear, anger, pain, sex) and other motivational forces such as free will and love can be channeled to create appropriate behavior. "Appropriate behavior" is whatever behavior is appropriate to achieve the individual's goals of success and happiness in any particular situation. This "appropriate behavior" might start off as a primitive "fight and flight," but has to be constantly refined to handle social situations where neither fight nor flight will create the desired outcome.

My model of appropriate behavior is Martin Luther King. In the face of extreme persecution and provocation, he was able to accomplish his goals by simply standing his ground and resisting the urge either to fight back or to give in.

This programming is necessarily a growth process, and ideally should go on throughout life. As one grows older, as the brain develops physically, as one is better able to differentiate, as one acquires knowledge and experience, one is always able to write a better program, approaching something that can be called "wisdom."

The ability to differentiate, or know the difference, is the most important element in the fine-tuning of this mental circuitry. For example, in my dream of the white wolf, just because he CAN kill me doesn't mean that he WANTS to.

At a crude level of differentiation, one believes the broad-brush smear, and sees members of other races, religions, nationalities, and political parties as slovenly, dishonest, and vicious. But as one becomes better able to differentiate, one is better able to see individual human beings, and see that members of other social groups are no more likely to have these faults than members of one's own group, or (gasp!) oneself.

When I was dealing with my fear of dogs, a huge dog came suddenly out of the bushes and grabbed my right hand in his mouth — and then looked up at me. He really didn't want to tear my hand off. He was just testing me to see if I was afraid of him.

The ability to differentiate is the ability to see the nuances and the subtleties in all situations. The better one is able to differentiate, the more finely tuned the mental circuitry is able to be.

The ability to differentiate, in turn, gets better as the physical brain develops. So it is necessarily a growth process. It also improves as one's knowledge and experience increase, so it is a growth process that can continue throughout life. But unlike physical growth, this growth process isn't automatic. It doesn't happen unless the individual actually uses these abilities.

The creation of this mental circuitry is the most important human creative activity. It is more important than art or architecture or music or any of those other things we recognize as "creative," because here we are creating human beings.

But this programming normally doesn't go on throughout life. It stops for some reason, usually during the childhood years, at some point where the individual feels comfortable or uncomfortable.

"Daddy got killed in the war. Mommy has gone all to pieces emotionally. Therefore I have to be very grown up and take care of Mommy."

This is incredibly heroic, probably the most heroic thing this person ever did in his life, and he remembers, and identifies with, and admires greatly his three-year-old self for doing it, but in doing this, there is a danger of arresting the psychological growth of the "self" he identifies with to the limitations of his three-year-old programming. The way he thought then, and felt then, rightfully feels good, and that can prevent him from abandoning the three-year-old self in favor of more advanced programming.

Or, in the more normal case, people stop their programming when they outgrow their parents psychologically, or the culture around them, usually around age ten. It is easy then to download some mass-produced software which not only works for life, but also gives one a feeling of belonging to some social group.

I am not saying that all aspects of a human being stop growing psychologically in childhood, but only a central part, one that includes the "self" that one identifies with. So, as a person who was psychologically four years old, I was able to graduate from Harvard, serve in the Army, and have normal sex with adult women. The main difference was that the four-year-old just couldn't see himself as a "Daddy," and feared that if a woman became pregnant by him, he would just have to run away and hide somewhere.

PSYCHOLOGICAL AGE

In my psychological development, I have caught glimpses of what I call "psychological age" and its relationships to the human potential — the 4-year-old who needs a mother and can't imagine himself as a "Daddy," the 10-year-old who is normal for the culture, the 14-year-old who has reached the psychological age of puberty and is ready to give and share and sacrifice self and become a parent, and the 18-year-old who has reached the psychological age of adulthood and is comfortable as an adult. I would like to introduce my concept of psychological age to the culture, for whatever it may prove to be worth.

Defining "psychological age:"

What I have seen in pictures and patterns I am now trying to translate into words. The words are not the thing. I am only trying to represent the thing.

Intuitively and internally, "psychological age" is the age of the childhood "self" that one identifies with.

"Psychological age" is the potential for human psychological development at a given age.

"Psychological age" is the level of psychological development that one would reach at a given age if allowed to develop naturally without one's psychological development being arrested.

People at certain levels of psychological development behave in certain characteristic ways. A person at psychological-age-10 is more likely to be motivated by competitive self-interest, whereas a person at psychological-age-14 is more likely to be altruistic. This characteristic behavior can be taken to be a reflection of the psychological programming on which it is based. Much of this information may be already in place, in the huge amount of material already available on psychological development.

It would be hard to know the psychological potential of an individual at any given age, but the normal for any given age could be determined, and then the individual measured against that. As with IQ, some individuals may prove to be way ahead of their age group.

Unlike IQ, which involves continuous growth up to age 16, psychological growth can be arrested at any point. So the mathematics of determining what is natural unarrested psychological growth may be tricky. I visualize a cluster of people developing at a "natural" rate, that cluster diminishing in size as individuals stop growing psychologically. Once tests are devised to measure psychological age, longitudinal studies will show this pattern.

The difficulty in creating tests to measure psychological age is that people know what morality and maturity are, and have learned to fake these attributes — but not really. "Maturity," to most people, means behaving as the grownups behave. And adult behavior is not always psychologically mature, but is sometimes an act where they themselves are faking adult behavior. Much of authoritarian behavior falls into this category, where people are trying to be very grown up, like Mommy and Daddy used to be. This false-adult behavior can be identified, and questions can be devised to trap people who are trying to fake it.

Individuals can be tested for psychological age, without calling it "psychological age," by testing their likes and dislikes, their attitudes, their heroes, and their ways of dealing with situations. Twelve-year-olds of all ages are attracted to each other. A person who has reached the psychological age of puberty is boring to a person who is still psychologically 12 years old. It is hard to elect a President who is psychologically mature, because people relate better to somebody who is nearer to their own level of psychological development.

To avoid completely the problem of people faking psychological maturity, people could be tested on their ability to differentiate. The ability to differentiate is an indicator of one's level of psychological programming, and, like intelligence, is not something that can be faked.

Tests of psychological age (PA), like IQ, could be useful in many ways, both for the individual and people evaluating the individual, like colleges and employers and (!) potential marriage partners. If

Harvard had been able to tell my father, "This boy needs psychotherapy before he is eligible for Harvard," I would have been eternally grateful.

From my simple intuitive observations, there is a long way to go before reliable tests can be created, starting with a furious debate over what constitutes "maturity." But just for a start, here are my few simple intuitive observations:

Psychological-age-4: Boy still needs a mother to shelter and protect him, psychologically sub-normal.

Psychological-age-10: Boy learning combat lessons of physical warfare, homosexual, authoritarian, psychologically normal for the culture, each person working in his/her self-interest.

Psychological-age-12: Mental warfare, cultural leaders, boy still not ready for puberty.

Psychological-age-14: Psychological age of puberty. "Human nature" as self-interest gives way to an equally natural desire to give and share. Discovery of the spiritual reality and one's spiritual nature. Boy is ready to be a father and raise a family. I estimate that 5% of the people reach this level.

Psychological-age-16: "The hog age." Boy thinks he knows everything, writes his philosophy.

Psychological-age-18: Psychological age of adulthood. Boy becomes a man, is certain and authoritative about things, no doubts about adult stature. I estimate that 1% of the people reach this level.

Richard Kieninger added psychological-age-28 as the ultimate in human psychological development, involving clairvoyance and a level of awareness that I can only imagine. The Brotherhoods say that one person in 2500 reaches this level (Kueshana, 1982, page 295).

My concept of psychological age is not the same as Freud's or Erikson's stages, or Maslow's hierarchy of needs, or Kohlberg's stages of moral reasoning, nor is it derived from any of those systems. It has the advantage over all those systems in being numerical, so that it can be used for measurements and in mathematics — for those who want to develop it. I am only the explorer who has caught a glimpse of it.

PERCEPTIONS

The source of all our knowledge is perception. Everything that we know, all our evidence that anything exists at all, comes to us through our perceptions. In the computer analogy, these are the input devices. Without any input, the computer has no data to work with.

My psychology text (Bernstein et al, 1997) differentiates between "sensation" and "perception," where "sensation" refers to the senses themselves, and "perception" refers to the process of the brain interpreting the data. I am not getting into the technicalities of how it all works, and I am using the words "perception" and "senses" interchangeably.

I notice that the text recognizes more than the "five senses" (hearing, vision, smell, taste, and touch). It breaks down the "skin senses" into touch, temperature, and pain, and adds the proprioceptive senses — kinesthesia, the sense that tells you where parts of your body are, and the vestibular sense, or sense of balance, that tells you about the position of your head. The text doesn't tell me how I sense a stomach ache or an orgasm, and it definitely limits itself to physical senses.

There are two other physical senses I would add to the list. The first may simply be the proprioceptive senses, already recognized. Philosophers have made a big issue out of "How do you know you're not dreaming?" When I am dreaming, many times I think I am awake. Sometimes I think I have woken up from a dream, only to find myself in another dream. But when I am awake, I know I am awake, and I am sure I am awake, because I sense it. This may be just the proprioceptive senses, telling me the positions of my body and head, or it may be some other "sense of awakeness."

The other sense I would add is my sense of time. I have an internal clock that gives me a sense of the passage of time, even when I am sleeping. There have been times when I didn't have an alarm clock and was able to wake myself up, fairly accurately, by setting this internal clock.

The few times this internal clock was most noticeable was when it was absent, when I was anesthetized for an operation. In the most serious operation, they were starting the anesthesia at about 6:40 AM, and in the next instant, in my awareness, it was about 3:30 PM, and they were wheeling me into the recovery room. For me the intervening time did not exist. I had been spared any awareness of the whole horrendous procedure.

This gives me an alternative theory of what happens to me after I die. If I simply cease to exist, then my sense of time ceases to exist, and the eternity of time for me is nonexistent. This, to me, is much less scary than having to go to some spiritual place and deal with spiritual beings.

Descartes, mistrusting his senses to perceive his own existence, said "I think; therefore I am." But how did he know he was thinking unless he first sensed it?

I have already described the "mental senses," by which we are aware of what is going on in our own minds. We "see" the proof of a logical proposition by comparing images we have created in our minds. We also "see" the output of intuition. We "see" items of memory as we retrieve them (or "hear" or "feel" or "smell" or "taste"). We "feel" feelings of joy, sadness, anger, and fear in our minds, as distinct from physical feelings of pain and pleasure. When we dream, we "see" and "hear" and "feel" a whole theatrical production.

These mental senses are normally able to differentiate (and sometimes not) between something observed in physical reality, something observed in mental reality, like a dream, and something created in the imagination.

Previous cultural terms, like "introspection" and "the mind's eye," don't make a clear distinction between the ability to create and the ability to perceive things in the mind. I am using the expression "mental senses" to make it clear that I am referring only to the ability of the mind to perceive itself.

We all have these mental senses, to a greater or lesser degree. The ability to perceive our own mental processes is something that has been called "consciousness."

These are the normal mental senses. There are also abnormal mental senses which have been employed by seers throughout history and have been verified by researchers in parapsychology like J.B. Rhine since the mid-20th-century. The expression "extra-sensory perception (ESP)" is of course a contradiction in terms if "perceptions" and "senses" are equivalent, and parapsychologists now use the term "psi" to refer to paranormal perceptions.

These, of course, are what the culture calls "the sixth sense." Psi abilities that have been demonstrated successfully in the laboratory include precognition, or the ability to see the future, clairvoyance, or the ability to see or sense things that could not be detected with the physical senses, such as things happening at great distances, and telepathy, or the ability to detect what is on the mind of another person. The interesting thing about the research in parapsychology is that most of it has been done with normal people. Yes, gifted people do better, but most normal people have shown some ability to use these psychic perceptions (Feather, 2005).

I got the idea, from seeing diagrams of the "conscious" and "subconscious" parts of the mind in psychology books, that these were fixed parts of the mind. Maybe that was just my misunderstanding, because as I went through psychotherapy and dream analysis, my subconscious receded, and more and more of my mind became conscious. I experienced it symbolically as the raising of a window shade, or the waters receding and revealing a beautiful but formerly unknown land, full of trees and flowers.

Even what I had previously thought of as "consciousness" was improved. I realized that formerly I had been only partially conscious, as I became more fully conscious of things.

I could see things, as they crossed the threshold into consciousness, first as only glimpses, like fish at the bottom of a deep pool. Then gradually they would emerge, more and more clearly, as they came to the surface and finally into full consciousness.

So "conscious" and "subconscious" are not fixed places in the brain. It is possible to roll back the shade of the subconscious and bring that area into consciousness. "Consciousness" is only the ability to perceive one's own mental processes via the mental senses.

To what extent one's subconscious can be made conscious, I

don't know. Some yogis can control their heartbeats and other "automatic" functions. And it is possible to bring into consciousness those perceptions that are normally subconscious, like the various psi abilities.

Artificially expanding the consciousness through drugs can be traumatic and potentially harmful, as in my dream of being half insane, or my experience of dead people coming into my dreams after smoking marijuana. Things are subconscious for a reason. The mind protects us from things we aren't ready to handle.

So if you are looking for instant enlightenment through LSD, consider the risks of a "bad trip" — fifteen years of sheer terror, clinging to Jesus for dear life, followed by five years of psychotherapy, bringing you to the stage of enlightenment you probably would have reached in that time naturally, without the pain.

For those gifted few who have made it to enlightenment, there are also "spiritual senses," by which one perceives the spiritual reality. Instead of calling this "mysticism," as the word has been used to discredit Carl Jung, I would call this "evidence." I would say that all founders of religions have had visions or revelations through these spiritual senses. I think the courage and "faith" of the saints is because they have actually seen the spiritual reality and know for a fact that it is true. And I think that the "faith" of ordinary people comes from the spiritual senses buried in the subconscious. They aren't really aware of the spiritual reality, but on some level they "sense" that it exists. From time to time ordinary people catch glimpses of the spiritual reality, as I did with the "big 'I' in the sky" and the death experience.

If the only way that we know anything is through our perceptions, some clever person could turn that around and say that there is no reality independent of our perception of it, or even that we create the reality by our perception of it, and it would be very difficult, if not impossible, to prove them wrong. Some clever person has already done that — George Berkeley, more than two hundred years ago. Of course Berkeley is dead now, but he argued that the reality exists because SOMEBODY has perceived it, and that is what is so difficult to disprove. Philosophers since Berkeley have felt they had to take Berkeley's argument into account. In fact, most of present-day Western philosophy seems to be people answering other people's arguments, or answering answers to arguments, or answers to answers to arguments, ...

I don't want to fall into that trap, but how can I avoid it?

I don't design computer software by debugging all the competing software previously written. I just write my software and bring it into the marketplace, and see who uses it. I take that same approach with the works of philosophers like Berkeley. Let their followers support their products in the marketplace, and I will support mine, and let's see whose product works best.

Psychologists have shown that children by the age of two have figured out that there is a reality independent of their perception of it. Children know by that age that when their mother has left the room, she has not ceased to exist. How do they know? I don't know. But I do know that they are never disillusioned in their belief. Since this belief has never failed us, I see no reason to turn it around.

Another philosopher creating confusion here is Immanuel Kant. Kant argued that we have "a priori" knowledge, knowledge that precedes the evidence of the senses, like our concepts of time and space. As I see it, (along with many Western philosophers), the concepts of time and space are abstractions that we build upon countless perceptions of the senses (not to mention cultural education).

Also I have identified an internal time clock as one of my "senses." I have heard that Kant was very punctual. I would guess that he had a very precise sense of time, but didn't recognize it as a "sense."

As with Berkeley, let the followers of Kant promote his system and show that it is accurate. I hold to my relatively simple view that the raw data upon which all our knowledge is built comes through our perceptions first, and is then processed in our minds by the other faculties.

Another problem that has baffled the philosophers throughout the ages is that our senses are unreliable. There are optical illusions. There are people who are color-blind. There are people who are totally blind. Even at their best, our senses don't perceive the ultimate reality. Reliable or not, our senses are all that we have to perceive the reality, so what can we do to make them work?

In computer technology, people have learned how to build reliable systems out of unreliable components. This is nothing new. People have been doing this with the senses ever since they had senses to do it with. We combine the input of our various senses with our reasoning ability to create a more accurate picture of the reality. If you can't see the tree, you can touch the tree. What might be a mirage in the distance is resolved when you get up to it, and can see more reliably the water, and can feel and taste it — or not. Or you just learn by experience that heat waves create the illusion of water in the distance.

Philosophers and holy men alike have complained that our senses give us only a crude perception of our immediate environment, and don't show us the ultimate truth. Our senses don't show us the cells of the body, or the atoms and molecules and sub-atomic force fields. Holy men have told us "All is illusion." Well, if the ground the holy man is standing on is all illusion, then why doesn't he fall through into nether space?

Our senses may not perceive the ultimate and absolute truth, but they give us relative truth, relative to our environment. The table-top is hard; my elbow is hard. I relate to the table-top in a certain way. The ground is solid, solid enough to support the weight of the holy man. The more we learn about these relationships, the more we know, not of ultimate truth, but of relative truth.

The environment is everything we relate to. And if the environment is everything we relate to, then what else, really, do we need to know? To start with, our senses have evolved because they have enabled us to survive in a physical environment.

Besides, our senses are all we have to perceive the reality, so they'll have to do. If all we had was a single antenna to grope our way around the universe, we would have to make do with that.

Consider the computer: The basic computer circuit can only count to one, and yet with these circuits combined in an intelligent design, the computer can do complex mathematics, calculate pi to thousands of decimal places, make logical decisions, store documents, play games, and play back music and movies. In the same way, our crude senses, when combined with our ability to reason and to build instruments, can perceive more and more subtle intricacies of our environment in a relative sense, as it relates to us.

If the senses are all we have to perceive the reality, then why are these people telling us to reject the senses? Do they have something better to offer? Usually the answer is that we should ignore our own perceptions and believe instead on the authority of these people.

DREAMS

I just want to make the point here that dreaming is an important human mental activity. Freud recognized dreams as "the royal road to the unconscious." Carl Jung improved upon Freud's knowledge by recognizing that dreams were a correction to, or compensation for, the conscious attitude. Jung also knew about the self-steering process in 1931, but did not publicize it as I did, or seem to recognize its importance.

Certainly the self-correcting aspect of dreams is very important. What other human mental faculty has a self-correcting function built in? Science is accurate because it includes a correction mechanism, replication, which works on the principle that two minds (or more) are better than one. But with the self-steering mechanism, actually, one mind is better than one.

And how does the self-steering mechanism work? What aspect of the mind is so accurate that it can correct the conscious mind and educate it with this awesome display of wisdom? I originally assumed that my subconscious mind was doing the correcting, with 20 times the mental power of the conscious mind, until I talked to the Catholic priest at the dream conference. Now I'm not so sure. Maybe dreams do come from God. Maybe Swedenborg was right. Or at least maybe I am receiving an education from some spiritual source, tapping some universal Mind while I am sleeping, and becoming conscious of that through my dreams. I don't really know how dreams work. All I know is that they do work, and that they gave me an education in the winter of 1966-67.

I have had precognitive dreams, and I had the dream of my grandmother's death, received at a distance of 350 miles from the source. These dreams defied all present laws of physics. Therefore what we know as "laws" of physics need to be revised to incorporate this information. My simplest explanation is to postulate that there is another dimension in the universe, a mental dimension, that is independent of space and time. I can pick up messages from that dimension when I am dreaming.

I also have this little tidbit from Richard Kieninger supporting my "mental dimension" theory:

> ... Egos of great advancement are able to converse mentally with their counterparts on the other planets; so They have no need whatever of physical space ships to acquaint Themselves with human activities elsewhere.
>   (Kieninger, 1971, pages 2-3)

Implied here is that this mental dimension is totally independent of physical distance, and that once one's mind is developed fully, one is able to communicate consciously and accurately via this mental dimension.

I am receiving messages through this mental dimension all the time, but my conscious mind is only crudely aware of them on an emotional level, becoming "manic" or depressed depending on whether the news is good or bad. I become manic or depressed when the stock market goes up or down. When people are being murdered in my mental environment, I get horrible feelings, and when good things are happening, I become elated, all in advance of receiving the news through my physical senses. But it is only in my dreams that I am able to actually see the message.

I see dreams as experiences in this mental dimension, while we are asleep. And through this mental dimension we are able to receive messages from spiritual dimensions, which may be more distant than the farthest planet (as implied in my death experience), or as near as the very center of our being.

All this speculation aside, our dream experiences while we are asleep are an important complement to, and commentary on, our real-life experiences while we are awake, for the development of knowledge and wisdom on this earth (even if you don't believe in the soul's continuing education through reincarnation).

This is a long way from the physical scientists with their expensive equipment doing brain scans. I see them as being in the first grade, as far as their knowledge of dreams goes. The people who have actually observed dreams with the mental senses have gone much farther in their knowledge of dreams. So while the physical scientists are spending their "many lifetimes" (and they may yet succeed in getting a recording of a dream), I am hoping more people will study dreams by the time-honored method of observing a dream and writing it down. And I am hoping that society will learn to recognize that the evidence of the mental senses is "evidence."

On the subject of "evidence," I took a course in atomic physics and we never once observed an atom. Modern physics deals with entities so minute that really all they are testing is theories: "If such-and-such a theory is true, then we should see an energy change at this level." There is a huge structure of logic in between what is actually observed and the "findings" of modern physics.

In many cases they are dealing in metaphors. For example, sometimes sub-atomic entities behave like particles, and sometimes they behave like waves. Obviously the metaphor isn't accurate. Maybe they behave like mayonnaise.

In chemistry class, we studied balls and sticks. The balls were atoms, and the sticks were chemical bonds holding them together.

So the physical sciences deal with highly theoretical objects, objects which aren't actually observed in reality, but their effect can be observed in reality. And if the observation of these effects of theoretical objects can be accepted as "evidence," then certainly, with no less stretch of the imagination, the observations of dreams, presented in an orderly theoretical framework, can be taken as "evidence."

One dream, taken by itself, can be taken as a random firing of the brain's memory contents (more or less), just as one atom may travel in a somewhat random, senseless pattern. But taken in a series, a collection over a long period of time, dreams show patterns, just as the random atoms define the shape and size of an object. Carl Jung recognized the importance of a series of dreams, as opposed to an individual dream. A dream-series, given the self-steering process, can be a highly accurate source of knowledge, as accurate as any method we know, including science.

Within this theoretical framework, dreams can be taken as "evidence" and can be a source of knowledge, just as chemistry and physics give us knowledge within their respective abstract theoretical framework.

HYPNOTISM

I told myself that I would have to study hypnotism before I would be ready to write this book. Then I read *The Great Psychological Crime* by J.E. Richardson, describing hypnotism as a major invasion of another person's mental space, for which there are serious karmic consequences. I didn't want to take that risk, either to be hypnotized or to hypnotize another person. So somebody else can pursue that subject.

But I have made a few observations of hypnotic "suggestion" (actually "command") in effect in daily life. Some of these things I'll be discovering in the next chapter. I am including hypnotism here because it is part of the mind, as I see it, and an important part of the mental environment.

A friend in Nova Scotia used to talk about "the New York mindfuckers." I am sure there are more of them in New York than Nova Scotia, just as there are more people in New York. About the time of the drug revolution, people discovered that they could implant hypnotic suggestions in other people's heads, I suppose because the drugs made people more open to suggestion (Cohen, 1967), but it works even without drugs. By "hypnotic suggestion" I mean an idea that somebody puts in your head that you accept as true, even though it is false according to everything you know and your conscious reasoning ability. Or, put the other way around, it is a thought that bypasses your critical faculties and is accepted by you uncritically. I can't tell you the examples of "mindfuck" which succeeded with me, but here are a couple of examples of when it failed.

I was pulling into the parking lot at The Moors, which appeared to be full, except for a couple of spaces right in front of the door. Just then, a couple came out of the restaurant and said, "There's a parking space there in the back," pointing to the farthest row away from the restaurant. I thanked them and parked in front of the door, but with some hesitation (checking to make sure there was no "handicap parking" sign).

I was getting on the train at Philadelphia bound for New York. I could see that the front cars were full as it came into the station, so I headed towards the back of the train, looking for a seat. When I asked a young woman, "Is this seat taken?" she said, "There are plenty of seats in the front of the train." I answered, "I don't know that." What I really meant was "I know that that isn't true," but I don't always get it right in real time.

So here are two deliberate attempts at misinformation by people I can reasonably assume are from New York.

And then there are the processes I call "mind-jamming" and "mind-scrambling." Some people, when they are in an argument with me, have the ability to block my thoughts. This I call "mind-jamming." Others have the "mind-scrambling" ability, the ability to scramble my thoughts so that I can't think straight. Some people can do both. When I am out of their presence, or "force field" as I think of it, I am able to think straight again. I remember telling a former boss, who was exceedingly brilliant, "Just let me think about it overnight, and I'll tell you in the morning." And of course, given the chance to remove myself from his force field and think about it clearly, I was able to see the many errors in what he was proposing.

In my most recent place of employment, there were about half a dozen people within whose force field I wasn't able to think straight. This wasn't in any kind of an argument, because we all had a friendly and cooperative relationship, just helping each other to get our work done. I think it had more to do with sheer mental power, because I sincerely believe that most of the people there were smarter than I was. It was more like a louder radio station drowning out a less powerful one.

In TV court dramas, you see stuff that I don't think would be allowed in a real courtroom. For example, the lawyer says, "Isn't it true that you picked up the axe and brutally hacked the victim to death 29 times?" This isn't really a question but a hypnotic suggestion that is being planted in the minds of the jury, and everybody in the courtroom. The image of somebody hacking somebody to death is so powerful that it comes into the mind and sticks, regardless of any attempt of the mind to say "This is only a question," or of the judge to say "The jury will disregard the question."

There are also tactics used in politics and the sleazy press, like "We're not saying that Bob Gebelein is a child molester or a mass-murderer, but ..." And of course logically and legally they aren't saying it, but really they are saying it, because that hypnotic implant has made its way into the minds of everybody in their audience.

Stage hypnotism and medical hypnotism, where a person surrenders completely to the powers of "suggestion," are really only the most dramatic examples of a process that goes on constantly in our daily lives, influencing our thoughts and shading our beliefs.

THE MIND IS NOTHING BUT THE PHYSICAL BRAIN

A well known scientist appeared before me one day on television, looked me straight in the eye, and said (as best I can remember it), "There is not one shred of evidence that the mind is anything but the physical brain." It doesn't matter who the scientist was. He was echoing an opinion that has been heard many times, from many scientists.

The key to that statement is the word "evidence." If you accept only the evidence of the physical senses, most likely you will see only physical phenomena. Present-day scientists don't even recognize that there are mental senses or spiritual senses, much less accept anything detected by those senses as "evidence." They accept as evidence only what has been detected by the physical senses, and "explain away" the rest. Explaining things away was one of the first things I learned to do in science labs. Scientists are very good at this.

Not only do scientists accept only physical evidence, but also, because they have the status, they make the rules that govern how observed phenomena are to be interpreted: Any possible physical explanation is to be accepted over any non-physical, especially spiritual, explanation. That really seems to be the ultimate in bias. Couldn't physical and spiritual interpretations of things be given equal weight? The answer is "No." For many scientists, spiritual explanations of things simply can't be allowed. Everything must be explained in physical terms.

And scientists have the status to enforce this. Not only do scientists make the rules, but scientists are the judge and jury to decide what is accepted as knowledge, or not. This doesn't seem fair, that scientists should be the judge in a debate in which they are one of the adversaries.

So I think I'll take the issue to a higher court: I decide what I believe, and you decide what you believe. We don't need scientists to decide these things for us. We can look at scientists as consultants or advisors, to tell us what is probably true, but we don't have to give them the authority to tell us what to believe. I say "give them" because that authority is yours and mine, to keep or give away as we choose. And especially since many scientists appear to be highly biased against the possibility of a spiritual reality, this is a good reason to keep them in their place: Where the issue is purely physical, science is highly reliable, but when the subject crosses the line into the area of the mental or physical, the opinions of scientists are suspect.

Even with only the evidence of the physical senses being acceptable, the parapsychologists have managed to demonstrate the reality of precognition, clairvoyance, and telepathy, by the strictest rules of physical science. But the physical scientists got them at Step 2, where any physical explanation is preferable to any non-physical explanation. Insinuations have been made that the parapsychologists have used bad science, or their experiments haven't been replicated, or they have been duped by magicians' tricks, and even though these insinuations are false, they are accepted over the non-physical explanation by the physical scientists because, Step 3: These same scientists are the court by which the issue is judged.

And the idea that the mind is nothing but the physical brain is a verdict of that court.

So, starting with Step 3, I would like to see issues like this ruled upon by an International Court of justices, independent of the people arguing on both sides. When I say "ruled upon," I mean only offering some kind of an official opinion, not binding on anybody. It is still you and I that decide what to believe for ourselves.

At Step 2, I would put things into whatever bin — physical, mental, spiritual — that seems most appropriate. I think that is the most reasonable and sensible way to do it.

Let us postulate that there are physical, mental, and spiritual dimensions in the universe. Let us put into the appropriate category whatever observations we might have. If we have no observations of a particular category, then that category can be empty, but let us at least set up the structure to allow it.

I welcomed science when I was first introduced to it, because it gave me a means to combat the moral judgments of religion and the authority of the Bible. Part of that is to deny the existence of the

spiritual, to take away the power of religion. I think other people
have embraced science in the same way. What I am proposing now
is not to go back to the authoritarian rule of religion with its moral
judgments, but to extend science, in the spirit of science, asking not
what is "good" and "evil," but only "What is?" I want to extend the
scientific rules of evidence to include the evidence of the mental
senses and the spiritual senses. I want to build on the discovery of
Carl Jung that it is possible to learn spiritual truths not just from
Holy Books written thousands of years ago, but on the basis of
evidence, obtained in a scientific way. This is not moving back to the
past, to religion, but ahead, to a new kind of scientific understanding
of the universe.

Do I have a complete picture of this physical, mental, and
spiritual universe? Certainly not. I am only reaching out from my
small understanding to a slightly larger understanding, one step at a
time.

I am reminded of Columbus, who sailed across an ocean and
discovered the island of San Salvador, and thought he had reached
the East Indies. He was wrong, and he only discovered a small
island, but he had proved his point, and he was followed by many
more explorers who discovered more. In the same way, little
independent discoveries can add up, until we have a comprehensive
view of the mental and spiritual dimensions.

So I would present to the International Court for their approval,
first of all, the hypothesis that there are physical, mental, and
spiritual dimensions in the universe.

Second, I would present my definition of "evidence," that it
should include all human perceptions, including those of the mental
and spiritual senses. The Court can decide what is a "hallucination"
and what is a true "vision" of the spiritual reality, and who is a
reliable observer or not.

Third, I would ask the Court to accept the "most reasonable" rule,
that things should be put in the category most appropriate, and not
explained away as physical by every possible stretch of the
imagination.

Then I would present my evidence that the mind is more than the physical brain. I am only listing these things here, because I have already described them:

The conviction from age 4 that I had always existed. This conviction came from somewhere, something I "sensed" in my subconscious.

The big "I" in the sky that I "saw" with some inner sense, when I was 9.

The dream of my grandmother's death, which I received at a distance of 350 miles from the source.

My precognitive dream of the psychiatrist greeting me at Grand Central Station.

The scientific evidence of precognition, telepathy, and clairvoyance assembled by researchers in parapsychology.

Carl Jung's discovery that there is information that comes out of the subconscious that wasn't put there in this lifetime — that the subconscious is a source of information and wisdom, not just a garbage dump. It could be argued that I could have been exposed to a great deal of wisdom in my education that didn't consciously register with me. There is plenty that I could have observed subconsciously, just as people discover when they are hypnotized. But by the "most reasonable" rule, this isn't a reason for rejecting this point, but only assigning it the status of "possible truth."

Carl Jung's discovery of "original experience," that it is possible to discover the spiritual through evidence, and not just Holy Books.

My dream experience:
The education I received from dreams, the self-steering process of dream analysis, uncovering the traumatic experience the psychiatrist missed, reaching the psychological age of puberty. If the dreams were giving me all this knowledge, then why would they deceive me into thinking there was a spiritual reality? They were definitely presenting the spiritual reality:

My grandmother and Tada coming into my dreams.

The dream of the large ship being resurrected, definitely pointing to reincarnation. Steering a big "S" course out into the harbor, obviously standing for "Spirit" or "Soul." The oppositeness of "spiritual" dreams, like a cold wind blowing from the south, making it easy to differentiate spiritual dreams from other dreams.

The lessons of love, learning the meaning of love, the symbol "light" meaning "love."

Then the supreme Light, the supreme Love. Certainly, if not a supreme being, this represents a supreme power in the universe, and that power is spiritual, and that power is Love.

The dream of the spiritual teacher, clearly pointing out the physical laws and the spiritual laws, and explaining that both sets of laws are equally precise and equally binding.

The dream of the camera car, definitely teaching me that it is possible to see into the future.

Dreaming of my friend coming to visit, he arguing that it could be a case of telepathy, of me reading his mind as he made plans to visit.

Dreaming of the car not starting, definite evidence of precognition. Here was a mechanical device that had a malfunction that nobody knew about until I dreamed it.

The self-steering mechanism is monitoring all this: Never have any of the above interpretations of my dreams been corrected.

Replication: People who have successfully completed Jungian analysis have had essentially the same spiritual experiences in their dreams.

Edgar Cayce life readings: The first reading on reincarnation was unprompted. Reincarnation wasn't part of Cayce's belief structure; therefore he had to overcome a bias against it. All 2500+ life readings asserted the fact of reincarnation.

Books already written on reincarnation and karma, and more every day on spiritual subjects. Some of it may be deception — necessary to sort it all out.

People who went to investigate Edgar Cayce: Hugo Munsterberg, Harvard, 1912, failed to "expose" Cayce (Sugrue, 1967, pages 11-33). William Moseley Brown, Washington and Lee, 1928, "I can't expose it. ... I'll have to believe in it." (Sugrue, 1967, page 236)

My impression on visiting the A.R.E.: Nice Virginia lady showing me the library, very low key, no sales pitch.

People making insinuations about Edgar Cayce are requested to come before the Court with their evidence.

Ian Stevenson, *Twenty Cases Suggestive of Reincarnation*. This is a fine piece of research and should be replicated.

The death experience, 1969: I am transported up into the presence of the Light and the figure of Christ, who says "Get back to work." From that point on I am not afraid to die, and feel that my work is supported by higher beings.
Discovery of my spiritual self made me feel complete, where I had felt there was something missing after completing therapy.
Every society in the world has a belief in the spiritual. Is this evidence of a spiritual reality, or only of a mental distortion that we all share?

Columbus brought back an "Indian" to prove he had sailed to the "Indies." What do I have to show for my mental and spiritual explorations?
I have GERALD FORD CARTER printed in pencil on an old piece of cheap paper. Are there dating methods that would prove when this was written? It isn't much, but it's a start.

PART III

MIND POLLUTION

7. REPRESENTATION, MANIPULATION, AND MENTAL WARFARE

REPRESENTATION

I was first made aware of the idea of "representation" when I visited The Stelle Group in Chicago in 1971. They had a practice of not "representing" another person. First of all that meant that they had a town-meeting type of government, where the people each represented themselves, as opposed to a representative type of government. But mainly it meant that they didn't say anything about another person or pretend to describe another person, and this was the new meaning I was exposed to. They didn't say "You are this," or "He/she/they are this."

It was uncomfortable to start with, especially because they didn't judge me as good or bad, either. They didn't give me the expected ego-strokes of social approval, like "That's good."

And it is impossible to do, too, to never represent another person. Right now I am representing The Stelle Group. The best I can do is to keep that representation at a minimum and to make sure it is as accurate as possible.

The problem with representation is that it is usually misrepresentation. And many times it is deliberately derogatory misrepresentation, as in "Democratic dirty tricks," or "You are a jerk."

So, then, what I mean by "representation" here is not that Charlie Bass became my representative in Congress in 1994, or that Charlie Bass didn't represent my interests. What I am really talking about here is the way his campaign represented his opponent, Dick Swett, in 1994. It was, in my opinion, the dirtiest political campaign I had ever witnessed, at the time (but mild compared to more recent political campaigns). I never did learn what Charlie Bass represented, except of course that he represented the derogatory representation of his opponent.

I wanted to write my Congressman saying that there should be a law making it illegal to represent one's opponent in a Federal election, except for matters of public record and exact quotes and representations that were determined to be accurate by a court of law. But my Congressman was Charlie Bass, in a Congress dominated by Newt Gingrich, and what was the use?

Not long after that, in the winter of 1995, I joined discussion groups on the Internet, on the subjects of "world transformation" and "new civilization," and began learning first-hand, for the first time in my life, about representation, or what is normally called "politics" — people bashing each other mentally.

A friend of mine from Brooklyn once compared me to a delicate orchid, that wouldn't be able to survive in the "real world." So, for those of you who are street-wise, this may seem to be a really elementary education. But in my state of innocence I have learned things in full adult consciousness that other people may not have thought about much, and I am hoping that my insights may be useful.

I sent copies of *Re-Educating Myself* to the leaders of all these discussion groups, and one of them replied with a piece called "The Myth of the Self-Made Individual." It was a bunch of generalities punctuated by smear-words — "myth," "archaic," "pretensions," "erroneous out worn notions," "simplistic," "superstitions," "folkways," "irrational." There was no evidence that this person had read any of my book except for the title. The "self" in the title had triggered an automatic response well known in academic circles.

The self-made individual is a stereotype in America, the person who starts off without benefit of social position or money or formal education and makes it to the top. This person represents the promise and opportunity of America, "the American dream."

And somewhere along the line, somebody in academia pretended that this self-made individual was claiming to be exclusively self-made, without any social influences other than self. And in so doing, this academic person created what my dictionary calls a "straw man" — a fictional person who is easy to beat up on. It is very easy to show that nobody is exclusively self-made or self-taught. To start with, we all learn language from somebody else. We learn many things from other people. We read books. And so on. But this fictional self-made individual doesn't exist in reality, because nobody is claiming to be exclusively self-made or self-taught. Those self-made individuals are only claiming to have made it without the benefits of money, social position, and formal education.

Having this straw man in one's collection of stereotypes, it is then easy enough to spew out "the myth of the self-made individual" whenever anybody claims anything for "self." The "myth," actually, is the fictional straw man who does not exist in reality. And extending the myth to include "re-educating myself" is an even greater misrepresentation of the real person.

First of all, I never even claimed to be "self-educated." I was educated in some of the finest schools in America, and I give full credit to "the system" for that. But that education did not give me the necessary background to solve the cultural problems I faced in 1955. And it seemed that those problems, especially the threat of nuclear annihilation, were evidence of "systems failure" of the same culture that had given me the education. I needed a re-education, and I didn't see anybody to give me that re-education but myself.

When I say I am "Harvard educated," it is clearly understood that that doesn't mean that Harvard wrote all the books. Harvard only determines the course of study and decides which books I should read. When I say "re-educating myself," it means the same thing: I determined the course of study. It doesn't mean that I am claiming to have invented all the methods involved or to have written all the books.

I am dwelling on this because this particular straw man seems to be an entrenched belief in academia. He doesn't represent me, and he doesn't represent any real person.

There were many more misrepresentations of me on the Internet. I started off by saying that I believed that there was such a thing as "right" and "wrong," and I was criticized for my stance. (Am I "wrong," then?) It was represented that I saw everything in terms of black and white only, and that I was intolerant of other people's beliefs. Again, I was made into a straw person, easy to knock down.

When I argued against people's cherished books, beliefs, and gurus, some of them argued that I had a psychological problem that compelled me to be negative and destructive. The problem with this argument was that no two described the same psychological problem, and they all described psychological problems that more nearly seemed to represent themselves.

In one discussion group, my name, Gebelein, was compared to the name of Hitler's propaganda minister, Goebbels. In another group, a person invented the name "Gabbling," which I thought was very original and very effective, to portray me as "babbling."

I learned about "red herrings" in my prep-school English before I ever saw and smelled a real red herring, the summer I was seventeen. And I learned about smear tactics at the same time. In Harvard freshman English they drilled into our heads the difference between valid arguments and propaganda techniques. I think the people I worked with in the business world must have taken the same equivalent courses, because I rarely encountered these invalid methods of argument in my working career, and when I did, people recognized them for what they were.

But on the Internet, it seems, people didn't all have that equivalent education, and the invalid arguments were common — the smear tactics, misrepresentations, propaganda techniques, and character assassinations. I hadn't experienced these tactics in my personal life, either, since the eighth grade.

It was easy for people in the group to misrepresent me because nobody really knew me. American politics works the same way. Most of us know very little about the candidates. That makes it easy for an unscrupulous opponent to influence the voters very heavily by misrepresenting a candidate.

That's why I would like to go back to the system of Presidential Electors, in the original sense: We vote for somebody we respect and know locally, who also knows the political candidates, and then those Electors gather and choose a President. Now that the country has grown, it might work better on four levels — tribal, local, state, and federal. That way, first-hand knowledge is in control all the way, and misrepresentation has less of a chance of success.

I just want to pause for a moment and reflect on the fact that we choose our government, our most important institution, from among people we don't know, many of whom misrepresent themselves and each other in order to get elected. No wonder we mistrust them on things like UFOs. If they lie to us to get elected, of course they are going to lie to us when they are in office. I suppose at least that is better than having a mentally-deranged King born to the office "by Divine Right."

In representing their opponents, political candidates turn the attention away from themselves. We tend to pay attention to what they are saying and not what they are doing. We tend to look at the person the finger is being pointed at, and not the person pointing the finger. It is not so easy to see persons who represent others negatively simply as persons who represent others negatively.

In the political arena, it shouldn't be too difficult for people to understand, regardless of education or intelligence, that when one political candidate says something derogatory about the other, it is done in order to win votes, and should not be taken as true. What maybe not everybody knows is that some people in politics (as opposed to other professions) are allowed to lie. Joe McCarthy got away with his smear tactics because you can't sue a United States Senator for defamation of character.

The second thing that should be understood is that if Able says derogatory things about Baker, then Able is the kind of person who would say derogatory things about another. Able represents Able in that respect, and not necessarily Baker. Whatever Able says about Baker represents Able's character and not Baker's.

And so I learned on the Internet, and tried to point out to others, that the persons doing the talking were representing themselves. At least if we understood that much in American politics, we would be taking a step towards a new civilization.

In representing persons, there are three parties involved — the Speaker, the Target, and the Audience. When Person A says to Person C, "Bob Gebelein is weird," Person A is the Speaker, Bob Gebelein is the Target, and Person C is the Audience. The Speaker is making some statement which is supposed to represent the Target, for the benefit of the Audience, usually to influence the Audience's opinion of the Target.

These roles can also be combined, in all possible ways. The Speaker can also be the Target, as when I am saying things about myself. The Target can also be the Audience, as when somebody says to me, "You are weird," to undermine my self-confidence. The Speaker is always part of the Audience, always hearing what is said, and can be exclusively the Audience, as in trying to convince oneself of something. In all this it should be clear that the Speaker is always representing the Speaker and the Speaker's opinion.

I am the world's foremost expert on myself. I have known myself all my life — not only my outward actions, but all my innermost thoughts as well. And yet even my own representation of myself is not accurate. My knowledge is not complete, and my words are not adequate to express it. The representation of me by a person who has known me for ten years is likely to be less accurate. The representation of me by a person who has known me for only ten minutes, or has read only a few words that I have written, is surely even less accurate.

So I am the best qualified person to say whether a representation of myself is accurate or not. But you don't know me, or know whether I am lying. But you know yourself. And you are the best qualified person to know whether a representation of you is accurate. You know how you have been misrepresented, and so you can assume that when others are being represented, they are also being represented inaccurately. (This is replication. We don't all have to be observing the same gorilla.)

Without knowing anything about the person being represented, there are certain assumptions you can make:

Politicians representing their opponents are obviously trying to be derogatory. Even an exact quote may be taken out of context or may not accurately reflect the thinking behind it. I try to get the story from an impartial source, or ignore it.

There are certain levels of smear tactics. At the lowest level are just plain derogatory words like "jerk," "asshole," and "idiot," which obviously don't represent the Target, but certainly do represent the Speaker and the Speaker's willingness to use such words.

Then there are the pseudoscientific smear-words, like "pseudo-science," "folk-belief," "myth," "supernatural," "superstition," etc. You can be sure that anybody using smear-words is not doing science.

At the next level are the pseudo-psychological diagnoses, like "paranoid," "deluded," "anal," etc. At best, such a diagnosis would have to be made by somebody in the field of psychology/psychiatry, after having examined the person over some period of time. These findings would be confidential unless ordered by a court of law. And in the final analysis, psychologists/psychiatrists can't really observe a person's mental state unless they are clairvoyant.

And I am always on the lookout for psychological projections. People giving psychological descriptions of others are often describing themselves. Also people using certain words like "judgmental" are describing themselves.

Then there is the preemptive mode of projection, like "Democratic dirty tricks," where one side accuses the other of exactly what they are doing themselves before the others can accuse them, so that if the others then accuse them, it looks like retaliation and not the truth. I suppose this is a carefully thought-out strategy, maybe even documented in textbooks.

At the highest level are the plausible representations, the ones that might possibly be true. Did Freud have sex with his daughter? Did 25% of the people in the Clinton Administration do drugs? Was Anita Hill's representation of Clarence Thomas accurate? When you eliminate all the representations where obvious smear tactics are being employed, there aren't many of these plausible representations left. And even at this level the words don't mean much, because the only way to find out the truth of the situation is through some kind of evidence.

With this understanding, it would be foolish for one person to represent another, except as a witness of specific simple actions or exact quotes in context. It is not necessary to pass a law saying "Don't represent others." Instead of the commandment, we have the statement of fact: "You don't represent others." An informed public will recognize this, and those who try to represent others will simply lose credibility.

Maybe we need laws, to start with, to make it clear that this isn't the way we want to do politics. But ultimately the answer lies in educating the Audience to recognize the inaccuracy of these tactics. I envision that the Audience in a new civilization will see the people who pretend to represent others as some kind of crazy people, just howling at the moon.

When I was young and didn't have the conscious self-knowledge that I have now, I listened to people's representations of me. Sometimes they were better representations than I had of myself, and sometimes they were very misleading. For example, my math teacher told me I was the laziest student he had ever had, when I was 14 and getting a straight "A" in his course, because I didn't do the extra problems that he thought I might enjoy doing. And I went through prep school and college with the idea that I was lazy — not just ordinary lazy, but super-lazy, the laziest student this teacher had seen in 20 years or so.

Self-knowledge is self-defense in the area of representation. The more you know about yourself, the better you can recognize when you are being misrepresented. And for the young people who really don't know themselves well, you can just assume you are being misrepresented, unless something really rings a bell.

Getting back to the Internet, a guy joined the discussion group and began telling us we should abandon the intellect and follow his way, which was something like the mystical path. Immediately I took issue with him, and he replied:

```
Date: Feb 25 1997

It is clear that you are unable/unwilling to question
the rationality of your intellect.
```

Obviously he didn't know the first thing about me, that I had re-examined everything I had ever been taught to believe, and in reply I sent him this paragraph from *Re-Educating Myself*:

> One of the first questions I asked myself [1955] was whether I could use logic. It seemed that logic was a man-made artificiality, a product of the civilization I was questioning. But without logic, I couldn't get anywhere. If what was true could also be false, then I had no way of knowing anything. There would be no point in saying anything now, if the words could also mean their opposites. In order to proceed at all, I had to use logic, whether it was artificial or not.
> (Gebelein, 1985, page 20)

None of this seemed to register with him, as he persisted in holding his same opinion of me. But this exchange gave me an insight: Here was a person who knew absolutely nothing about me, except that I had challenged him, and yet from his position of almost total ignorance, he was pretending to know something about my thought process. From this experience I identified the practice of "preemptive misrepresentation."

Some people, when they don't know very much about you, will make up stuff to fill in the gaps. That is preemptive misrepresentation. Whenever you are not well known, as in somebody meeting you for the first time, there is an opportunity for the people who do this kind of thing to jump in and make up things about you. It doesn't have to be derogatory. It works both ways. For example, psychological tests have shown that when young men are shown pictures of beautiful women, they assume these women have wonderful qualities of character as well.

People who see me as a stereotype are doing preemptive misrepresentation. Racial, ethnic, and class prejudices are based on preemptive misrepresentation. Most misrepresentations are preemptive, before one has even had a chance to tell the truth about oneself.

Preemptive misrepresentation can also be used as a ploy to get at the truth, as in "You had sex with her, didn't you?" But I think more often it is just used to create fictional characters that fit more neatly than real people into somebody's belief structure or satisfy somebody's psychological needs.

In the eyes of the law, anything you say can and will be held against you. But with preemptive misrepresentation, whatever you DON'T say can and will be held against you.

In another exchange on the Internet, I was comparing my views to those of the New Age, and I was met with the following line of questioning:

```
Date: Jun 11 1995

. . .
Next Bob says:

>4A. Combining logic with perception, I decided to
use the method of science and to accept everything
proven by science.

and somebody else supposedly says:

>4B. Rejection of science

Well, are you saying that you will only accept what
is proven by somebody with scientific credentials?
And you will accept everything that such a person
proves?

. . .

Bob says:

>5A. Psychotherapy is THE way to a new civilization.

Somebody else says:

>5B. "Psychiatrists are tools of the Establishment."

So, are you saying that only people who get
psychotherapy are allowed in a new civilization. What
```

will you do with the people who have other
approaches?

And are you saying that psychiatry always is good and
helpful? Are you saying that lobotomies and Prozac
are the way to a new civilization?

. . .

Obviously all of these questions convey derogatory ideas. I was
struggling trying to figure out how best to answer these questions,
when the thought struck me: "These aren't questions. These are
suggestions."

Yes, they are phrased as questions, but they include specific
representations of me, representations that are inaccurate and make
me look bad, and these representations are implanted as suggestions
in the minds of the Audience.

"Science" is turned into "somebody with scientific credentials,"
and the word "only" is inserted to narrow my viewpoint even more.
Emphasis has been shifted from the word "proven" to the "person"
of science.

On psychotherapy, "are allowed" and "What will you do?" are
creating the suggestion that I am some kind of an authoritarian
person, making rules, and possibly disposing of people who don't
comply. I realize now that the implied assumption here is that a
"new civilization" is a new kind of government. I didn't see that at
the time, because the assumption, being implied and not stated, was
invisible to me, while at the same time acting as a suggestion to
block my thinking. (Of course my view of a new civilization is
totally different — something achieved by a majority of people
reaching the psychological age of puberty. Those people would then
determine the government, which I assume would treat with
compassion those individuals who hadn't reached that level of
development.)

The suggestions that I am saying that "psychiatry always is good
and helpful" and "lobotomies and Prozac are the way to a new
civilization" are other inaccurate and derogatory representations of
me implanted in the minds of the Audience.

If I treat these suggestions as questions and answer "No" to them, my answer will have very little effect. The "No" is nowhere near as powerful as these very specific representations of me which have already been implanted in people's minds. Besides, the Audience expects me to deny them, so they have already discounted my answer.

The way to deal with this, I decided, was to let the Audience know, each time it happened, that they had been the victims of a hypnotic implant. The Audience needs to know, to become consciously aware, that they are under constant bombardment by hypnotic implants. Once aware of hypnotic implants, the Audience will learn to identify others.

This was my initial discovery of how much our daily lives are full of hypnotic suggestions, or hypnotic implants. Going back over all the representations of me on the Internet, I realized that many of them contained hypnotic suggestions — unfounded assertions that don't need any supporting argument, because they are already in people's heads just from the act of being said.

I think I said it all better at the time:

```
Date: Sep 11 1995
From: bobgeb

From another mail group, I have just received the
statement (and I believe this is true) that if
somebody labels you a "fascist," a "racist," or a
"pervert," or smear-words to that effect, it does
create an image in people's minds — an image that is
immediately perceived to be true, and lasts for a
long time, and is hard to get rid of. Call it the
"zap" factor. The first example that comes to mind is
Ayn Rand being labeled "right wing," or Carl Jung
being labeled "a mystic" (right in my psychology
textbook).

The experiment I think has already been performed
many times with public figures whose popularity or
reputation has diminished as a result of name-
calling, and the experiment has been proved with the
well-known success of "dirty tricks" in the political
arena. "DUKAKIS WILL TAKE YOUR GUNS AWAY." Not true,
```

```
but it cost Dukakis votes in Texas, and I'm sure
there are still people in Texas today that believe
that Dukakis would have taken their guns away (that
which no President has the power to do).

But you might perform the experiment with a well-
known public figure and a definite lie proclaimed
publicly, and take polls of public opinion before and
after. I don't have to do that. I am convinced that
suggestion, or hypnotic command, plays a major role
in our daily mental lives.
```

And here is a very good reply:

```
Date: Aug-Sep 1995

Find me the poor soul that is hypnotized by
assertions? Who, specifically are you talking about?
I have more confidence in people than that, and I
invite you to trust peoples intelligence and bigness.
They can handle more than you can imagine.
```

This is a nice political move, first flattering people, and then insinuating that I am insulting all people, instead of trying to share a valuable insight with them. The inaccuracy here is that this person is sliding off from the word "hypnotic" to "hypnotized." I am not saying that anybody is "hypnotized" by assertions or that this is "hypnotism," as in having one's mind totally dominated, as in theatrical demonstrations of "hypnotism." I am using the word "hypnotic" to indicate that these assertions get implanted in the mind through the same process by which hypnotism works:

You hear the words and then your mind registers the thought: "The Moon is made of green cheese." The thought has to be in your mind and in your memory before you can evaluate it and say "Ridiculous!" That doesn't get rid of it from your mind. The memory of having heard it and having registered the thought is always with you, although now with the label "Ridiculous!" and probably buried at some subconscious level.

The thought always enters the mind first, before the mind has a chance to evaluate it. In stage hypnotism the critical/rational faculties are somehow turned off, so that the thought becomes part of one's belief system. But in a normal, non-hypnotized state, if you aren't really paying attention or taking the time to evaluate it, the thought, which has already been implanted into your mind, can escape into your belief system at some subconscious level. And even if you reject the thought, the memory of it is always there.

The mind is not usually dominated by these hypnotic implants, but it is <u>influenced</u> by them in some way, creating inaccuracies. I know highly intelligent people who didn't read Ayn Rand because she was labeled "right wing," or Carl Jung because he was labeled a "mystic." And I'm sure Dukakis lost votes in Texas because of the fear that he would take their guns away. And I know that politicians wouldn't use those kinds of tactics if they didn't work. And I think that the best defense against hypnotic implants is not to deny their reality and their effectiveness, but to be totally aware that these things are coming at you.

My examples of misrepresentation (etc.) may not be very good, because I don't do this stuff myself and I have to rely on the few examples that have been thrown my way. For some really great examples, wait until the people who do mind pollution start criticizing this book.

MANIPULATION

I said I was against "manipulation," and somebody replied, "But you are trying to manipulate us. You are trying to influence our opinion to agree with you on some things and be against other things."

True, I was trying to influence people to think my way, and I was being forceful at it, but I didn't think of it as "manipulation." My methods were different. I was trying to be as accurate as possible, and present a factual and logical argument. "Manipulation," to me, meant some kind of inaccurate or dishonest means of influencing people. But I didn't have any clear definition in my mind.

So I looked up the word in *The Shorter Oxford English Dictionary* (1964 edition):

Manipulate 1. To handle, esp. with dexterity; to treat by manual (and, hence, any mechanical) means 1831. 2. To handle or treat (questions, artistic matter, resources, etc.) with skill 1856. 3. To manage by dexterous (esp. unfair) contrivance or influence 1864.

Manipulation ... 4. Dexterous (esp. unfair) management of persons or things 1828.

I have in my mind this stereotype of the British as knowing exactly what the rules are and therefore knowing exactly what is meant here by "unfair." But I don't really know, so I looked up "unfair." And it said "not fair." So I looked up "fair." And among many definitions I found these:

Fair ... A ... III ... 2. Free from moral stain, unblemished ME. 3. Free from bias, fraud, or injustice; equitable, legitimate ME.
    (Oxford 1964)

"Fraud" implies lies and misrepresentations. "Bias" implies inaccuracy, usually caused by emotional forces. "Moral stain" implies cheating, lying, stealing, trickery, and other types of "foul play." Now we are getting a handle on what it means to

151

"manipulate" people — not the honest argument with accurate facts and logic, but some kind of deceit and trickery.

My Merriam-Webster (1996) dictionary adds the word "insidious," which they then define as "treacherous," "seductive," and "subtle." That about sums up "manipulation:" It is treacherous, involving some kind of lie, it is seductive, involving some kind of emotional pull, and it is subtle, meaning that you probably aren't aware that it is being done to you.

Manipulation is getting you to do things for false reasons. It usually involves misrepresentation. But it can also mean having your buttons pushed, or having somebody make you react emotionally, without involving any element of truth or falsehood.

For example, a young woman I was very much attracted to was asking me if I could fix her record player. I was honest with her and said I wasn't very good at fixing things like record players. She said, "That's OK. John will fix it. He's good at things like this." John was her serious boyfriend. Just the mention of the competition triggered an emotional reaction in me. Without thinking, I leaped up and went over to the record player, realized I didn't know the first thing about it, and then immediately realized that I had been manipulated, magnificently.

There are many kinds of emotional buttons that can be pushed. In addition to sexual attraction, as was used on me here, there is courage (as in "You're chicken"), patriotism, normative pressures (as in "You're not cool," or "You're a tweak"), love, money, authority, anti-authority, ego, maturity ("Grow up"), intelligence ("Don't be stupid"), psychology ("You are paranoid"), or anything that can exert an emotional force.

Manipulation can be harsh, as in "You're a whore!" Or it can also be very subtle, as in the "Jewish mother" jokes. ("It's OK. I can just sit here in the dark.") And it can include more refined techniques that haven't been invented yet — and better ones are being invented every day. I would hate to give a definition of "manipulation" that was limiting.

Going back to the first two definitions of manipulation, "to handle with dexterity or skill," manipulation means treating human beings as objects, to be handled with skill, to act according to the will of the manipulator, instead of as human beings acting on their own free will. It brings to mind puppets on strings, being controlled by somebody else.

So when I am arguing something with you, no matter how forcefully, I am treating you as another human being who can think about what I am saying, with your own mind, and can agree with me or not, of your own free will, and not exploiting you as an object whose strings can be pulled or buttons can be pushed.

The mother says to the child, "Don't play in the street, or you will get hit by a car."

This is not manipulation. The mother is just teaching the child the cause-and-effect of what the environment is like.

The mother says to the child, "Don't play in the street, or I will hit you."

This is not manipulation, either. This is "coercion." The mother is becoming a force to alter the child's environment, so that the child, of the child's own free will, chooses not to move in the direction of the street. The child is still acting out of free will, but the environment has been altered to steer that free will in a given direction.

Coercion is part of all our legitimate social institutions. It is with us all our lives. Parents use rewards and punishments to steer their children into socially-approved behavior. The schools continue with prizes for some and ridicule for others. The law needs to be enforced by coercion — guns and prisons. Your company can give you a raise or fire you, depending on whether you do what they want you to do. In all these institutions, human beings become a force to change the environment of other human beings, so that of their own free will they will move in certain directions. Everybody is aware of coercion — that forces are being applied to us to behave in certain ways — and there is no attempt to disguise it.

Now the mother says to the child, "If you play in the street, I won't love you any more."

Now the mother's physical force has been replaced with the child's own emotional force, in wanting to be loved by the mother, and this makes it more subtle. The child is probably not aware that this force has been expropriated to serve the mother's interests instead of the child's interests, or even that there is such a word as "expropriated."

Also an element of deceit has been introduced: The mother will always love the child, but the child doesn't know that. The child trusts the mother to tell the truth. The mother may even act unlovingly, just to convince the child.

When this element of deception is added, "coercion" becomes "manipulation." Manipulation always involves some kind of inaccuracy. The person is made to believe some kind of a falsehood, or the person is unaware that he/she is being coerced, or both.

I remember a friend I had in the Army, a white guy from the South. We spent many an evening together, drinking beer and arguing about why he couldn't invite a black person to his house for dinner. Evening after evening, he spouted his moral and righteous reasons. Finally, maybe just from exhaustion, he admitted, "OK, if I had a black person to dinner, the men in the white sheets would burn the house down and kill us both."

So here were these social laws in the South at the time, which people obeyed for the highest social reasons ("It just isn't done"), and people had ceased to become consciously aware of the forces of coercion enforcing these laws, until this was brought back into consciousness after a few evenings of beer-therapy.

I am complaining about manipulation, as opposed to plain and open coercion, because of the false belief systems that are created in people's minds to support or disguise the manipulation. So we have people in the past believing that the sun traveled around the earth, because that was the highest truth and the Word of God, and not because they would be burned at the stake if they claimed otherwise.

People in the present become members of a peer group, and they are told by their peers, "Play in the street. It's cool. It's not what your mother taught you."

There are two forces operating here: First there are the social pressures of the peer group, the normative pressures, to conform to their behavior. They are telling you what is "cool," what will give you respect and status in their group. That may or may not have anything to do with the wisdom of playing in the street. It is easy to confuse the two ideas, and most people do. They don't go around thinking, "Yes, I know it's stupid to play in the street, but I am gaining respect and status in the group by doing this." It is more like, "All the kids are doing this," and, implied, "I would die of humiliation if I didn't." The cause and effect of playing in the street fades into the background and maybe even into the subconscious, because the social forces applied are so much more powerful.

The second force operating here, a force that was irresistable to me, at least, is the force of rebellion from the legitimate coercion of parents and schools. Parents and teachers are pressuring you to do what is "good." Peer group leaders are promoting what is "bad," and this is emotionally appealing to all kids, to question the "authority" that has been imposed on them — to rebel against it, and to try the "bad" things.

But instead of just experimenting with the "bad" things to find out why they are bad (or not), some kids will decide that the "bad" things are "good" because they give them status and respect within the peer group. Some people make that peer-group approval a criterion for knowledge throughout their lives.

If you belong to any social group, you must conform to their social laws. You must act as they act and think as they think — or at least pretend to. The social laws are enforced by what I call "social manipulation." It starts out as obvious coercion, like the threat of being punched in the face. Then it goes to less obvious coercion, like being called "chicken," or being called a "dwek" — you aren't really sure whether you are being coerced, or whether your peers have all (in unison) accurately identified some flaw in your character.

Eventually it is just a matter of being "cool." If you are "cool," you have friends and social pleasures. If not "cool," you don't. And what is "cool?" It goes around quickly like some social disease, and everybody knows what it is — everybody that is "cool," anyway.

"It goes without saying." Social manipulation usually operates below the threshold of consciousness.

This social group you belong to, you may think of as your "friends." But have you chosen these people of your own free will to be your friends, or are you just all being manipulated by the same strings?

To sum up "manipulation:" Manipulation is getting you to do things you would not ordinarily do of your own free will. Manipulation is getting you to do things for the wrong reasons. Manipulation always involves some kind of inaccuracy or misrepresentation: Either there is a deliberate lie, or emotional buttons are being pushed, or you are not aware of the social pressures being applied, or any combination of these things. Manipulation treats people as objects, to be handled like puppets on strings. The legitimate coercion used by our legitimate social institutions differs from manipulation in that it is totally honest and makes it totally obvious that social forces are being applied. Manipulation is insidious, treacherous, seductive, and subtle.

MENTAL WARFARE

Misrepresentation and manipulation are the two main ingredients in what I call "mental warfare."

"Mental warfare" means the use of the mind as a weapon of battle to destroy, defeat, diminish, demean, or discredit an opponent. Accurate and valid arguments are not included. Generally mental warfare is destructive to the opponent. But I would say that mental warfare has the same objective as ordinary warfare, in the words of the U.S. Military, "To destroy the will to resist."

Warfare is important. It determines who lives and who dies and who rules and whose bias is reflected in the history books, and what we call our country, and what language we speak, and what we are allowed to say or do. It may ultimately put an end to the human species.

But warfare doesn't have to determine what we think and believe. Accuracy is not determined by warfare. The social forces operating on us to manipulate us are very real, and they can pressure us into believing things that are inaccurate. But might definitely does not make right. Just because warfare is a powerful force [SAID THAT] doesn't mean it has to shape [SAY IT OVER AND OVER] what we think and believe. Our thoughts and beliefs are private. No ruler can control them.

According to *African Genesis*, warfare is older than the human species itself. The reason why human beings don't have claws and fangs and armor plate and other mechanisms of survival is because we evolved from the ape already with a weapon in our hand, to kill other creatures and also to kill each other. More basic than that, we live in an earth environment where the basic law of survival is that creatures must kill each other to eat and to defend themselves against being killed, and our most basic drives are ingrained to that end. Killing members of one's own species would seem to work against the survival of the species, but human beings have such a huge survival potential relative to other species, a potential to overpopulate the earth, that killing off a large percentage of each new generation doesn't seem to hurt.

Other species sometimes do warfare against members of their own species, usually males fighting for domination or territory or females. What makes human beings exceptional is that they organize to do warfare against their own species. Tribes fight against tribes. Nations fight against nations. Somebody a long time ago figured out that the more warriors you have, the more powerful fighting force you have.

The other ingredient of warfare is technology. Sticks become spears. Spears become swords. A man on horseback could travel faster than a man on foot. A man on horseback could wear a full suit of armor. Guns could shoot through armor. Gunpowder broke down castle walls. A motorized vehicle became a tank. Airplanes could drop bombs. Ships could be designed to operate under water. Rockets could carry missiles to far countries. Atomic energy could be used for super-destructive purposes. The whole history of warfare is a history of "Right makes might," as superior technology has won out time after time.

And then, at Kent State University in 1970, a mob of student protesters had a confrontation with the National Guard. The National Guard had guns, and the students had no guns. Four students were killed, but the side with no guns won the battle. It was deemed socially unacceptable for the National Guard to use their guns to kill people in a situation like that. Public sentiment ran against them and in favor of the students.

Here is another kind of force operating in warfare — not physical power but mental power. It wouldn't work with a brutal ruler like Hitler or Stalin who wouldn't have hesitated to have killed off thousands or millions, by the Machiavellian formula that if you kill off enough people brutally, you can rule the rest by fear. But in a country like the United States, where we have a tradition of dissent, and where we value each individual human life, and where the majority rules, this kind of brutality was unacceptable to the ruling majority.

Make no mistake about it, the students without guns were doing warfare. They were violating existing laws established by the majority, and testing the power of their new methods of social manipulation, to see if they could overcome the social forces enforcing those laws. And they succeeded.

Mental warfare, like physical warfare, is destructive. You aren't killing people, or forcing them into physical slavery, but you are doing things to them mentally and emotionally to cause pain, damage their reputation in society (and hence their survival potential in a social setting), undermine their self-confidence and sense of well-being (raising doubts in the minds of the National Guardsmen that their job was an honorable one, and causing many to drop their guns and defect to the other side), and generally being destructive psychologically to another person, using lies and hypnotic implants and whatever particular talents you have to be mentally destructive.

I remember the story a female co-worker once told me about a guy she met in a bar.

"You are a Sagittarius," he said.

She was impressed. He was right.

"You have a job in a technological field," he said.

Again he was right, and she was even more impressed.

"You are going to die a violent death," he said. And then he walked out.

This left her, of course, in a state of shock and anxiety. She believed him.

I told her, "He was just doing a number on you." I hope that relieved her anxieties. The Hippies were famous for doing "numbers" like that on people, and I was more familiar with the subculture than she was.

Life is not organized by categories, and this story belongs in many places, as an illustration of many things. Maybe I should have included it with "hypnotic implants" as the most vicious case of "mindfuck" I have ever been aware of. I refer to it under "Logic" as an illustration of logical deception. It belongs in the chapter on the Drug Revolution, as an illustration of "doing a number on" somebody. But mostly I think it belongs here as an instance of mental bullying, because bullies are sometimes just plain cruel, and this is just plain mental cruelty.

Just as there is mental warfare, there is also mental bullying, which works the same as physical bullying, where individuals of superior mental powers use those mental powers to do destructive things to people of lesser mental powers, like ridiculing them, damaging their reputation, damaging their self-esteem, or just causing them emotional pain.

My great-aunt Tada, who grew up in the 1800s, used to say to me:

Sticks and stones will break my bones,
But names will never hurt me.

And I used to disagree with her strenuously, because names hurt me terribly. In my state of psychological underdevelopment and lack of self-knowledge, the hypnotic suggestions got through to me and gave me doubts that maybe I really was what those names were calling me.

In the 1800s, men were brought up to be insensitive, hardened to heat, cold, pain, exhausting work, and all kinds of suffering. Their lives demanded that they be "tough." But when you harden yourself to be tough and insensitive, you are blocking your awareness. Sensitivity and awareness are the same thing. If you want to be aware, you have to be sensitive.

A totally-armored man I once knew said to me once, "Don't let it get to you."

And I replied, "It has already gotten to me. Now what do I do about it?"

Instead of armoring, which blocks my input and therefore blocks my awareness, I want to deal with these hypnotic implants. First of all, I want to be aware that there are these hypnotic suggestions constantly bombarding all of us in ordinary social life. Once aware of them, I can evaluate them to see how accurate they are. I can identify the source as one who does mental warfare. With awareness, I open up a whole new dimension I never had when I was simply armoring myself against all derogatory statements.

So I recognize that names really can hurt you. The solution is not to deny it, but to learn how to deal with it.

If you come up with a better argument or a better product than your competition, that is not mental warfare, even though your better argument may defeat your competition in court, or your better product may defeat the competition in the marketplace and throw thousands of people out of work. To be mental warfare, it has to be primarily destructive to the competition: You lie in court to destroy your opponent's credibility, or you spread the rumor that your competition's software has bugs in it.

In the movie *Amadeus*, Mozart clearly wrote better music than his rival Antonio Salieri. That is not mental warfare. But then Mozart also ridiculed him. That is mental bullying.

Mental warfare includes, but is not limited to, the practices known as "defamation," "libel," and "slander," under the law.

Where defamation is limited to false statements, mental warfare includes true statements which are destructive. For example, *Time* Magazine said that Howard Dean went to a prep school that cost $30,000 a year. True, but why else would *Time* mention that, except to alienate the working class from Dean? They neglected to say that Franklin Delano Roosevelt, who was the greatest friend the working class ever had, went to the most upper-class prep school of them all, Groton.

Defamation is limited to damage to a person's reputation. Where the Audience does not include anybody beyond the Speaker and the Target, that is not considered defamation under the law. So the guy in the bar has not done defamation by first setting up the woman, and then saying she will die a violent death, although he has certainly done mental bullying and caused her mental injury.

And certainly one can never prove or disprove a statement about the future until the future happens. This is another trick that people use to create chaos in our thinking.

With defamation you have to prove there was injury, and mental injury is often hard to prove when the only evidence that can actually be shown in court is the evidence of the physical senses.

Also defamation has to be directed at a person, or a legally identified "party," whereas mental warfare can attack an idea, a belief, or even a feeling (like the woman who told me "You are very disturbed").

So while mental warfare starts out looking like defamation, it includes much, much more, and the law doesn't protect us against most of it. The present culture is a pretty lawless society when it comes to mental warfare and mental bullying.

I haven't even mentioned propaganda, the best known form of mental warfare, using the mass-media to lie and manipulate and distort people's thinking. "Propaganda" comes from the word "propagate," and I guess there has been propaganda as long as there has been mass-media. I remember from World War II, the word "propaganda" was always used to mean what the enemy was saying. (Of course, our side never used propaganda, or so I was led to believe as a child.) In the second Iraq war, thanks to technology, we were actually able to see the Iraqi Information Minister on TV, telling us in English how the Americans were cowards and we were losing the war.

And Arabic television stations were inflaming their audience by saying we were conducting a "war on Islam." I am sure that the flow of angry young men into Iraq from other Arabic countries was largely a result of this propaganda. So the mental and emotional force of propaganda can translate directly into physical force.

I use the word "propaganda" loosely to mean any statement which uses the methods of mental warfare — misrepresentation and/or manipulation.

The question here is not whether warfare is a terrible thing. Warfare is a terrible thing. And people do it, and they determine the course of history. And people will continue to do it until we find a greater power to defeat it.

And I am not saying that we should ignore the power of warfare. Warfare is a powerful force, and we need to acknowledge that it is a powerful part of our environment, and shape our lives around it.

What I am saying here is that warfare is a major source of mind pollution. While we acknowledge the power of warfare on the one hand, we need to be careful that that power does not reduce the accuracy of our thoughts and beliefs. Just because we are forced to pay lip service to the conquerors and their beliefs doesn't mean we can't always have our private thoughts and beliefs.

It is easy enough with physical coercion, with a gun pointed at your head, to see that you are being coerced. But it is not so easy with mental and emotional coercion, as I have already pointed out. From "I'll pretend to think this way because it makes me accepted in the group" to "This isn't a bad way to think after all" isn't really a huge transition.

Back in the days when one's success and survival in warfare depended on one's ability to swing a battle-axe, women didn't have much of a chance at physical warfare. It seems pretty obvious that men came to dominate women because of that kind of superior physical strength. Up until maybe a hundred years ago, a woman was practically owned by her husband in our civilization. He was not only allowed to beat her, but he was encouraged to do so, to maintain the proper "discipline" in the household.

Mental warfare has enabled women to overcome the physical domination of men. And the Feminists have not hesitated to be openly and actively destructive to their adversaries.

I first read "All men are little boys" just after I discovered the psychological age of puberty, and I thought, "Oh, good. The women know what I know." And I thought the women were becoming more mature than the men. But not so. Equality for women just meant that women could do the same ego trips and power trips as the men. "All men are little boys" is only about 40% accurate. Most men are little boys, and most women are little girls.

Then there was the "male chauvinist pig." This was coined by female chauvinists.

Some feminists have portrayed all men as being totally preoccupied with dominating women — manipulating, invalidating, discounting women. Some men are like that. I remember guys I knew at Harvard referring contemptuously to their girlfriends at Radcliffe as "cunt." But not all men are like that. To claim that all men are like that is what my dictionary calls "sexist." But the feminists have already labeled men as "sexist." It's the old political game of preemptive finger-pointing.

The well-publicized leaders of the Feminist Movement have used a great deal of destructive rhetoric in their mental warfare. I really don't know how any intelligent and educated woman could follow that kind of leadership, with its smear tactics and psychological projections. But it does all serve to make us aware that women haven't had a fair deal in the past.

Why haven't I given credit to Gandhi and Martin Luther King for initiating mental warfare? Both of them were successful with nonviolent methods, before Kent State. But I hesitate to call it "warfare" because it doesn't seem that they were doing anything destructive to their adversaries. They were both great men, saintly men, and it seems that their greatness and saintliness caused them to prevail on a higher spiritual level than "warfare." They brought their adversaries up to a higher spiritual level, where they were able to see the evil of their ways.

But let's look at it more closely. I remember in the movie *Gandhi* a scene where the British machine-gunned more than a thousand unarmed civilians. And what did that do to the British? It made them look bad. It probably also made some of them feel bad. So it did something destructive to the British to be killing large numbers of people like that. And Gandhi forced them into a position where they were forced to kill or imprison possibly millions of people if they wanted to dominate.

The Nazis machine-gunned large numbers of unarmed civilians on many occasions. They didn't care if it made them look bad. The badder the better, because they ruled by fear. But the British were different. They thought of themselves as enlightened and civilized, and wanted other people to see them as enlightened and civilized. So it was destroying their own self-image as well as their public image to be machine-gunning people.

Was Gandhi doing anything destructive? No. He was just forcing the British to recognize that their own coercive methods were in conflict with their own self-image of being civilized. They could machine-gun a thousand people without thinking much about it, but to machine-gun ten thousand would have been what they considered an "atrocity." (Hitler wouldn't have hesitated, except for the cost of the bullets.)

There is a fine distinction between actually being destructive and creating awareness in people's heads that lessens their opinion of themselves.

The Civil-Rights Movement in America worked the same way. Nobody was machine-gunned, but the police were bashing people on the head. That works to control individuals, but when the police are doing it to large numbers of people, it makes the police look bad. Southern law-enforcement officials were made to look very bad, and of course this was highly publicized by the Northern press. And again, this was destructive not only to the public image but also to the self-image of the Southern officials, most of whom, I'm sure, thought of themselves as good Christian people.

So yes, there was a destructive element in what Gandhi and Martin Luther King were doing, but they did not actually DO anything destructive. They won by the saintly method of raising the consciousness of their adversaries.

If you are calling the law-enforcement officer "Pig," when he is just trying to do his job, that is mental warfare, but if you are just saying "We shall not be moved," that is not.

MACHIAVELLI WINS

I decided that I could make a positive contribution to a new civilization by pointing out misrepresentation, manipulation, and mental warfare in the discussion groups, and making people aware of these things as they were happening to them. Some people were complaining that we were just talking and not doing anything towards a new civilization. Here was a way of doing something towards a new civilization while we were just talking — by cleaning up the talking.

In one group I was not allowed to say "This is derisive" when a member responded to my question in a derisive way. At other times I was labeled a "combatant," even though I was careful to explain that I was only trying to make people aware that certain tactics were being employed.

I had some degree of success until I met an adversary who was highly skilled in the arts of what I have described as misrepresentation, manipulation, and mental warfare. I am grateful to have encountered such a person and have his words recorded in email, as an illustration of the art of mental warfare.

I am calling this person "Guy." I have changed people's names to protect their privacy. If anyone wants credit for their input, I can do that in a future edition.

To pick up the thread of the conversation, we were trying to define where we were going with this new civilization, and people were talking vaguely about "the spiritual" and "spiritual development." I was trying to get people to define what they meant by "spiritual," and got answers like, "It can't be defined in words because it is spiritual." I was concerned because it seemed to me that nobody recognized the difference between the higher beings and lower destructive spirit entities posing as higher beings. I found my opportunity to present my views when one member presented an outline of what the new civilization should represent, including specifics of spiritual education and collecting facts about the spiritual.

So I presented facts about the spiritual as I knew them, starting with the fact that some spirit entities are destructive, supported by references to Edgar Cayce and Richard Kieninger. I then supplied a list from my own experience, with a short explanation of each: "Ouija Board NO, Automatic writing NO, Channeling NO, *A Course in Miracles* NO, Spirit possession NO, Ego YES, Tarot NO, Astrology NO, Yoga (reservations), Psychedelic drugs NO, Meditation (I don't know), Out-of-body-travel (I don't know), Dream analysis YES, Psychotherapy YES, The Twelve Great Virtues YES, Believing on faith NO, Mentalism NO, The Protective Prayer YES."

These things represent my viewpoint as I have already explained it in Chapter 5. I am not reproducing the whole statement here because it is five pages long and not relevant to this discussion of mental warfare. Only the last part of it is relevant and will be important to the ensuing discussion:

```
The Protective Prayer -- YES -- Richard Kieninger teaches
      that we shouldn't pray indiscriminately to spiritual
      forces for "help" or "guidance", because we could pick
      up lower spiritual entities who would like to guide us
      down into the mess they are in. We should pray only to
      "Christ" and only for "protection" from such
      interference:

      Dear Christ, please protect me.

I invite other people to create similar lists of which
spiritual practices they support, and why.
```

There was a long reply from the person I respected most in the group, disagreeing with me on many points, but doing it in a way that would lead us to a greater degree of accuracy, citing evidence and experience. And then there was this:

```
From Guy to Group 8-15-97
Subject: RE: definition
```

```
Dear Bob, All !!

Your LONG discourse is, to me, a mixture of truth of a high
order, partial truth of a lesser order, and delusion based in
personal religious beliefs which have nothing to do with
spirituality except in how they lead (or not) you PERSONALLY
into spiritual experience and enlightenment.

Let us not debate religion here. I will forbear to correct
what I perceive to be partial truths and inaccuracies and
attribute these to your particular religious beliefs.

I prefer that we be inclusive of persons and philosophies
that may be of spiritual nature regardless of RELIGIOUS
slant.

<EDITED>
```

This is, in my critical opinion, such a truly great work of art that it is really hard to comprehend all that has been said and its effect on the Audience. First of all, he has changed the subject. He has dismissed my subject and has substituted for it a personal attack on Bob Gebelein, known as an "ad hominem" attack. For this purpose he has created a "straw man" by misrepresenting me as some kind of a deluded religious person. This all serves as a "red herring" to create a stink, to draw attention away from the subject. He has all the classic elements here.

The word "delusion" is one of those pseudo-psychological misrepresentations. But not satisfied with that, he slams me down from "truth of a high order" to "delusion" in a single sentence, to have the maximum destructive impact. In not saying which are the truths and which are "delusion," he creates doubts about everything I have said without having made a single specific accurate criticism of anything. And the implied premise here, which he is trying to slip past an Audience who isn't paying attention, is that he is really qualified to judge what is "truth of a high order."

The next stop here is the word "personal," which gets amplified as the word "PERSONALLY" (shouted). The word "personal" is a common tactic used by manipulators, especially the authoritarian kind, to put down other people. Everybody's opinions are personal, including the Speaker's. By asserting that my opinions are "personal," the Speaker is here diverting attention away from himself and the fact that his statements are also "personal."

Then we get to "religious beliefs." This is the gross misrepresentation of me, out of which he is creating the straw man. I am not coming from any religious indoctrination. I rejected religion in 1956. My view of the spiritual is the result of an open-minded search for answers, with the operating principle, "I don't care what I believe, as long as it is true." He doesn't know that. In his ignorance he is making up this fiction about me. This is preemptive misrepresentation. Whatever I haven't said can and will be held against me.

He leans heavily on the words "religion," "religious beliefs," and "RELIGIOUS slant" (shouting again), pushing cultural buttons. Religion is a sacred subject. You don't discuss religion or politics. This can have the effect of making me look bad to the Audience.

" ... which have nothing to do with spirituality ..." — the authoritarian pronouncement. He is only making an assertion. The things I am saying have a great deal to do with both the "School of Spiritual Development" and the "Spiritual Database" as proposed by the previous speaker: What kinds of things should we research? accept as facts? teach in the school?

" ... except in how they lead (or not) you PERSONALLY into spiritual experience and enlightenment." The "or not" is more put-down, more ad hominem attack.

"Let us not debate religion here." He is already debating. I am just trying to share my knowledge.

"I will forbear to correct..." He is already correcting, or presuming to correct.

"I prefer that we be inclusive..." He is implying here that I am not being inclusive, without even having to say it. He ignores the fact that I have already invited other people to create similar lists.

This all came at me so fast and so neatly in three short paragraphs that it was impossible to comprehend at the time everything that was being communicated, never mind trying to answer it. All these things have just slowly dawned on me in weeks of solitude.

In the next post, he continues:

Spiritual is NOT spiritism, not ouiji boards, not black
ritual demonological invocation....

Please try not to be too alarmist or promotional of narrowly
held religious views.

It is important for us to bring the highest and best of our
selves to this FLOW of creative energy...

This is more misrepresentation, for the benefit of the Audience,
portraying me as "alarmist" and "promotional." He is insinuating
that I am not bringing the highest and best of myself to this
discussion.

From Guy to Group 8-21-97
Subject: Spirituality?..... PERSONAL !

Bob, much of your discussion of "spirituality" seemed to be
coming from a fear based space of needing to define others'
spirituality and "codify" what is and is not "acceptable" to
be "taught"...

[CUT HALF A PAGE]

I don't know where he got the idea that I was trying to limit the
discussion to ideas that were "acceptable" to me. First of all, he
would have had to totally ignore my statement inviting other people
to share their views. Second, he would have had to totally ignore the
fact that I had thanked the other person for his long reply, which
differed from my view in many ways.

Again, given years of separation and weeks to think about it, I
can see that he is the one who is trying to limit the discussion and
remove my viewpoint from it. This is a case of preemptive finger-
pointing. And if I didn't see what was going on at the time, I don't
suppose other members of the group did, either.

I never did find out why he was trying to remove my viewpoint
from the discussion. I was hoping he would reveal himself, but he
never did.

From Bob to Guy, Group 8-21-97

```
Subject: Re: Spirituality?..... PERSONAL !

>Bob, much of your discussion of "spirituality" seemed to be
>coming from a fear based space

Yes, a fear based space

>of needing to define others' spirituality and "codify" what
>is and is not "acceptable" to be "taught"......

I am trying to share my knowledge with the innocent that
there are dangers in the "spiritual" just as there are in the
physical. I think the manipulative technique of trying to
make people feel that they are somehow inferior because they
fear things is leading us away from truth and into danger.

The word "acceptable" in quotes is a manipulative device
trying to link me with such things as censorship, when really
all I am trying to do is warn people of danger.

[CUT ONE PAGE]
```

Perhaps I should have said "misrepresentation," which is what it was. But my thinking leaped ahead to the fact that by misrepresenting me he was manipulating the group into rejecting my viewpoint.

```
From Guy to Group 8-22-97
Subject: RE: Spirituality?..... PERSONAL !

Dear  Bob: The terming of another person's attempts to
communicate as manipulative should quite easily shine through
as being 100:1 more "manipulative" than placing a word within
quotes for attention and emphasis.

[CUT 2.5 PAGES]
```

So he turns my criticism of "manipulative" around, returning it 100-fold to me. Then he follows with a barrage of derogatory misrepresentations about me. I don't even know strong enough words to describe it. But again, in the perspective of years and weeks, I can see that most of this is preemptive finger-pointing and is describing exactly what he is doing himself:

```
you have clearly linked YOURSELF to censorious tendency
you have extrapolated wildly
"characterizing" my purely well intentioned communication
    in such negative light
completely totalitarian and fear based
someone whose communication borders on insult
your control freak identification
locked into a fear based state with relation to ...
    other's opinions of him
pontification
your dogmatic viewpoints
denunciation/denigration
pitifully small and judgemental
you baited me
ad-hominem attacks such as you made
```

So when I point out his more subtle attempts to manipulate, he responds with this full-fledged attack, and my obvious response is to point out to the Audience, including himself, that this whole attack is evidence that makes it pretty obvious what he is doing.

```
From Bob to Guy, Group 8-22-97
Subject: RE: Spirituality?..... PERSONAL !

Thank you, Guy, for providing in your long post ample proof
that you are a manipulative person. It's too bad you don't
see it yourself.
```

This serves to subdue him somewhat, sending him back to his more subtle smear mode. But I'm sure the message is not lost on the Audience — that if they oppose him, he will attack them in the same way. People are going to criticize him privately, but not in the public arena.

What I think was lost on the group were the specifics of what he was saying, because it seems like so much of a rant. This is part of the art of mental warfare. When people aren't paying close attention to what is being said, and aren't critically examining it for accuracy, a message can be implanted in their minds which isn't accurate. So in this case what appears to be a rant is actually taking advantage of psychological principles to get a message through into people's heads. Later on I will be accused of "baiting" him, where that was actually his accusation and not really what I was doing. Some of the other representations also may have worked their way into people's heads.

There was no payoff in confronting Guy with his derogatory behavior. He slammed anybody who said anything unfavorable about him, just as he slammed me. So some members of the group turned on me, saying he couldn't help what he was, and he was angry, like a wounded animal, and it was my fault for baiting him.

I don't know that he was angry, or wounded, and I don't know that he had any psychological problems. What I do know is that he was a master of these techniques of put-down, manipulation, and mental warfare. He was able to draw negative inferences about me that were just plausible, from the facts I presented. He had that air of certainty which drove his opinions into people's heads with authority. And he created such a stink that he got what he wanted: The discussion of the dangers in exploring the spiritual stopped right there.

The list of the techniques he is using goes on, beyond my ability to understand what he is doing. He uses my name 8 times in his long post: "Dear Bob," "So, Bob," "you, Bob," etc. I know there is a reason for that, but I don't know what it is. Maybe he is trying to get to me on a more personal level, where I might be more vulnerable.

He is not making it clear why he thinks I am displaying religious intolerance. I can't argue with him if I don't know what he is referring to. Finally he comes out with this:

```
... not to mention your [Christian] cant and
denunciation/denigration of practically all of the various
religions of the world, which is quoted at the end of this
post?

... you have shown yourself to be beholden to views that I
feel are pitifully small and judgemental such as:

B:    We should pray only to "Christ" and only for
"protection" from such interference:
Dear Christ, please protect me.
```

So I suspect that he is complaining about "Pray only to Christ." But I don't know this for sure. The two statements above aren't together, and the last isn't at the end of the post. So he is forcing me to confess to this in order to defend myself. Thus I am rendered defenseless — another magnificent strategy.

Actually I am glad I didn't try to defend "Pray only to Christ." It is so easy to attack, and so difficult to defend. I would have been hopelessly defensive.

First of all, "Pray only to Christ" was offered in contrast to praying indiscriminately to spirit entities, some of whom are destructive. Guy left this part out, changing the meaning of my quote by taking it out of context.

He also left out "Richard Kieninger teaches." Both Guy and the Audience are probably ignorant of who Richard Kieninger is, who the Brotherhoods are, and who Christ is, except as the various Christian religions teach. This mutual ignorance provides the perfect setting for preemptive misrepresentation. In fact, preemptive misrepresentation always comes out of ignorance, and can only be sold to an Audience who are ignorant.

And the only way I can see to defeat this preemptive misrepresentation is to give the Audience an education, which might be boring to them, and might be more than they want to know, and certainly will take longer to explain than the assertion that "Pray only to Christ" means religious intolerance. So my adversary has not only forced me to "confess," but has also forced me into a position where I have to explain the whole cosmology in order to defeat this viewpoint based on ignorance, for an Audience who is already primed to discount everything I am saying as "retaliation."

Richard Kieninger teaches what the Brotherhoods taught him, and the Brotherhoods don't represent any religion. They are scientist/philosophers. They have placed Christ (not Jesus) at the head of the hierarchy because they have observed Him there, just as I have in my dream experiences.

This is not "religion." This is "how-to," based on what works for me. This is not "Christian" dogma; this is theory to be tested. This is not "intolerance." I invite other cosmologies and other theories, with supporting evidence. This is not "religion." This is the beginning of "knowledge" about the spiritual.

Having tried to make me into somebody "religious," Guy is now trying to take that one step further into religious intolerance. But the fact that I am giving my viewpoint does not make me intolerant of other people's viewpoints. This is just bad logic, and this kind of bad logic is used quite often by those who would make others look bad. There is not even an ambiguity here to seize upon. I make it quite clear that I am giving my viewpoint only as an "example," and again my statement, "I invite other people to create similar lists of which spiritual practices they support, and why," should cover me against any charges of "intolerance."

Richard Kieninger, facing these same kinds of pressures, added "or Mohammed or Buddha or Moses." But I am not going to go that way, because if anyone is intolerant of my viewpoint, then they are the ones who are intolerant. This is just one more example of preemptive finger-pointing.

And when Guy accuses me of "denunciation/denigration" of religions, this is just more preemptive finger-pointing, drawing the Audience's attention away from his own denunciation/denigration of my views: "... views that I feel are pitifully small and judgemental..."

```
From Kent to Bob (private) 8-23-97

... It's a page from [a famous politician's] book of
campaigning; [he] is quoted to have said, "Call your opponent
a pig-f***er; then watch him deny it."
```

Another person reminded me of the story of the "Tar Baby:" The more you became entangled with him, the blacker you got.

I recently received a local political advertisement, correcting a smear from the 2004 campaign, and then saying that it took something like 572 words to correct it. I have taken more words than that trying to clear my name from the charge of religious intolerance. And that is only one of the many accusations thrown at me. It is so easy to smear, and so hard to show that it is a smear. And every word I use in my defense can be used as a springboard for further accusations.

So it seems to be accepted as political wisdom that you don't answer these kinds of accusations. But if I ignore the accusations, the Audience is left with these strong derogatory statements about me loudly ringing in their ears — establishing in their minds a false image of me, which for lack of contradiction becomes the only image of me they have: Bob Gebelein, pig-f***er.

As an example of what happens when you don't answer the accusations, Guy accused me of stealing time from my employer, because I was doing this on company time. Actually it was none of his business what arrangement I had with my employer. I thought of referring him to my boss, knowing that my boss would tell him exactly where to go, but then I didn't want to waste my boss's time with this. So I didn't answer this accusation at all. Some time later I received from Guy the most perfect and complete example of preemptive misrepresentation I have ever seen:

```
From Guy to Bob, Group 10-24-97

...
When you made several conspicuous statements about using your
employers time and equipment to do your email, you may
remember that I asked what that statement had to do with
anything.
Since you failed to answer, I did assume you were stealing
time from your employer.
Now that you have answered that you are using your employer's
time and equipment with their permission ...... after not
responding to the original question about WHY you kept
mentioning the fact that you were on company time.... I won't
need to be concerned.
However to say that such a statement was a "lie" is a lie in
itself. It was an assumption based on reasonable evidence at
the time.
...
```

You are presumed guilty until proven innocent. Whatever you don't say can and will be held against you. Silence will be taken as a confession of guilt.

It is clear that the methods of "dirty politics" are going to win, whether you respond or not.

The authority on dirty politics was Niccolo Machiavelli, who wrote *The Prince* and *The Discourses* in the 1500s. His methods have been known to work, and are very much in use today.

I remember Machiavelli's advice to his Prince, words to this effect: "Appear good and kind and virtuous on the surface, but don't ever be so foolish as to really be that way." I remember scenes on TV of Saddam Hussein smiling and patting little children on the head, and speaking great platitudes of goodness and warmth and high spiritual purpose — this same man who had tortured and killed thousands, maybe even millions. I remember Machiavelli saying that if you brutally kill off the leaders of the opposition, the rest then can be ruled by fear. Again, this is exactly what Saddam Hussein did. It was my impression that Guy did the mental equivalent of this by slamming me and silencing the rest.

I have been known to say that Machiavelli is the only Western philosopher worth reading (until Bob Gebelein, of course), because his methods work.

Richard Christie and Florence L. Geis, in their book *Studies in Machiavellianism* (1970), have identified what they call the "Machiavellian orientation" in people. First they derived tests to measure to what degree people agreed with statements "believed to be theoretically congruent with statements based on *The Prince* and *The Discourses*" (Christie and Geis, 1970, page 10). They then classified as "high Mach" those people who pretty much agreed with Machiavelli, and as "low Mach" those people who were mostly in disagreement with him. Christie and Geis, along with others, have then been able to devise scientific experiments showing how the high Machs do vs. the low Machs in various interpersonal situations resembling business and politics, and demonstrating leadership ability. Basically the high Machs lie, cheat, connive, and manipulate, in the time-honored tradition of Machiavelli, and the low Machs are basically honest. And what these scientific experiments have shown us is what politics has shown us all along — that the high Machs usually win.

For example, in one experiment there are three participants — a high Mach, a middle Mach, and a low Mach. The object of the game is for two of the participants to enter into a coalition to divide up ten dollars, leaving the third person out. These are ten real one-dollar bills, and you can pocket your share at the end of the experiment. After this game had been played by 7 different sets of participants, the high Machs figured in all 7 coalitions and took home an average of $5.57, the middle Machs were in 5 coalitions and took home an average of $3.14, and the low Machs were part of 2 coalitions and took home an average of $1.28 (Christie and Geis, 1970, page 165).

I, myself, am sort of a middle Mach, agreeing with Machiavelli about half the time. I agree with P.T. Barnum that "There's a sucker born every minute," but I also feel that "Honesty is the best policy."

Something the book doesn't mention, that I observed in my encounters with Guy, is that the Machiavellians are very good at making their opponents APPEAR to be the Machiavellians, lying and manipulating, while they, the Machiavellians, are innocent and pristine. And the thing that amazed me was how successful Guy was in actually getting people to believe it.

So we get the idea of what kind of a person this high Mach person is, in terms of morality (their word), views, and tactics, and that there is a payoff for this kind of behavior, both as demonstrated in politics and proved in the scientific laboratory. I suppose the smart people just become Machiavellians, when they see that it is a winning strategy. But I don't want to live that way. So, the question is, how can we defeat these kinds of tactics?

In actual Machiavellian politics, your opponent can kill you, but in mental warfare the worst the Speaker can do is to make the Target look bad to the Audience. There is always this third party involved, the Audience. In a one-on-one confrontation, Machiavelli wins. But this third party can tip the balance of power. If the Audience can recognize when Machiavellian tactics are being employed, and then speak out and identify the inaccuracies, I think these tactics would be defeated.

First of all, the Audience always needs to keep in mind that the Speaker represents the Speaker and not necessarily the Target.

In my short exposure to local politics, I learned to say to people who were misconstruing my words, "That's your fiction, not mine." People in politics are always afraid of how their words or actions are going to be construed. The Audience should understand that this is totally beyond the control of the person who is the Target. Construing is the action of the person doing the construing, and the Audience should understand that it reflects totally on that person. Anything can be construed to be anything, if enough inaccuracies are applied.

So I am adding to my list of known misrepresentations the cases where people construe the words of another, as Guy did with my statement "Pray only to Christ." Such construing should always be considered the fiction of the Speaker, unless there is conclusive evidence presented by an independent third party to support it.

It would also help if members of the Audience would speak up on behalf of the Target, as independent third parties, so that it can't be construed that the Target is retaliating. I got very little of that kind of support — probably fewer people supporting me than accusing me of creating a disturbance.

The person I respected most in the group said that he just went ahead and did what he was doing, regardless of what was being said about him, with confidence that sooner or later people would recognize him for who he really was. I totally agreed with him on this. But again, this was something the Audience had to be able to do — to recognize the difference between what I was being called and what I was actually doing. And what I was doing was pointing out mental warfare.

I pointed out that Guy was doing misrepresentation, defamation of character, and smear tactics, included in my definition of mental warfare:

From Bob to Guy, Group 10-21-97

Guy said:

>Sorry Bob........

>Smearing and pecking and all of the other problems you have
>are just not mine ;)

Just for the benefit of the group, I feel I should state that
this is a serious misrepresentation of me. There is no
evidence to support it. In fact it should be obvious to
everybody that it is a projection of Guy's own tactics.

>I don't think too much of your highly bragged about
>psychotherapy if it hasn't yet enabled you to be free of
>your paranoia and such delusions as your stating that I have
>"lied"...

Again, when you pretend to represent me, you better have
clear-cut documentary evidence of "paranoia" and "delusions".
In this case I require an opinion of 2 or more
psychotherapists chosen by an impartial third party.
Otherwise what you are doing is defined in the old
civilization as "defamation of character." I expect that in a
new civilization that people would recognize it for what it
is, and not give people who do these things any credence.

If there are other people in this group who are aware of what
"smear tactics" are, and agree with me that smear tactics are
basically lies, and believe that Guy is using smear tactics,
and who don't want such lies as part of this discussion, I
wish they would speak up.

People were complaining that all this arguing was interfering with
"the work." I explained why mental warfare was not a good thing in
a new civilization:

From Bob to Doug, Group 10-22-97

Doug said:
>With Guy there, the challenge might be to overcome our
>differences and co-create for the higher good. All input is
>welcome.

The issue that I am dealing with is not "differences," which
I respect, but people doing deliberate derogatory
misrepresentation of other people. It is a significant part
of the old civilization that I would like to get rid of. It
is an important factor not only in political elections, where
it keeps us from getting the best people in office, and leads
to a general mistrust of government (because if they lie to
us to get into office, then of course they are lying to us
once they are in office), but also in the academic world,
where it reduces the accuracy of what is considered
"knowledge," in the business world, where it keeps us from

getting the best possible product, and in every aspect of our
old-civilization lives.

My approach to derogatory misrepresentation, which I call
"mental warfare," is to encourage it to happen, and even
provoke it to happen, and point it out for all to see, so
that an informed majority can discount it as basically false,
so that it will no longer have an impact on our government,
our education, our business, and so forth.

One person supported me here, saying:

From Matthew to Group 10-23-97
...
Let us continue this conversation as this IS the work.

Guy turned it all around and called it "Bob's Mental Warfare."

In a post of 10-24-97, I said, "If I say 'lie', that is the same as
saying 'inaccuracy' or 'misrepresentation', but it takes less letters to
type."
And Guy replied, "Moronic. Get a dictionary. Look up lie. Look
up inaccurate .... Etc......."
People who lie (I had encountered this before) know that "lie"
implies the intention to deceive, and that one's intention is not an
easy thing to prove. I remember that when I lived in New York City,
everybody who short-changed me apologized and said they had
made a mistake. Not living in New York City, I can't remember
anyone making that same kind of "mistake" in the last 40 years.
People who lie are obviously deliberately trying to deceive,
because "mistakes" have a whole different character and quality. It
reminds me of the old Peter Lorre joke, "I was cleaning my knife,
and it went off six times."
Actually, definition #2 of "lie" (verb) is simply "to create a false
or misleading impression," with no mention of "intent to deceive"
(Merriam-Webster, 1996). But I know that Guy is doing this
deliberately and with malice, so how do I get him for "intent to
deceive?"

Of course, if I can't prove that it is his intention to deceive, then neither can he prove that it isn't. It is simply his word against mine. But I think I can do better than that.

First of all, he supplies no evidence, or insufficient evidence in the case of "Pray only to Christ," to support his representations of me. So it appears they are pure fiction that he has just made up.

Second, and most important, just the fact that the put-down is always "down" — always derogatory — shows intention. If they were "mistakes," one would expect that half of them would show me as better than I really am. The probability of 20 consecutive "mistakes" all being on the "down" side is one in 1,048,576. That is way beyond anybody's requirement for "proof."

Third, if these are truly "honest mistakes," he would admit his errors and back down, and even apologize maybe, when faced with corrections. Instead, when I correct him he refuses to be corrected, but bounces off my corrections, taking them as a launching pad to say more negative things about me.

Actually, his refusal to back down makes him more formidable as an adversary, if one is only doing warfare, at the same time as he is becoming less credible because of his inaccuracies.

Guy dominated the mail by volume in this particular discussion, from 10/17/97 through 10/29/97, sending 37.3 pages, compared to my 9.2 pages, and 35.4 pages for the whole rest of the group combined.

A few people supported me, but most of the people seemed to deplore the "unhealthy" state the discussion had descended to. Many saw it just as a stereotype of males fighting. A few saw it as my fault, that I was the one provoking and baiting Guy, and he was not responsible for his actions. One person said that we should "look normal," so that we could deal more effectively with organizations of the old civilization.

So Guy was not only able to make individuals look bad, but he also could make the group look bad, just by his presence and his smear tactics. And when I pointed out his mental warfare, he escalated his level of mental warfare, creating a supreme stink that made the group look even worse. By this power tactic, he was able to manipulate the group to obey his will. If we just let him dominate, he would do a minimum of social pecking, and the group would "look normal." But if anybody (not just me) disagreed with him or tried to correct him, he would create this stink that would make the group look bad in the eyes of the world. The group was powerless to deal with this, and just had to concede to his domination.

At least one member asked the group leader to remove this guy from the group. But this was supposed to be an "open forum." And I wanted it that way, too. I welcomed the chance to deal with a person like this who was really expert at these kinds of tactics. One person said of me, "... he has provided a high level of service to us," but I would turn that around and apply it to Guy.

Guy sent 8 consecutive messages, most of which were derogatory to me, on Friday, October 24, 1997, after I had left the office. There followed a long discussion over the weekend, which I had no part in. One person seemed to understand what was going on and what Guy was doing:

From Leanna to Group 10-27-97
Subject: Re: Mental Warfare, (Do we need it?)

... Guy has successfully used these kinds of tactics to attempt to oust someone from the list and I think it is unfair....he is acting out the very tactics that he accused Bob G of using...

****

From Leanna to Group 10-27-97
Subject: Mental Warfare

...[Guy] has regained his control of this list and I do not feel that he is using his power compassionately or that he is really truly receptive to anyone else's viewpoint.....Who will be the next one that he BLACKBALLS from the list... There is no place on this list for me or any other woman or visionary person.... Guy wants a ... list that he controls and that is what he seems to be getting... Your fear of mental warfare has brought it about because no one can reach you in any other way.....You are the one who needs a separate list....just call it Guy's list.....it is time for very straight talk here...

She was supported by the females in the group, but shouted down by most of the males. It seemed that, if not the consensus, then at least a majority wanted me to stop what I was doing. It was all emotionally overwhelming for me, anyway. So on Monday, when I came in and read all the mail, I unsubscribed. I was out of there, just in time for Halloween.

I sat watching the World Series and thought to myself, "They don't pick just ANYBODY for their team." With the degree of excellence required to create a new civilization as a group, it seemed very unlikely that such a thing could be created by such a group that allowed just anybody to participate.

I felt that the group had failed this exercise in identifying mental warfare. Only Leanna really seemed to understand what I was doing and what was going on. But mostly I give credit to Guy for his exceptional skills at the art of mental warfare.

I enjoyed several months of peace until Guy became visible in another group. He was insulting a newcomer to the group, and I said "Guy doesn't represent the group." That started another round of attacks, starting with "Are you claiming to represent the group?" (more bad logic) He had followers in this group who were giving him credit for many good works. He was openly calling me a liar and a negative influence on the group, and his followers supported him. When I claimed he was a disruptive influence, he claimed that I was the disruptive influence, and people believed him. Whatever he was, he could turn that around and say no, that's what I was, and people believed him. This was a whole new experience for me.

The group leader issued a very mild statement saying that Guy was disruptive and his tactics were undesirable. That's about the only support I got.

I was steered into "arbitration," even though I made it clear that I had no dispute with anybody, but only with certain tactics. The "arbitrator" was a newcomer and seemed to be highly biased in favor of Guy. Guy wasn't there, of course, saying "Bob needs arbitration, not me."

Guy was sending huge posts, with replies to replies to replies, etc., making it very unclear who said what. It was really impossible to straighten out the mess. So I just gave up.

Again I felt that the group had failed me.

There was too much material to plow through every day. I wasn't accomplishing anything. At the same time, I had an enormous amount of work to do, allowing no time for this Internet stuff. So, mostly out of exhaustion, I unsubscribed. The Machiavellian tactics had won.

At least there is one important difference between physical warfare and mental warfare:

Sticks and stones can break my bones,
But names will never KILL me.

8. LOGIC, PSYCHOLOGY, AND SORCERY

LOGIC

After the 9/11 attacks, President George W. Bush said, "Either you are with us, or you are with the terrorists." Immediately, within a minute, three different members of the media represented this statement as, "the with us or against us rule," and "the for us or against us rule," and again, "with us or against us."

If you don't see anything wrong with any of these statements, and/or you see them as equivalent, you need a lesson in logic. You may not <u>want</u> a lesson in logic, but you <u>need</u> a lesson in logic.

First of all, there are probably many people in the world who are neither with us nor with the terrorists. There are Tuaregs and Eskimos and tribes in the Amazon jungle who may not know or care what a terrorist is. Since the terrorists seem to be attacking the United States ("Death to Americans!") and our allies, there may be vast numbers of people in the world who are really neutral on this issue.

And while it is true that if you are with the terrorists you are certainly against us, being with the terrorists is not the same thing as

187

being against us. I'm sure there are vast numbers of people in the world who are against us but not with the terrorists. They may have different issues, or they may not support the methods of the terrorists.

An Egyptian newspaper editor and also a high-ranking official of another Arab country both pointed out these logical errors — both in perfect English, of course. They know, even if we don't.

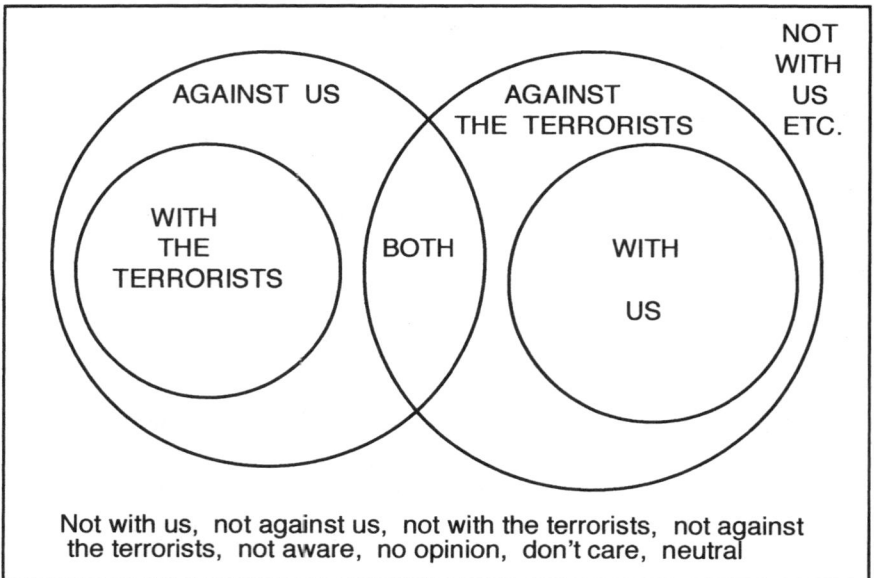

I have drawn this diagram to illustrate this logic. The smaller circles labeled "WITH US" and "WITH THE TERRORISTS" represent two more limited viewpoints within the larger viewpoints "AGAINST THE TERRORISTS" and "AGAINST US." The space labeled "BOTH" covered by both circles represents people who are both against us and against the terrorists. The space outside all circles represents those who aren't for or against either side.

And then there are nuances which are not covered by this diagram. For example, I am personally against the terrorists but not with the way President Bush handled the situation. So I am "with us" if "us" means for the greatest good of humanity, but not if it means the Imperial "We."

And what if I am curious to know why they hate us so much? What if I am ready to accept some real reason that they hate us? The Arab sheik was trying to start that dialog with the Mayor of New York, and the Mayor of New York just gave him back his check for $10,000,000.00. That seems to be the American political thought on the subject.

But what if I am with the terrorists to the extent that they are human beings and they are so angry that they are willing to kill themselves in order to hurt the people they hate? And if one could find out why they are so angry, and do something to make them less angry, then that would eliminate terrorism, and that would be in the best interests of the United States.

So I can be both with us and with the terrorists. And that means I am with the terrorists but not against us.

So the diagram above is really an oversimplification. To draw a diagram that would represent all the possibilities of human thought would really be impossible.

Closely related to the "with us or against us" logic is what I call "packaging and labeling." Because Carl Jung was not totally "scientific" in that his evidence did not all come from the physical senses, he was considered "unscientific" and therefore was packaged with everything considered "unscientific," including mysticism, which is just the opposite of science, and he was labeled a "mystic," along with people at the extreme end of this range. In other words, if you aren't totally with us, you must be totally alien to us.

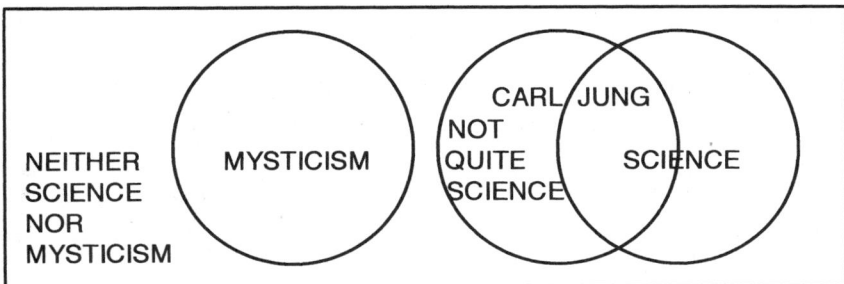

Bad logic is a major source of mind pollution, coming at us from all sides, not only from political propaganda, but also from philosophers and scientists, and internally from the fun-house mirrors of our own psychology.

I think we would be less vulnerable to bad logic if logic was taught in high school. I had a hard time in geometry because I never really understood what it meant to "prove" something. If I had had a course in logic, I think I would have understood. So logic should come before geometry, ideally in the ninth grade, when students are just beginning to exercise their reasoning ability.

In school, students can learn good logic, but they also need to know about the bad logic. I have already given many examples of bad logic in the preceding chapters:

There is the thinking, "If we can't study it scientifically, then it doesn't exist."

There is the authoritarian pronouncement, "No such things (UFOs, Bigfoot, Angels) exist," based upon incomplete information, because one would need a complete knowledge of the relevant universe to be able to make such a statement with certainty.

The errors that Freud made do not refute the accurate and important (profound, culture-changing) discoveries that he made.

The fact that I am expressing a particular viewpoint does not mean that I am intolerant of other viewpoints.

The fact that I have said nothing when accused of stealing from my employer does not mean I am guilty.

I learned about straw men and red herrings and smear tactics in the 11th grade. I think the bad logic could be taught along with the good logic in the 9th grade.

What can we ever know with certainty? The ancient Greeks asked that question, and Western philosophers are still asking that question.

We can know man-made systems like logic and mathematics with certainty, systems of abstract thought that people have created and people have defined to work in a certain way. Two plus two is always four, absolutely and unquestionably, even when $2 + 2 = 11$ (base 3). Arithmetic works in all number systems and is translatable into all number systems. If you are doing logic, "A" and "not-A" are always mutually exclusive. But if you are doing LSD, "I am the chair" and "I am not the chair" can both be true at the same time. What I am saying is that only within that system of abstract thought, logic or mathematics, can we be absolutely certain of accuracy. When we try to extend it to the real world, things get fuzzy.

Certain things can be calculated with a high degree of precision, like the movement of the planets, and other things can't be calculated, like the exact number that is going to come up on the dice, or how a human being is going to behave in any given situation. So we have this concept of "randomness," which means that we don't know exactly what the outcome is going to be. Nothing is really "random" in the universe. Everything behaves exactly according to the forces applied to it. But the concept of "randomness" is a convenient way of dealing with things and predicting an outcome, when we don't know exactly what those forces are, or the exact equations to represent them.

And to deal with "random" events we have probability theory. Probability theory was developed in the 1600s in response to gambling problems: What are my chances of drawing to an inside straight? And if the payoff is even money, what are my expected winnings in the long run?

Questions involving cards and dice and roulette wheels, where the numbers are defined precisely and mathematically, can be calculated precisely and mathematically. But in most real-life questions the probabilities are not so precisely defined. "She loves me, she loves me not, ..." You might as well pluck the petals off of a daisy. But still the concepts of randomness and probability are useful in everyday life.

This is an improvement over the ancient Greeks. The answer to their question is that nothing is known for certain, except within systems that people have created and defined to operate in a certain way. But all is not lost, because we have these concepts of randomness and probability to deal with the real world. But I think that many Western philosophers are still tied to the legacy of the ancient Greeks, and still looking for certainties.

So I approach life as a gambler, asking myself, "What is the probability?" of something being true. And where I can't calculate the probability, I estimate my knowledge as "certain," "almost certain," "probable," "possible," "not likely," or "impossible." Very little, outside of the absolutes of logic and mathematics, is either "certain" or "impossible," in my view. And if I can't rank something on this scale, I ask myself whether one possibility is "more likely" or "less likely" than another.

I think that high-school students should also be exposed to probability theory, and I see that they are already. I see it as a logical extension of logic, for dealing with an uncertain universe.

One thing I have noticed, living in a generally uncertain universe, is that arguing from the particular to the general isn't all that bad. If I have seen only one swan, and that swan is white, then it is logically inaccurate to conclude, "All swans are white." But if I have seen only one swan, and that swan is white, there is a greater probability that all swans are white than that some swans are not white. It is not a much greater probability, but still, if I was betting even money on it, I would say that all swans are white. Of course, the more swans I have seen, the more certain I can be, and the better my odds become. So here is a philosophy where I can build out from ignorance towards a greater certainty, and never have to worry about absolutes (except of course the accuracy of my logic here).

One of the tricks used by those who would deceive us is to intersperse true statements with the false. Then those of us who think in terms of probabilities will think, "Well, all these things that I know about are true, so this thing that I don't know about must also be true." An example of this is the woman who met a guy in a bar who told her she would die a violent death. The first two things he told her about herself were true, and that made the third more believable.

In logic, the entities we are dealing with are words, and one source of bad logic is the words. Abstract words are ambiguous — they might mean one thing and they might mean another, unless precisely defined, as in mathematics. So abstract words mean nothing to me. For example, in describing Freud's viewpoint as "deterministic," does that mean that childhood experiences CAN determine adult behavior, or that childhood experiences ALWAYS DO determine adult behavior, or that childhood experiences ARE THE SOLE DETERMINANT of adult behavior? These are three different logical entities, and people can shift from one to another, with the ease of an automatic transmission, under the umbrella of "determinism."

Contemporary Western philosophy means nothing to me because there are too many abstract words and few, if any, precise definitions. People just start out and assume, I guess, that everybody is going to know exactly what they mean when they use words like "will" and "love" — never mind the more abstract words like "determinism." No wonder that the English philosophers have claimed that the French philosophers aren't doing "philosophy," and vice-versa.

Getting back to the "with us or against us," the word "we" is a convenient and simple abstract word that can mean any of the combinations of six billion human beings. As used by President Bush, it can mean Bush and any collection of one or more other human beings that he is associated with — his immediate family, his administration, his church, his political party, his country, and so forth. By switching meanings of the word "we," it is possible to be both with "us" and against "us," as for example with humanity and against the Bush Administration in their dealings with humanity.

I think the slickest use of the ambiguity in the word "we" was the rationale given by President Bush for his invasion of Iraq. He said that "we" were only resuming hostilities because Iraq had violated the cease-fire agreement. Of course the "we" that had the cease-fire agreement with Iraq was the United Nations, and the "we" that was invading Iraq was the United States and its allies, acting totally outside of the United Nations. The whole issue of "weapons of mass destruction" was irrelevant, or a red herring, because that too was an issue for the United Nations, not the United States. How many people were not fooled by the "we?" Raise your hands.

An enormous amount of our mental environment is made up of logically inaccurate statements. A logically accurate statement is called "valid." A logically inaccurate statement is "invalid."

It would seem that anybody can prove anything using logic. This isn't true. What is true is that anybody can prove anything using logic inaccurately. The trick is to make the inaccuracy so subtle that the Audience, and preferably even the Speaker, can't detect it. This is what is known as "rationalization," which I define as follows:

A "rationalization" is an argument that is not quite accurate and not quite valid, but is accurate enough and valid enough to convince somebody who really wants to believe it.

And this leads us into psychology.

PSYCHOLOGY

A major cause of mind pollution is people's psychological problems. The people who are deliberately trying to deceive others I believe are outnumbered by the people who are deceiving themselves and don't know it. And these people are more convincing because they themselves sincerely believe in what they are saying.

We have had 2300 years of Western philosophy before Freud, with brilliant people trying to convince others of the rightness of their beliefs, with no idea of whether those arguments are in defense of some psychological prejudice. We have had rulers and religious leaders forcing their beliefs on people, again with no idea of whether these beliefs are psychologically sound. And all this has defined a culture.

I remember, in psychotherapy, spending hours and hours and hours spinning long-winded arguments to justify my actions and my psychological state. My psychiatrist made me aware that this was rationalization. The longer the argument, the greater the chance of inaccuracies being slipped in along the way. So I became aware that long-winded arguments were most likely rationalizations, and most likely contained inaccuracies. Also I became aware that the more impassioned the argument, the more likely I was defending some weakness, some inadequacy. If I am certain of something, my system does not compel me to spend fanatic amounts of energy defending it.

I don't expect anybody to know what "rationalization" means unless they have been through psychotherapy, at least to the point where they have been able to observe themselves rationalizing. But a hundred years after Freud, brilliant people are still rationalizing, rationalizing that they don't need psychotherapy, and rationalizing that therapy is no good because "half the therapists are crazy themselves" and because Freud did "bad science." One guy I knew (brilliant, of course), in his first appointment with a top psychotherapist in New York, convinced himself that he should be a therapist himself, and immediately went up to Columbia to sign up for courses.

So what can you do? You can't say to anybody that they have psychological problems (unless they are ready to hear it, as I was). Their likely response is, "No, YOU have psychological problems."

If you tell people they have psychological problems, or go so far as to identify their particular problem, before they are ready to hear it, it causes them to put up defenses against that particular information, defenses which make it more difficult to solve the problem when they come to it (if they ever do). Under the law, you can be accused of defamation if you say anything about anybody's psychological problems. People's psychological problems are nobody's business but their own, not only legally, but primarily because of the power they have by having an exclusive view of their own mental processes.

So the best I can do is to talk about my own psychological problems, and hope that somebody gets the idea. No, I am not writing just to tell you my problems. I remember once trying to share my discovery of the self-steering process with a discussion group, and the guru said to me, "It is good that you are able to talk about your problems."

So the defenses are airtight.

But I know that all people with psychological problems are suffering some kind of pain. If they are not aware of pain in the daytime, then their dreams will give them pain at night. If they block out their dreams at night, then I don't know. But I think the pain reaches at least the vast majority of people with psychological problems. That's a start.

People who are hurt by their psychological problems (loss of job, loss of lover, etc.) tend to seek out psychological help. But the people who hurt other people as the result of their psychological problems don't usually seek help. They are doing just fine, usually in some high-ranking social position. And these are the people who are doing the most damage, in terms of social pain, and starting wars, and writing brilliant treatises which implant their inaccuracies into the minds of millions.

So how can these "successful" people possibly be motivated to seek psychotherapy? They are hurting people for a reason. Somewhere they have been hurt themselves, and it gives them some kind of satisfaction to be hurting people, a satisfaction that makes the pain go away, at least momentarily. But then they have to hurt people again and again, because the pain never goes away. The only way to make the pain go away is to go through psychotherapy and identify the reason for the pain, and eliminate it.

We can't solve anybody's psychological problems but our own, so we can't eliminate this source of mind pollution, at least until these people solve their own problems. But we can recognize the inaccuracies and protect ourselves from them. To start with, rationalizations that are subtle enough to fool people who are psychologically underdeveloped may not be subtle enough to fool people who are psychologically developed. As more people become psychologically developed, those who are psychologically underdeveloped will begin losing their credibility and their Audience, and will no longer have the influence on the culture that they once had. And then they might even be motivated to seek psychotherapy.

SORCERY

I know there is such a thing as mental telepathy because I have experienced it. I know there is such a thing as hypnotic suggestion because I have experienced it. I know there are such things as spirit entities because I have experienced them. And when Richard Kieninger mentioned the supremely evil entities called "Black Mentalists," I was ready to accept their existence because I had had a couple of dreams with supremely frightening black forces at work. So I accept the possibility and even probability that there are these supremely evil entities, so evil that they could not incarnate because they would self-destruct immediately, who are trying to drag down all humanity with them, and are trying to influence us from the spirit realm via telepathic suggestion.

This may be a little bit too much to swallow, for people who haven't had the same experiences I have had. One friend just called me "paranoid." But if you call me "paranoid," you will have to prove it. And then you will have to get into that argument of "There are no such things," which can't be proved unless you have a complete knowledge of the universe, in all its dimensions.

I think the first problem with the idea of malevolent spirits operating in our environment is that it is extremely frightening. I lived in fear for almost a year after gaining this awareness, continually reciting the Protective Prayer, and even now the idea makes my hair stand on end. And I believe that I would not have reached this awareness unless I was psychologically ready to handle it.

This then means that I can communicate the reality of Black Mentalists only to those people who are psychologically ready to handle it. The others will just block it out. But then, if you are not psychologically ready to handle the reality of Black Mentalists, why are you not being totally invaded by them?

Richard Kieninger emphasizes that the Black Mentalists have nowhere near the power of a human Master, or even a high-level Adept, and that these Masters and Adepts, which he calls the "Holy Spirit," aligned with the higher powers of Angels and Archangels,

protect the innocent and unaware from interference by Black
Mentalists. If you don't believe that there are any kinds of spirit
entities, high or low, then I suppose to you this is all a lot of hooey,
but you are protected anyway.

In a totally unrelated book, Sylvia Browne, in *Life on the Other
Side*, mentions "the dark entities of *Noir*" only briefly, and
emphasizes the protection we have against them:

> ... they have chosen to turn away from God. And they have the same
> mission that the Dark Side has on earth: to defeat and destroy as much of
> God's light in as many spirits as possible, because darkness cannot survive
> where there is light.
>
> Like Mystical Travelers, the dark entities of *Noir* are highly advanced and
> powerful. But there's not anyone or anything that is more highly advanced and
> powerful than a universe full of souls united in the divine white light of the
> Holy Spirit, and ... ultimately we foot soldiers in God's mighty army have
> *nothing* to fear.
>
> (Browne, 2000, page 169)

If you don't believe at all in a spiritual reality, I'm sure this just
reads like more hooey. But for those who might be inclined to accept
the possibility, I think it might be easier to accept if it were less
frightening, and Sylvia Browne, by minimizing the danger, has
perhaps approached the subject in a better way.

Richard Kieninger goes on to say that your primary line of
defense against the Black Mentalists is not to get on their
wavelengths at all, with greed, anger, fear, or the will to power. This
includes fear of Black Mentalists, which will also make you
vulnerable to them. For those of us who may be vulnerable, he says
to pray to the Holy Spirit for protection. In its simplest form, the
Protective Prayer is "Dear Christ, Please protect me." In the most
elaborate form I have seen, it is:

> Dear Elder Brothers, in the name of Christ and by the white light of His
> power, please allow into my environment only those influences that are for my
> greatest good and for the greatest good of all concerned.

But Richard warns that the Holy Spirit will protect you only from
intrusions against your will. If you try, of your own free will, to

contact these spirit entities and allow them to operate in your environment, then the higher beings withdraw their protection (because then they would be interfering with your free will). Why is *Faust* great literature?

What I am outlining here is not a rigid belief system but a working hypothesis to be tested. I am asking the skeptical here only to set up the hypothesis and ask whether it explains anything. For example, why has Western philosophy become so far removed from the subject it was originally intended to study, the living of life? Why has it evolved into an intellectual snarl that most people can't even understand? Why does Eastern philosophy encourage people to turn off all thought and emotion, and become oblivious to their earthly environment? Why are religions authoritarian, depriving people of their free will as much as possible? Why do brilliant people introduce so much confusion in the world? Is it only their personal psychology or are they influenced by forces that would like to make us all crazy? Why do so many people spread hatred in the name of religion?

For those who don't believe in spirit entities, the explanation for all these things has to be that they are caused by people's personal psychology. When mediums apparently contact spirit entities, it can be inferred that they are speaking from other personalities within their subconscious.

And so when I complained to the psychiatrist in 1968 that dead people were coming into my dreams, he concluded that I had some "deep-seated" psychological problem. But I had had enough experience with dream analysis at that point to be able to differentiate between an aspect of myself, like the anima, coming into my dream, and some external entity interrupting my dream. And it is that fine distinction I am trying to communicate here, if you are ready to be able to tell the difference.

Richard Kieninger defines "sorcery" as the interference into another person's thought processes by means of telepathic suggestion. This can be done by people here on earth as well as by discarnate spirit entities.

Even if one is not practicing sorcery, Richard teaches that "operating in the environment" (meaning "mental environment") of another person, without that person's consent, can be karmically disastrous. For example, when I visited The Stelle Group in 1971, I was warned by one individual that interpreting other people's dreams was "operating in their environment." When I explained that I was only teaching people to interpret their own dreams, that was considered OK.

I see 3 levels of interference here:

1. ordinary suggestions
2. telepathic suggestions
3. telepathic suggestions coming from Black Mentalists

Telepathic suggestions operate the same as ordinary suggestions that come in through the physical senses, with one important difference: You may not be aware that these ideas are coming from the outside. You may think they are your own. So you may not look at them as critically as you would with ideas you know are coming from the outside. Here is a reason to keep an open mind to the possibility of telepathic suggestion. You need to ask, "Is this really me?" If it isn't, you might file it away as a possible example of telepathic suggestion.

I differentiate between "psychology," or inaccuracies caused by psychological problems caused by conflicts purely within the individual, between the conscious and the subconscious, and "sorcery," or inaccuracies caused by other entities interfering with the mental processes of an individual below the threshold of consciousness.

I make this distinction between "psychology" and "sorcery," but I can't tell whether a person is influenced by one or another, except perhaps in myself, where I am intimately aware of my own mental processes — if I can't explain something by psychology, then maybe it is sorcery. And sometimes in social situations I say a quick Protective Prayer, "Dear Christ, please protect me," to myself, and the people who are creating the stressful situation back off. That's about all I know about it.

It is difficult enough to recognize the influence of sorcery in myself, and it would be that much more difficult to recognize it in somebody else. So I see sorcery, like psychology, as a person's own personal business.

According to Richard Kieninger, when Black Mentalists are operating in a person's mental environment, the color black is visible in that person's aura. So I suppose that if we have a judge and a jury all skilled at reading auras, we could have a witch trial. But I would hope that any society thus evolved would treat with compassion any persons thus afflicted.

I would not want anything I am saying here to be taken as authority to support anything as foolish as a witch trial. What I am saying here is intended for the personal growth and awareness of the individual, and not to point an accusing finger at anybody else. I feel that it is necessary to present this disclaimer, before I even use words like "Satan" or "witchcraft."

"Satan" is a word that has been used by religious people to describe anybody who doesn't agree with their particular beliefs. Freethinkers, heretics, members of other religions, people who enjoy sex, insane people, sorcerers, and diabolically evil people are all lumped together in one category and all considered to be under the influence of Satan. Maybe I shouldn't use the word "Satan" at all because it has so much past history of prejudice associated with it. But the idea of "Satan" and "fallen angels" seems to fit the description of the Black Mentalists, and maybe this is where the idea of Satan came from in the first place — except that they aren't fallen angels, but only fallen human beings.

These Black Mentalists, who are so evil that they are never again able to incarnate, and thus never able to redeem themselves, and want to drag down all humanity with them, fit the description of an Evil force in the universe that can be called "Satan." I am not going to define "Evil." I am only saying that whatever is for the good of the individual and for humanity, these entities are working against it. I capitalize the word "Evil" only to refer to these spiritual forces, and never to earthly forces, no matter how evil they might be. Similarly I use the word "Satan" only to refer to these discarnate entities, and never to any persons or organizations or governments here on earth.

If people on earth can be influenced by these Satanic forces, can people then be "possessed," meaning completely taken over by them? I don't think so, because the body thus possessed would probably self-destruct immediately, as a body legitimately occupied by that spirit entity would if that spirit entity tried to incarnate. But people are influenced by these spirit entities, to some degree or another, from zero to the point where they do self-destruct.

This is a more specific definition than the historic definition, or non-definition, of "Satan." Again, this is only part of a theoretical structure I am setting up. I am only beginning to find evidence to support it.

I was once communicating with a person on the Internet who was doing Wiccan. And I asked her, "Isn't that witchcraft?" She was trying to explain to me that it wasn't witchcraft, but we had no precise definition of witchcraft, so it was hard to tell. I still don't know what Wiccan is, but I have since come across a more specific definition of "witchcraft," specifically that people who do witchcraft have sworn allegiance to Satan. Given a more specific definition of "Satan," we can have a more specific definition of "witchcraft." Note that this definition does not limit the practice to women.

These more specific definitions should be more accurate to work with than the religious prejudices of the past.

Sorcery, like psychology, is a major source of mind pollution. If you haven't experienced telepathy or spirit entities, I'm not going to argue with you if you want to think of these influences as all coming from a person's personal unconscious. But for those of you who already accept the spiritual dimension, these are influences that come from outside one's personal psychology.

As with psychology, it is probably not possible to remove these influences from every individual that is affected by them, but at least the rest of us can be warned that such influences may exist, and can be looking for evidence that supports their existence.

Quoting the Jesuit priest from the movie *Bless the Child*,

"The Devil's greatest achievement is that people don't believe he exists."

9. DOMINATION, STATUS, AND AUTHORITARIAN SYSTEMS

DOMINATION

Domination starts from the moment we are born. We start off completely dependent on our parents and completely dominated by them. As we grow older, we gradually become less dependent and less completely dominated by them. Up until a certain point in my life, my parents could just pick me up and put me where they wanted me. And then there was another period in my life when an adult had to be with me at all times. I wasn't completely independent of my parents and their domination until I was actually earning my own living and had an apartment of my own.

And along with this dependence and domination, we are fed whatever beliefs our parents have, which we absorb almost automatically as small children and perhaps more skeptically as adolescents. We absorb an enormous amount of information, life-shaping information, as children, not because it is right, but because we accept the authority of the people who are feeding it to us.

In school, again, we are dominated by the teacher. We are required to memorize whatever the teacher teaches us, not because it is accurate, but because if we don't, we won't get a very good grade. At least what the school teaches us is usually factual, and usually accurate, as opposed to class prejudices, racial prejudices, and religious prejudices our parents may feed us.

Sometimes the child receives conflicting information from parents and teachers. I remember being taught in school that Cape Cod Light was the most powerful lighthouse on the East Coast (1944). But Tada had taught me that Highland Light was the most powerful lighthouse on the East Coast. I think what they told me at home was "Go along with what the teacher says in school, but at home we know differently." Nobody at the time seemed to know that they were all talking about the same lighthouse.

And it never occurred to me at the time to find out the truth for myself. Truth came from some "authority," and I was just bouncing back and forth between the two "authorities."

Children enjoy this authority and eagerly absorb everything they are taught, if the adult doing the teaching is psychologically mature. And conversely, if the adult doing the teaching is still psychologically a child, children resent it. They are being cheated, actually, although I don't think they are aware of it. (I wasn't, anyway.) And this is the more normal case.

So children build up a resistance to this adult authority, sort of like the French "Resistance" against the Nazis in World War II. It is a secret underground, with its own code of behavior. The teachers are the enemy, imposing their domination, and not thought of as good people who are doing their best to educate children. The first thing I learned from the other kids was that I wasn't supposed to like school. And the next thing I learned was the code, never to be broken, that I was never to tell the teacher when anybody did anything bad. This was called "squealing" (as in "little piggie," I guess), or "ratting on" somebody.

I remember, in the Charles Manson movie, where they were all saying "Snitch," "Snitch," "Snitch," at the "snitch." And then the body of the "snitch" was found cut up into little pieces. That's what will happen to you if you are a "snitch," or so the bullies would have small children believe.

And then, at some point in school, the young Attila the Hun emerges. Not only can he beat up everybody, but also he is a superb manipulator, exploiting everybody's resentment of authority so that they submit to his authority. Not satisfied that he can beat up everybody, he assembles his gang around him to help him do it. The school authorities look the other way, because they believe that it builds character for children to have to submit to bullying.

Domination is not taught in school, but it is learned in school. It is also the ruling principle behind everything that is taught.

In adult life, beating up people and verbally abusing them are criminal activities, called "assault and battery." The code against "squealing" on people is one of the rules of organized crime, not normal adult life. Where children have been taught by their parents to be "good," they are now learning to be "bad," to live by a criminal code, and to ingest harmful substances into their bodies. Older kids are not only stealing lunch money from younger kids, but they are probably also manipulating younger kids into doing drugs in order to support their own drug habits. (At least that's what the anti-drug TV commercials are telling me.) Because of the potential for permanent damage to children from drugs, I would look for the influence of Black Mentalists here.

And all this is supposed to build character? I think that is an age-old rationalization by school administrations that created the problem in the first place and are now powerless to stop it. There is a whole genre of high-school movies portraying inept school administrations. These movies reflect what the kids believe, anyway.

And there are also the movies where one good teacher turns the whole thing around. Of course that is fiction, but I think that school officials who are psychologically adults could turn it all around:

"OK, kids, we are learning to be adults here, and in adult society assault and battery are criminal behavior. You WILL go to jail for it. And people who witness crimes report them to police. And police have witness-protection programs. There is no such thing as a 'snitch,' unless you are in organized crime. If you want to be in organized crime, we will identify you and send you to a special place, so that the rest of us can grow up to be adults."

And there should be a special place. You can't go to school if you aren't toilet-trained. And so you shouldn't be allowed in school if you constantly abuse other children, physically or verbally. I'm not talking about the occasional fight. I'm talking about kids who are constantly and compulsively bullying, picking on younger and smaller kids. This behavior is probably learned in the home, so kids like this are probably better off being removed from the home, as well as the school, and sent to a withdrawal facility. And what would be the authority for this? Simple — criminal convictions of children for assault and battery on other children.

The withdrawal facility would have clear discipline, but it would also have loving kindness, compassion, and psychotherapeutic help. It would recognize that these childrens' desire to injure others comes from having been injured themselves. It would redo their upbringing. It would use older children who have been "converted" as role models for the younger children.

The withdrawal facility should be way out in the boonies — the last place a city kid would want to go — and that should be enough of a threat to keep kids from misbehaving if at all possible. Being way out in the boonies, it should not cost the taxpayers much — far less than the cost of keeping these kids in jail later on — and so it would be politically attractive. It would also be politically attractive to cut down on drug use, not make children go through Hell at school, and prevent other tragedies like the Columbine massacre. How about it? Can we get rid of institutionalized bullying in our schools?

Even without Attila the Hun, there are pressures applied in any social group, to think as they do, and believe as they do, for their approval or their scorn. In any group, people tend to go along with those who are most dominant, I guess so they don't have to fight with them. And after going along with them for a while, they tend to agree with them. And after agreeing with them for a while, they tend to believe them — all because of domination. Nowhere in any of this is any consideration of accuracy, but only what people who are able to dominate you want you to believe.

As a child, I enjoyed the domination and authority. I particularly enjoyed my years at summer camp, with its military-like routine —

reveille at 7, march to flag-raising, dress-right-dress, inspections, and all that stuff. Our days were all planned for us, with assigned activities. And instead of loving parents, there were counselors who didn't particularly love us, enforcing the rules.

But by the time I got to prep school, at age 14, I began questioning the system:

"Sir, why do we have this rule?"

"We have always had this rule, and we will continue to have this rule."

"But Sir!"

"No buts."

And of course when Harvard gave me official permission to think at age 18, it was a great moment in my life. I realized that I didn't have enough knowledge to disagree with professors who were experts in their fields, and of course my teachers were still the authorities doing the grading, but this was a major step away from the teacher being the "authority" to assuming the authority myself, in my own mind, to decide what to believe.

Ideally as the child becomes an adult, the child has the same equivalent knowledge as the adults, and can argue that knowledge with adults as an equal, and doesn't have to accept anything on their "authority." At that point the child has become free of domination, at least in respect to knowledge.

I didn't actually take that step until I saw the need to create a new civilization. Then I began questioning everything I had ever been taught. "Sorting out the baggage," I called it.

I wonder how many people actually do that? Some people seem to think that all education comes from domination. I remember when I was trying to describe on the Internet my process of re-educating myself, one heckler called it "Circular." This implies that there have to be two parties involved, one doing the teaching and one doing the learning. I guess this person never read what I read many years ago — that the way to study philosophy is to go out in the world with a notebook.

It has been theorized that it is impossible to break free of one's culture. If this is another variation of the self-made-man argument, then of course it is impossible. But if it just means to break free of the domination of parents and teachers and peer groups, then it is possible, and I have done it. My methods were psychotherapy, withdrawal, and dream analysis. It was a long and difficult process that took me 17 years. In the end, my dreams taught me things that were outside the culture.

So it seems that I have just replaced the authority of the culture with the authority of my dreams. Well, yes and no. First of all, the dreams are not just dictating to me. They are giving me riddles which I have to figure out and interpret in my own mind, and it is in the analysis that I develop my beliefs. My own mind is telling me what to make of the dream.

But then if I don't get it right, the dreams will correct me. So the dreams represent some kind of authority — the authority of my own deeper mind, or of God sending me messages. In either case, these messages reflect the authority of natural law, or "the way things work." Natural law is an authority to which all things including people must conform. Our freedom is limited by natural law. For example, I can't just float to the moon. There is the law of gravity bringing me back to earth. I have to develop an equal and opposite force, or figure out how to neutralize gravity, as in levitation or an anti-gravity device.

The dreams are giving me lessons in natural law. I can test these lessons in real life and see that they work. For example, my sex life became better when I reached the psychological age of puberty, and better yet when I reached the psychological age of adulthood. The dreams are not teaching me some dogma which I am coerced or manipulated into believing, by the authority of human beings to dominate other human beings. The authority that dreams represent is the authority of natural law, which dominates us all. All lessons need to be tested in real life, to see if they are consistent with "the way things work." And where the lessons taught under the authority and domination of other human beings conflict with natural law, there is what I am calling "mind pollution."

STATUS

Animals establish a "pecking order" by biting, pecking, clawing, cuffing, butting, and generally fighting each other. It is like a tennis ladder — whoever beats whom takes the higher place in the rank order, and the leader is the one who is able to beat all. This rank order is established by domination. One's status is one's position in the rank order. So, in a group of animals of a given species, status is determined by domination.

In human society, it isn't that simple. Physical fighting does not always lead to domination. Mental warfare and mental bullying play a very important part — name-calling, insulting, put-downs, making one's opponent look bad if he were to resort to physical fighting, and various other manipulative tricks. And the kind of domination that comes from fighting, either physically or mentally, is more likely to lead to status among children and primitive people and those who are psychologically underdeveloped than among people who are psychologically developed.

Mature human beings are more likely to give status to those people who show some kind of merit at some kind of human endeavor — art, music, athletics, sex appeal, professional ability in general — not just those who show a high degree of skill at warfare or the ability to dominate. There are also people who gain status because of general qualities, such as their character, wisdom, or service to humanity. Also the amount of money one has, or the length of time one's family has had money, give people social status.

Also human beings organize, and within the organizations they create, status is not determined purely on the basis of domination. Certain positions in the organization require certain specific skills. Yes, it helps if a manager is able to dominate when the situation requires it, but more important is the ability to coordinate the various people under him/her to accomplish the specific function within the organization.

There are various levels of status in the organization. There are unskilled workers and skilled workers. There is the boss, and there is the big boss. You don't get to be the CEO by punching out the big boss. Everybody is dominated by somebody in the organization, even the CEO, who has to satisfy stockholders and customers, and even the President of the United States, who has to get the votes. And this domination, and the status that goes with it, are determined not by fighting but by the importance of one's job in carrying out the goals of the organization.

But this status is within the organization only. It doesn't carry over into the world at large, except by "bragging-rights." When you go to the country club, you can say, "I am a doctor," or "I am a lawyer," or "I am a vice-president," and everybody smiles and nods. If you said "I sweep floors," they would probably all turn away.

And of course with status there are higher salaries. And with more money, people are able to buy things to show other people that they have this status — "status-symbols."

But really, individual human beings have very little status in the culture at large. The organizations have the real status, starting with the United States government, the Catholic Church, other major religions, other major governments, television as a group, academia as a group, and so on down the line. Somewhere way down the line individual human beings start appearing — Jane Fonda, Robert Redford, Charlton Heston, Arnold Schwarzenegger — because they are known to the public as movie stars or sports stars or pop-music stars, or because they have appeared on television. But if I am looking for the greatest doctor or the greatest lawyer, I really have to be in an inner circle to know who they are.

When I was a child, my father taught me how to pitch. But I couldn't be a pitcher, because the pitcher had to be the guy with the highest status in the social group. That usually meant the guy who could beat up everybody else, not the guy who was the best pitcher. The infielders were those with the next highest social status. I always felt more comfortable in the outfield, as one with a low social status — meaning that I couldn't beat up anybody, except for the very weakest guys.

I had the same kind of experience in football. One day I ran back a kickoff fairly well with guys hanging all over me, and the coach asked me if I would like to be in the backfield. "Oh, no, I couldn't be in the backfield," was something like my reply. Again, in the social code, the guys with the highest status got to carry the ball, not because they were good at it, but because they could beat you up. And I knew it was just not my "place," socially, to be in the backfield.

Eventually I saw that my "place" was in the backfield, because I could run fast and didn't weigh much. The influence of the coach is important here as one who is trying to match abilities to positions on the football team, as opposed to the group leader saying, "I'm going to carry the ball, and the rest of you guys get in the line and block."

And so it seemed natural that the guys who were able to beat up everybody would go on to become leaders in later life. At least they had experience at it, and they had confidence in their ability to lead, whereas those of us who had had their faces pushed in the snow day after day had our doubts. I suppose that's what builds character — to be able to overcome that kind of adversity and rise to the top. But on the other hand, I think a number of people who are better qualified to be leaders in later life are being defeated too early in life. And do we really want eighth-graders to be our leaders?

I always admired the guys who were oblivious to peer-group pressures and were able to grow up to be just what they wanted to be. But for the rest of us, again, I think the adults in the educational system have the responsibility, and need to have the ability, to minimize at least the permanent damage done to children by the pecking of the pecking order.

At the top of the status-heap is Government. I capitalize the word "Government" to mean the whole structure of government we have in the United States, from the federal government on down to states and counties and localities. The whole idea of government of course started with the pecking order and the guy who was able to defeat the others in warfare becoming the leader and telling the others what to do. And the leader became a Chief, and Chiefs swore allegiance to a King, to form a two-level pecking order where those in power could do pretty much what they wanted to those under them.

Then along came the bad King John, who was so bad that the Chiefs, the nobles, made him sign a document, the Magna Carta, agreeing to subordinate himself to certain rules of law. From that beginning, we have the rule of law today, where the law governs, and no person is above the law.

And with the rule of law comes the idea of "rights," where those persons of lesser status than the Government are allowed certain powers and certain freedoms which cannot be taken away by those of greater status. Note that these "rights" are not God-given. What God gave us was a jungle, where the adult male alligator eats as many of its young as it can, and where people have to fight for every little bit of power and freedom that they get. These "rights" were created by people and won by people, in hard-fought battles like the American Revolution. In many, perhaps most, countries today, the idea of "rights" is very foreign.

But in America and other advanced countries today we have this invention called the "law" which has a greater status than any person. And this invention, sort of like a software system, declares that all people governed by it have equal rights. Well, actually, it started off giving all white male property-owners equal rights. That still hasn't been extended, really, to all races, all genders, all belief systems, and all economic levels, but at least the ideal is there, and we are working on it.

And this Government is determined, "governed," if you will, by the voters, who are, again ideally, all American citizens age 18 and over. So the Government isn't really doing the "governing." The voters are calling the shots, telling it what they want it to do (within the Constitution, of course). Government is more like a service organization. It protects our "rights" internally with a police force and externally with the military. And note that these "rights" always have to be defended by force against those who would take them away. Government also provides other social services like highways and schools and support for the aged.

So instead of looking to Government for "leadership," as in telling us what to do, or "ruling," as in bossing us around, I see Government as a service organization. This is just a way of looking at it.

If people running for public office did so with the idea that they are going to serve people, instead of having power over them, Government would be more in tune with its ideals. A person loses no status by being a "servant" in a country where all people are equal under the law.

Under the law, we are all given equal status. In organizations, our status is determined by our specific skills and the needs of the organization. But in our social groups, we still retain vestiges of the old animal pecking order. Certainly in a free country, people are allowed to be in a pecking order, if that's what they want. I myself prefer not to. I don't want to dominate or be dominated. I am uncomfortable with people looking up to me or looking down at me.

Status, whether it is the old animal kind or the new organizational kind, creates inaccuracies in our beliefs. We tend to accept what persons of greater status have to say, and discount what persons of lesser status have to say.

One day when I was five years old, the grownups were having some kind of a problem by the side of the road near our house. I forget what the problem was — something to do with the board fence and a car, maybe stuck in the mud. All I remember is that I saw the solution, and I tried to tell the grownups, but they just said, "Don't bother us now. Can't you see we have a problem?"

And then finally the grownups solved the problem exactly as I was trying to tell them. I was furious that nobody had paid any attention to me, but I couldn't say that. I just vowed that some day I would show them how smart I was.

And so I rewrote the civilization, and still almost nobody paid any attention to me. Only four people liked my 1970 manuscript.

It was then that I remembered my five-year-old experience and realized that the child is not listened to because the child has no status. Even an adult with no status is ignored or dismissed or laughed at, not because his ideas have no merit, but simply because he has no status.

So I set out to get some status for myself. I went back to work as a computer programmer, hoping to make a name for myself in the computer field. I wrote the key commercial software (sorting, file indexing, report writer) for the Wang 2200. The only problem was that I didn't put my name on it, because I didn't want my phone to be ringing constantly. Within the company and to a few software developers, I had status, but to the world at large I was still "nobody."

I had to self-publish *Re-Educating Myself* — again, missing out on the status of having an established publisher's name on the book.

When I sent out flyers offering the book to philosophy departments at a discount, the few responses I received were mostly from colleges and universities I had never heard of, sometimes with a personal check from an individual. One would have thought that the more heavily endowed institutions would have more money to spend to explore everything written in their field, but no. I said to my friends, "It all has to do with status."

And they replied, "Of course it all has to do with status. Didn't you know that?"

When I sent out flyers offering free books to philosophy departments, I got a better response, but still not from any of the Ivy League universities or any other university ranked in the top 30. So evidently the rules of status are very strict, where one would be embarrassed to request even a free book from a person of no status.

Ideally, books and ideas should be judged on their merit. But it is clear to me that status comes first, at least among persons of status. There are exceptions, and I am thankful to those individuals for their support. But I think that most persons of status are dominated by the social laws and the fear that somebody above them in the pecking order might ridicule them for being seen with the "wrong" kind of book. So merit is judged only if one has status to begin with.

And it took me several more years to realize that persons of status don't have to be right — they are believed simply because they have status. And my friends again said, "Well, of course — didn't you know that?"

I have already discussed the mechanics of how status creates inaccuracies, in my section on "The Status of Science." I'll be giving more examples of status in operation in future chapters.

AUTHORITARIAN SYSTEMS

I was telling my psychology professor that I had precognitive dreams, and he asked me, "Can you prove that?"

I have proved it to myself, but his question made me realize that I can't prove it to anybody else. All my life I have been proving things to myself — telepathy, spirit entities, the self-steering process, and so on. That is the primary way by which I "know" anything, and, arguing from the particular to the general, I believe that that is the primary way by which anybody knows anything. I see the evidence for myself, in my own experience, and you can also see the evidence for yourself, in your own experience.

The idea of proving something to somebody else is something else. I know that this is what science does, but what is it?

I prove something to myself because I see the evidence for myself. You prove something to yourself because you see the evidence for yourself. I prove something to you by showing you the evidence. But if you weren't there to see this evidence, how do you know that what I am saying is accurate?

Science provides a method, not for showing people the evidence, but for convincing people that their findings are accurate. In some cases, we do see the evidence, as with the atomic bomb. And in many or most cases, the findings of science can be verified by individuals. But that isn't the scientific "proof." The scientific proof is done in laboratories, where only scientists see it, and replicated by other scientists, and reported in scientific journals, to create what has been called "certified knowledge." The assumption here is then that people are supposed to believe it, that it has been proved to the world. But really we are believing it on the authority of science — that their methods are accurate, that their observations are accurate, that their reasoning is accurate, and that they are all telling the truth, and not one great conspiracy to deceive the public. And because we are believing it on the authority of science, science is what I call an "authoritarian system."

An "authoritarian system" is where somebody figures out answers to apply to everybody. This is "authoritative" knowledge that people can just download into their own minds.

As children, we start right out with an authoritarian system, with our parents teaching us things which they know, and which we are supposed to believe, and are ready to believe, on their authority. The whole educational system is an authoritarian system, insofar as students are expected to accept things as "knowledge" upon the authority of their teachers. I am not surprised that some people go through life thinking that the only kind of education is the authoritarian kind.

But I remember the story of the parent who was so tired of telling his small child, "Don't do this," and "Don't do that," that finally in exasperation he said, "And don't EVER put peas up your nose." And soon after that the child had to be rushed to the Emergency Room with peas up her nose.

So actually we are testing things for ourselves, right from the beginning, in the face of all this authority.

Religion is another authoritarian system. People are telling us that they have the ultimate truth from the ultimate source. With most things, as we grow up and have the same equivalent knowledge as our elders, it is easy to dispute their authority, but not in regard to religion, because nobody ever has the ultimate knowledge to be able to dispute the teachings of religion. So religion is an authoritarian system that tends to stay with people all their lives. Religions teach us to believe on their authority, without evidence, and without any argument, because "Reason is error."

Science is more modern in appealing to reason and the senses for its authority, giving people an opportunity to see for themselves why certain things have to be true. But still it is an authoritarian system, insofar as the findings of scientists are to be considered "authoritative." And then with such claims as "objective" knowledge, they go beyond authoritarian into authoritarianism, with the idea that their knowledge is untainted with the errors of human perception and therefore must be believed.

I use scientific methods for myself, to prove things to myself. I don't expect anybody to believe anything on my authority. I expect you to prove these things in your own experience. I think this is a better system than the authoritarian systems, one which will result in more accuracy for everybody.

Astrology is another authoritarian system, trying to find out personal aspects of individuals from the positions of the planets. I do think there is some degree of accuracy in it, which could be easily tested in unbiased scientific experiments. So far the experiments I have read about seem to be coming from people who are just out to disprove it. I mean, really, how can the movements of planets millions of miles away possibly have anything to do with a person's character and personality?

I was seriously into astrology at one time. I sold my catamaran (1968) and took up farming (1969) when I discovered I was an earth sign. But I had one experience that really steered me away from astrology.

I have a book, *Heaven Knows What*, by Scorpio (Scorpio, 1935), that gives passages that describe a person's characteristics for each planetary aspect that they have in their birth chart. With this book, anybody can do a horoscope for anybody, given that they know that person's birth date.

I was having fun doing horoscopes with this book, until I came across a particularly bad aspect for one friend of mine. She was very upset and angry, and she insisted that this did not represent her at all.

So I backed off and realized that I really didn't know whether it represented her or not, but that I knew of a method — dream analysis — which will tell people the most intimate and accurate details about themselves. So if I have dream analysis, then who needs astrology? And I have never done astrology since.

I think there are a great many aspects of learning which have authoritarian systems in mind, like Carl Jung showing that there are universal symbols in dreams. If you can show that anything is universal, then it applies to everyone, and it fits in with the authoritarian approach to learning. Although I have experienced the universal symbols in my dreams, I think that the basic language of dreams is a personal language, drawing on one's own personal experience for its symbolism, and that this knowledge is beyond the reach of any authoritarian system.

People earn a living from authoritarian systems. If they can convince society that their system applies to everybody, then society will pay them to implement it. This is a possible source of bias. I don't think that people who are just trying to find the truth for themselves usually earn a living from it. But maybe what they learn is more accurate.

PART IV

THE CAMPS

10. ULTIMATE TRUTHS FIRST

In 1999, I saw an advertisement in the magazine *Free Inquiry* for a conference on the subject "Why Does Religion Persist?" I promptly responded with a paper describing how, through a process of free inquiry, I discovered God and a spiritual reality. But I was wrong.

"Religion" is not just a belief in the spiritual. Religion is a WAY of believing in the spiritual, a WAY of approaching a knowledge of the spiritual. Religion is a rigid belief system that claims to know the ultimate reality. It is an authoritarian system, to be believed on the authority of sacred writings that were written thousands of years ago and can never be changed.

I am not talking here about any particular religion. I am using the word "religion" just to mean a particular way of thinking that has influenced the culture and created inaccuracies, and I am criticizing only those aspects of religion that have created the inaccuracies. I am using the Christian religion as an example because this is the religion I am most familiar with.

Religions start out with the spiritual perceptions of highly evolved individuals. Great and gifted souls catch glimpses of spiritual truths — maybe not the ultimate truths, but enough beyond the perceptions of ordinary people so that they are to ordinary people as adults are to children. And ordinary people follow their teachings, and document them in sacred writings, and preserve these glimpses of higher truths.

The first problem of accuracy is that these books weren't written during the lifetime of these great souls, and therefore weren't written from first-hand experience. I have read that the Christian Gospels were written decades after the life of Jesus, based on other people's accounts, and that the life of Buddha wasn't documented in writing until centuries after his death. So what is written is really a legend, passed down by hearsay.

The second problem of accuracy is that religious and political authorities over the years can change these sacred writings, despite dire warnings not to do this. For example, reincarnation was declared a heresy in 553 AD by the Fifth Ecumenical Congress of Constantinople, dominated by the Emperor Justinian (Langley, 1965, pages 6 and 35). The statements in the Bible implying reincarnation (see Langley, 1965, pages 47-50) are clues indicating that more obvious statements about reincarnation were removed to comply with the official belief.

The third problem, and probably the most serious one, is that the ordinary people preserving the teachings, and teaching the teachings, are as children trying to represent adults, in trying to represent the great and gifted souls upon whose insights the religion was founded. These ordinary people interpret the original teachings according to their best understanding of them, which can't possibly be enough, and which changes what is taught. Their interpretation then becomes the teaching, and is perpetuated as such, although the teachings have probably lost a great deal of accuracy in their departure from the original.

Certain standard interpretations are adopted over the years, so that the religion can have one particular belief, and not the chaos that would result if different teachers were each teaching their own interpretation. The early Christian sects had many different beliefs, which had to be resolved, sometimes with loss of life, in order to create one unified Christian Church. Different interpretations were labeled "heresy" and punished by death or excommunication from the religion. For example, the Gnostics, who believed in

reincarnation, and also believed on the basis of knowledge, or
gnosis, and not "faith," were persecuted and driven into secrecy
when the early Church leaders decreed that belief had to be on the
basis of "faith."

In modern times, different interpretations have become the
different Christian denominations, all drawing on the same original
teachings.

Again, I am trying not to criticize any particular religion here, but
only those aspects of "religious" thinking that have created
inaccuracies.

One approach to knowledge is that one must know the ultimate
truths first, like a fixed picture frame defining the limits of "reality,"
and then filling in the picture from there. If we are living strictly
according to "the law of the jungle," maybe it is a good thing to kill
people. But if there is a God passing judgment on us, then maybe it
isn't a good thing to kill people. So it seems that in order to know
anything at all, one must first know the ultimate truth, as a
framework for one's whole system of belief.

But you can't know the ultimate truths first, any more than you
can build a building from the top down, or solve differential
equations before you learn simple arithmetic. It just doesn't work
that way. We all start off with fundamental truths, like "Mommy"
and "big toe," and build our knowledge of the universe outward
from there.

Since we can't know the ultimate truth right away, we reach out
to somebody or some source of knowledge that appears to know
something about ultimate truth, just as children reach out to parents
and teachers, and believe things on their authority.

Religion fills this social need for "authorities." Somewhere along
the line, the original glimpses of spiritual truth are extrapolated and
exploited to fill this social need for ultimate truth. These glimpses
are probably much closer to ultimate truth than most of us are
capable of reaching in this lifetime, but still they are only glimpses.

These glimpses, as interpreted, become perpetuated in a dogmatic
belief system, claiming to represent the ultimate reality, and which
never can be changed, of course, if it represents the ultimate reality.

The teachings and the teachers are claimed to represent the authority of God. All this is preserved and maintained by a large organization that maintains a uniformity of belief throughout:

"This is the way it is — this is what God is, this is what God wants of us, this is what we must do to please God and avoid God's wrath, and this is the ultimate and unarguable truth, as is written by God in Holy Scripture.

"If you believe everything in Holy Scripture and follow its teachings, you will be one of God's chosen few. Just believe on the Authority of Holy Scripture. Don't question it. Reason is Error. The evidence of your senses is Error. What you perceive with your senses is all Illusion."

This is religion, as a way of thinking, as I know it. As religion claims its teachings to be ultimate truth, this is a source of inaccuracy in our culture. As religion claims that the authority of its teachings comes from God, this is another source of inaccuracy.

Religion is a man-made system of thought that people have created to represent God and the spiritual reality. The Bible is not God's Word. The Bible is really People's Word. People wrote it, about people's experiences, in people's languages. Many of the people written about were great and gifted individuals, but still they were people, and not God. God is represented as God was able to communicate through them, to the best of their ability to comprehend, and not as God speaking to us directly.

Religion has invented words like "heresy" and "blasphemy," words which meant a death sentence in historical times, to describe anybody who doesn't go along with the authority of the Bible and its approved interpretation. But God won't strike you dead; People will strike you dead. People enforce the authority that People have created in religion.

And then we have this thing called "morality," which includes attributes of psychological maturity on the one hand, and sexual restrictions on the other, and allegedly is how God wants us to behave. But really the moral laws are just part of the social laws. They are laws that People are enforcing on us, by their social approval or disapproval, in the name of God. They will scorn you, shun you, stone you, or say nasty things about you behind your back, all in the name of God.

When we are asked to believe on "faith," there are two meanings of the word "faith." One is faith in the existence of God and a spiritual reality. The other is faith, or trust, that the teachings of religious authorities are accurate.

The problem with believing in "authorities" is that you don't know whether the "authorities" are right unless you know as much as they do. You may not be getting the truth, but how would you know?

The teachers don't know, any more than you do, whether the beliefs they are teaching are accurate. They are only preserving the belief structure that has been taught to them by other people who didn't know any more than they do, and so on.

I don't have to know as much as Buddha or Jesus or Moses to question these teachings. I only have to know as much as the teachers.

As one group of people follows one spiritual leader, other groups of people follow other spiritual leaders. And as the glimpses of the spiritual leaders are made into ultimate truths, each group thinks it has the ultimate truth. The only problem is that all these "ultimate truths" are different. Since they are all different, at most one can be right. And each religion believes its own beliefs are right and the others' are wrong. Most likely they are all wrong — none of them have the ultimate truth.

This is the first step towards religious intolerance. But just because I believe I am right doesn't make me intolerant of other people's beliefs that are different, because I don't claim to know the ultimate truth. I could be wrong, or we could be looking at different aspects of the reality, like the three blind men and the elephant. But if I have it on the highest authority that my beliefs are the ultimate reality, then I may just start thinking, "You must be really stupid," if your beliefs are different.

If you and I have different beliefs, we can discuss it, or argue it, or try to persuade each other that our view is more accurate. But if we both are convinced that our view is infallibly accurate, based on the highest authority, then there isn't much we can do to reconcile our viewpoints. If we further believe that reason is Error and the evidence of the senses is Error, and that the only source of truth is our own particular holy teachings, then there is absolutely nothing we can do to resolve our differences. We can either kill each other or agree to a "peaceful coexistence," as was advocated by Pope John XXIII.

But this air of absolute certainty is not the only ingredient in religious intolerance. There is an element of hate in intolerance. I don't hate anybody for being different, or even for being wrong. I accept Richard Kieninger's definition of "tolerance:" If I were that same person in that same situation, I would be doing exactly the same thing. What reason is there to hate somebody for being different?

Religions preach "good" and "evil." They teach that if you believe absolutely in their teachings and do exactly what they say, you are "good," and as you stray from their teachings, you are "evil." So then if you were doing or believing what these people from another religion are doing and believing, you would be doing evil. You would hate yourself for doing or believing these things, and so you hate these other people. As you would judge yourself, so do you judge others. Thus the element of hate completes religious intolerance.

There is one more logical step needed to make people ready to kill each other: Those others who are different and therefore thought of as "evil" are thought to be under the influence of Satan, or the supreme forces of Evil in the world. So it is easy to rationalize killing people if you can think of it as wiping out the forces of Evil in the world.

Religion has been a major source of mind pollution.

Religious intolerance has been a major cause of war.

And yet religion is a sacred subject. We aren't even supposed to discuss it. I think that's one of the problems with religion — the fact that it is sacred may have blocked honest and constructive criticism in the past. But at this point in history, with the absurdity that our species may itself create its own extinction, I think it is important to have a critical discussion of religion, because of its powerful influence on human thought and motivation.

God is sacred. Whatever God is, is, and we just have to live with it, as was pointed out in the Book of Job. But religion is a man-made system, and can benefit from criticism, and can be improved upon.

The only thing that makes me hesitate — and I have thought about this for a year now — is that people I love are seriously involved with religion, and I would not want to be too offensive to them. I guess the answer to that is that I have already said that I love you. I am only pointing out inaccuracies in a system of thought which you may already agree has serious flaws.

Religion has served a social need by communicating our highest human values and the teachings of the world's great spiritual leaders to large numbers of people. In criticizing the inaccuracies created by religion, I am not criticizing the central purpose of religion or the large numbers of people who feel comfortable following an authoritarian belief system. This is a totally necessary phase of human growth, just as it is necessary to go through the authoritarian phase of parents and teachers to acquire the necessary knowledge to question the universe on one's own. Nothing in this book should be construed as saying that a belief in authoritarian religion is any less valuable or important a learning experience than what I am advocating here, or that its believers should be treated with any less respect as human beings. And conversely, I expect that those people will simply ignore what I am saying here — unless of course it is threatening to them, in which case they might ask themselves why it is threatening.

I am writing here for those others, like myself, who have already questioned the "authority" of religion, and are ready to move beyond that "authority" to some other approach to knowledge. For all I know, this isn't even a "higher" stage of growth. We may revert back to "authority" at some point in our growth (as I have already accepted the authority of my dreams, because they have a built-in self-correcting mechanism).

Stephen Jay Gould, in *Rocks of Ages*, presents the idea of "Non-Overlapping Magisteria (NOMA)" — religion and science each operating in independent and non-overlapping areas of knowledge. Science operates in the physical domain, and religion operates in the spiritual domain. That is a fine idea for his culture, but my culture has now moved so far beyond his, by redefining "science" and "religion," that I have to bring up the conflict all over again, but coming from different angles.

"Science," as I see it, doesn't have to be limited to observations of physical phenomena with the physical senses, but can also include observations of mental phenomena with the mental senses and spiritual phenomena with the spiritual senses. Thus science can encroach on what was formerly totally the domain of religion. Gould equates "religion" with "faith," and that equation still holds true. But as Carl Jung and others have shown, it is possible to learn about the spiritual reality not only on the basis of "faith," but also on the basis of evidence. This brings the spiritual reality within the realm of science.

"Religion," as I have just defined it, is not just a belief in a spiritual reality, but a particular approach to knowledge of the spiritual — a rigid belief system based on Holy Writ. The attribute of being a rigid belief system puts it in conflict with science, where beliefs change as hypotheses are proved and disproved. Holy Writ never changes. These two systems are already in conflict on the physical facts of whether the heavens and the earth and all living creatures were created in 6 days in 4004 BC. And these two systems are more likely to be in conflict as science explores the spiritual.

The resolution of this conflict is that religion serves a constructive purpose where people feel a need for an authoritarian belief system, but that really science is the system to be used to move ahead and explore our universe, physical, mental, and spiritual. I think that religion needs to adapt to the discoveries of science. For example, the 6 days of Creation can be interpreted to be "days of the Lord," each lasting millions or billions of earth-years.

I am not able to study the spiritual scientifically because I am not able to observe the spiritual at will, but only in those few instances when it chooses to reveal itself to me. But I can at least take a few simple steps in that direction.

First of all, although it might be nice to have a neat picture-frame defining the limits of reality, it should be pretty obvious that it is not possible to know the ultimate truths first. And the various cosmologies presenting an ultimate view of things are meaningless to me, because I have no way of verifying their accuracy.

The way I know anything, the way most of us know anything, is starting with very simple truths, building an ever-expanding sphere of knowledge out from one's center of consciousness as one acquires more knowledge. This is not absolute knowledge. This is relative knowledge, as one fact relates to another. The more facts that are consistent with each other, the larger the body of knowledge.

The more one learns about these relationships, the more situations are covered by this knowledge, and the more secure one can be in this knowledge. We only "approach" the ultimate truth, as one "approaches" infinity in mathematics — at least until we know we have arrived.

If we must formulate views of ultimate reality, they should be seen as "theories" or "hypotheses," just as science has "the big-bang theory" to explain what happened "in the beginning." It should be understood that a theory is only a fictional construction, and the facts may not support it.

The cosmology of Eklal Kueshana is presented in this way — not as ultimate truth to be accepted on "faith," but as information to be tested. And in the spirit of science, I accept that cosmology — not as religion, but as a working hypothesis.

The second problem I can see with religions is that they are mutually exclusive. Wouldn't it be great if we could pool the insights into spiritual reality from all those great and gifted people who have founded religions, instead of having each one's glimpses confined to a particular religion? Why can't we see what Moses and Confucius and Buddha and Jesus and Mohammed shared in common, and accept these beliefs as a working hypothesis of what the spiritual may be like? We might then compare their insights with those of more recent people, like Mary Baker Eddy, Edgar Cayce, and Eklal Kueshana. Just as many explorers combined to give us our knowledge of geography — Marco Polo, Vasco de Gama, Balboa, Cortez, Magellan, Columbus, Cook, and many more — so might we combine the insights of many people to give us a better knowledge of the spiritual reality.

What do I know about the spiritual?

I don't take the Bible as evidence of anything. The Bible is legend. When all the holy books of all the religions agree on something, I'll take that as evidence. Every culture in the world has a belief in the spiritual. I'll take that as evidence that the spiritual exists, to be refuted only by conclusive proof that we are all suffering from the same delusion.

"Knowledge" to me is not what I have read in books, not even the Bible. "Knowledge" is what I have proved to myself through my own experience.

The most important thing I know about the spiritual is that I have free will here on earth. I know that because I broke the first four Commandments by allowing myself the thought, "God does not exist," and God did not stop me.

After the 9/11 attacks, people were asking, "How can there be a God, to have allowed this to happen?" I guess you can say the same about every atrocity in human history. How could a God have allowed a man like Tamurlane to assemble a horde of men and sack cities and kill all the inhabitants? How could God have allowed Hitler to come to power?

I would say that this is further proof of free will. God does not interfere with the exercise of our free will, but allows us to work things out within the structure of natural laws that God has put in place. Within that structure, it's up to us human beings to protect ourselves from the destructive power of other human beings.

And maybe God isn't an entity with a will, but only a Force in the universe, as my dreams showed me — the Light, which I interpreted to be Love, the supreme power of the universe. I don't know that this Light is a being, with an intention or a will or a design or the ability to create.

The second most important idea, after free will, is the theory of life as a learning experience. With our free will we interact with the earth environment and learn from it, as we experience pain or pleasure. I first learned this theory from Edgar Cayce, and then it was elaborated on by Eklal Kueshana, who said that our purpose here on earth was to learn everything about "the first four planes of existence," whatever that is. It necessarily involves reincarnation and karma, because it would not be possible to learn everything from all the different perspectives in one lifetime. I call it a "theory" because I haven't proved it to myself, although I have evidence to support it.

I was already working in line with this theory when I first set out to develop my potential as a human being. And I have proved at least that much of it — that developing my potential has in fact led to happiness. And I am motivated to continue doing what I am doing. I don't have to know what is at the top of the mountain. I just have to know that I'll get there, eventually, if I just keep going up.

I know that when I finished psychotherapy and my psychiatrist told me I was OK, I felt that there was something missing. That missing part was the spiritual, which I found later in my dreams, and then I finally felt like a whole human being.

As for reincarnation, I have my childhood conviction that I had always existed, supplemented by the evidence provided by Edgar Cayce, Ian Stevenson, and the Dalai Lama.

As for the Law of Karma, I believe it is the operating principle in personal psychology: You have to keep reliving a situation until you get it right, until your mind has resolved it, and you keep recreating that situation unconsciously in order to re-experience it. If you do reincarnate, then it follows that your unresolved problems would be carried over in your soul-mind from one incarnation to the next. But I don't think it is necessary to reincarnate or even to believe in reincarnation in order to see the Law of Karma in action.

So, then, some of the criticisms that I am about to make of religious practices lean heavily on the assumptions that we have free will and that the purpose of life is to experience and learn the earth environment. I have a fair amount of evidence to support these assumptions, but maybe not enough to make them the absolutes by which all else is measured.

My first criticism of religion is the one that was judged
"immature" and "far-fetched" in my freshman paper at Harvard:

The idea of a naked man and a naked woman together in the
Garden of Eden was so overwhelming to our sex-starved Puritan
ancestors that they thought that the story was all about sex, and that
"original sin" had something to do with human sexuality. They
missed the more subtle and perhaps logically-complicated point of
the story, which had to do with eating of the fruit of the tree of the
knowledge of good and evil:

> Genesis 2:16 And the Lord God commanded the man, saying, Of every tree of
> the garden thou mayest freely eat:
>   17 But of the tree of the knowledge of good and evil, thou shalt not eat of
> it: for in the day that thou eatest thereof thou shalt surely die.
>
> Genesis 3:4 And the serpent said unto the woman, Ye shall not surely die:
>   5 For God doth know that in the day ye eat thereof, then your eyes shall be
> opened, and ye shall be as gods, knowing good and evil.

And so the story goes, they ate, and their eyes were opened, and
they knew that they were naked, and they made aprons for
themselves out of fig leaves. This is all so familiar that I'm sure your
eyes are glazing over. But what is not familiar is the whole point of
the story: The thing that was forbidden by God was the knowledge
of good and evil. They judged themselves "evil" for being naked,
and had to cover themselves up. Is there anything inherently evil in
being naked? They thought so. But they weren't nearly as well
qualified to judge good and evil as God. They were only playing at
being God. For thousands of years, since human beings first lost
their innocence, people have been playing God by judging
themselves and others "good" and "evil," even though they lack the
necessary knowledge to make accurate judgments. And because this
is exactly what the religious leaders have been doing, they have
missed the message of this story.

I was sitting waiting for my car to be serviced, and this person
was ranting about the homosexuals. "God will judge them," she said.

I agreed with her, "Yes, God will judge them." What I didn't say
was "And God doesn't need your help."

When these religious types are passing moral judgment on people, they are just playing God. It is their particular fantasy, their ego-compensation. I just keep that in mind, to keep things in their proper perspective.

Why doesn't God tell us what is good and evil? Why don't we remember our previous incarnations? Why do we need "faith" even to know that God exists? God has been very mysterious about revealing the spiritual reality to us, revealing it only to the exceptional few. Why is that? Again, maybe God is only a Force in the universe. Maybe it is part of our learning experience to learn about the spiritual reality as we have learned about the physical reality — slowly, bit by bit, by trial and error. Maybe, as people once believed that gods were responsible for physical phenomena, we now believe that this God is responsible for spiritual phenomena.

My next criticism of religions is that they take away as much as possible of people's God-given free will, first of all by forcing them to submit to religious authority ("Obedience" as a virtue), and then by forcing them to take vows. A vow restricts a person's free will for the duration of the vow, usually for life. It would be fraudulent for me to take a vow, because I don't have the authority to represent my future self.

First of all, there are the marriage vows, "Forsaking all others, until death do us part." That prevents both parties from having relationships with half the world's population. Some people just naturally fall into life-long relationships with one sex partner. For the rest of us, the vow of fidelity is a serious violation of our free will. It also causes people to burn up enormous amounts of their life's energy, energy that could be put to better uses, either trying to repress their sexual desires, or concealing their covert affairs.

Along with the vow of fidelity comes the idea of "cheating." People feel that their honor has been violated if they have been "cheated on," if their partner has had sex with another person. Nobody is "cheating" if they don't take vows in the first place. Ideally one should be free to have sexual experiences which do no harm to others, without having to lie about it.

The social purpose of marriage is to provide a stable environment for having children and raising them. Instead of making vows to each other, the marriage partners should make "vows" for the benefit of the children, giving them support and education and a healthy environment to grow up in. Marriage should be a contract for the raising of children, much like a divorce agreement. There is no reason why the partners have to promise sexual monogamy, except to satisfy their sexual insecurities.

"Ah!" say the people playing God, "How can the children have a healthy environment when the parents are living in sin?" But actually it is the people playing God who are making it unhealthy by labeling it "sin." Perhaps the healthiest environments of all for the raising of children are those societies where everybody has sex with everybody, and all adults are as parents to all children.

I'm sure that good contracts for the raising of children can be devised: Lovers are allowed in the environment of the children only with the consent of both marriage partners. The biological father is determined by DNA testing. Both partners protect themselves and each other from the possibility of contracting AIDS. It shouldn't be that complicated.

Another violation of free will is the vow of sexual abstinence that priests and nuns have to take. At least with the marriage vow people have a sexual outlet, but here they have no sexual outlet, and have to spend an enormous amount of their life's energy, and prayers, just trying to restrain those powerful sexual forces. And some of them fail, with harmful results for children entrusted to their care.

There are certain commitments that have to be made in life. When I take on a job, I am obliged to finish it. The same goes for the raising of children, even though it will probably last 20 years or more. But there is no point in making a commitment for longer than is necessary to do the job, or for more than is necessary to do the job, like marital fidelity or sexual abstinence.

If people want to make a commitment voluntarily, to declare their love for each other or whatever, then they are doing this out of their own free will. They are sacrificing their free will as a token of their love for each other. But to require everybody to take vows if they want a certain status in society, that is a violation of their free will.

All these vows restrict human sexuality. In the strictest religious view, people aren't allowed to have sexual relations until they have taken a vow committing themselves to one sex partner for life. So the whole power of the sex drive is being used to force people into this restriction of their free will.

The Bush Administration, dominated by the Religious Right, has advocated sexual abstinence for teenagers. But they haven't said how they are going to enforce it. To offset the sex drive, you need a coercive force that is more powerful than the sex drive. In the olden days, women (not men, of course) were stoned to death for having sex outside of the sanctions of society. In the Victorian Age, a young lady and all her family were ruined socially if she had sex without social permission. There were manuals for young ladies explaining what a horrible thing sex was, and that unfortunately men enjoyed it, and how best to endure it. Shall we go back to the Victorian Age? I don't think that is possible now that women have discovered the orgasm. I think we'll have to go back to stoning people to death.

The Christian religion (I don't know about the other religions) has seriously repressed human sexual activity, to the point where the word "morality" is used more to talk about sexual behavior than Christian behavior. But I think we have come a long way towards sexual freedom since Queen Victoria died in 1901. First of all, Freud pointed out that people's psychological problems came from their repressed sexuality. Then we had "The Roaring Twenties." Then, in the 1960s, the birth-control pill was developed, and then we had the Drug Revolution, which liberated people sexually more than ever. Women discovered the orgasm. College dorms became co-ed. In 1973, the Supreme Court made abortion legal. In the 1980s, sexual freedom had a major setback with AIDS. The Religious Right claimed that it was God's punishment for homosexuality. How about the flu epidemic of 1918 as God's punishment for shaking hands? All I know is that sexual intimacy is a good way to catch another person's disease. There are obvious dangers in sexual activity, as with other aspects of life on earth.

Sexuality is an important part of our human life-experience here on earth. The challenge is to learn to deal with it, not to suppress it.

It is wonderful how wealth makes one indifferent to wealth. In the same way, people who are totally satisfied sexually sort of take sex for granted — they aren't preoccupied with it. I think if it really

is best for our spiritual growth not to be constantly dwelling on sex
and driven by sex, then we should be allowed total freedom to
pursue our sexual desires, in whatever way, and with whatever
partners, we are turned on, as long as we are not harming others.
And once we are totally satiated by it, our minds will turn naturally
to something else.

Religions teach us to suppress many things, in addition to
sexuality and free will. They teach us to suppress the intellect, the
mind in general, the emotions of fear and anger, the senses, and even
the whole life-experience, as Eastern religions encourage people to
become oblivious to it all, for the greatest possible bliss. If, then, this
earthly experience is our chance to advance spiritually, then it seems
that they are trying to take away from us as much of it as possible. I
would suspect the influence of Black Mentalists in all of this.

Some religions also control people's sexuality by coercing them,
once they are married, to have as many children as possible, and by
outlawing birth-control methods. This is simply not a good idea
these days when overpopulation is causing human starvation and
suffering, and contributing to the pollution of our physical
environment. I think that China has a good idea limiting the number
of babies a woman can have, and that this idea is contributing to
their prosperity, as opposed to India, where religions are still
encouraging women to have as many babies as possible, many of
whom will starve to death.

In advocating sexual freedom, I may be making a serious
mistake. Maybe there is a real reason why religions control human
sexuality, a reason that people who are highly evolved spiritually
understand and I do not. I could suffer serious karmic consequences.
This is risky business.

And it is risky business in general to exercise my free will here on
earth. I could advance spiritually, or I could screw up.

So I see that religion has a real purpose, giving people a set of
guidelines within which to exercise their free will. At least they can't
screw up too badly, whereas I, by rejecting these guidelines
regarding sexuality and free will, run the risk of falling to the bottom
of the bottomless pit.

But also there are people who lean too far the other way, who pray, "Thy will be done through me, O Lord," and "Make me an instrument of Thy will, O Lord." This is actually dangerous, because if God has given us free will, God isn't likely to answer these prayers, but these prayers could attract lower entities who want to use you to carry out their will.

So, to answer the question, "Why does religion persist?" Religion gives us glimpses of the spiritual laws of the universe from a God who isn't telling us what these laws are, but is leaving us to find out for ourselves. Religion preserves and teaches those glimpses, along with our highest human values. Religion also provides an authoritarian structure, very much like the educational system, where people can learn about the spiritual, until they are ready to break free and explore on their own.

But religion also contains inaccuracies which contribute to mind pollution and human discord. Religion does not know the ultimate truth, and is not qualified to judge any human being or any other religion. Religion is not sacred; it is a man-made system which needs to adjust to our expanding human knowledge from time to time. And because religion is the key to spiritual growth for most of the world's population, we need to be on the lookout for efforts by Black Mentalists to block that spiritual growth.

As for the *Free Inquiry* people, they are dedicated to scientism, the belief that nothing exists beyond the physical. This is like a religion itself, complete with its assertion about ultimate truth. So I think that the *Free Inquiry* people need to look at themselves to answer their question. Why is it, in trying to avoid religion, that people have created something like a religion themselves? I can't answer that question, but I'll be talking about scientism in the next chapter.

11. THE TYRANNY OF ACADEMIA

ABSOLUTE POWER

Power tends to corrupt; absolute power corrupts absolutely.
  (Lord Acton)

I wouldn't say that the power does the corrupting. But if the seeds of corruption are there, power certainly provides for them a fertile environment in which to grow. And power certainly protects the corruption and keeps it in place once it is there.

In Chapter 4, I explained how the status of physical science has become a social force in its own right, a force independent of science itself, enabling some scientists to get away with unscientific methods like argument-by-ridicule and authoritarian pronouncements, and enabling physical scientists to exert an influence on fields other than their own, as for example steering psychology away from the study of the mind. Social forces like ridicule can be much more powerful in influencing people than scientific methods. Where these unscientific methods have created inaccuracies in our cultural knowledge, I would call that "corruption."

In Chapter 6, under "The Mind Is Nothing But the Physical Brain," I explained how the status of science enables scientists to make the rules and also be the judges in a debate in which they are one of the adversaries. I would call this "tyranny."

When I say "science," I am not criticizing "science" the method, but "science" the social group. "Science" the social group is a subset of the social group "academia." "Academia" I define as those people whose function is to acquire, preserve, and disseminate cultural knowledge, and who teach or determine what is taught at the university level. As with science, I am not criticizing the legitimate function of academia, but the function of academia as a social group — the opinions, attitudes, and beliefs of academic people which are not based on valid academic studies or methods. Academic people qualify as experts in their own particular fields. But when they venture opinions in fields other than their own, they are likely to pick up the uninformed opinions of the social group. There is a profound difference between "peer review" and "peer-group pressures."

Why am I accusing all of academia of "corruption" and "tyranny" when I have shown these things to be true only for science? Because, first of all, science holds a position of domination in academia, from which scientists are able to peck, or influence, people in other fields, as for example when psychologists abandoned their mental science in favor of physical science. The leadership in academia needs to maintain the independence of all fields of inquiry, protecting them from social domination from people in other fields. But right now physical scientists are the leadership, so they are academia, in that sense. And second, I am going to try to show that academia itself has absolute power, or at least as close to absolute power as can be expected in the real world.

Because they share values, background, and work environment, it is natural that the persons of academia should become a social group, subject to all the laws of sociology, with status-ranking, and share certain opinions, attitudes, and beliefs, as determined by the leaders in that status-ranking. Academic people look outward at social groups as diverse as the gang on the corner and the Catholic Church, and have identified certain behavior patterns that apply to all, but I haven't seen much evidence that they have applied these laws of sociology to themselves.

For example, there are very definite opinions held in academia on the subjects of aliens, parapsychology, and non-physical reality. These opinions aren't based on academic knowledge, because these aren't generally considered to be areas of legitimate study. And why shouldn't they be areas of legitimate study? They are certainly areas that are largely unknown. And yet in deciding that they are not worthy of legitimate study, it has been determined (by nobody in particular, of course) that they are known, to the point where it can be said with certainty (or it goes without saying) that they are fictitious.

First of all, the sincere scholars should know that this chapter is not about them. This chapter, like the book, is about bad logic, domination, manipulation, and mental warfare, in this case as it is practiced among academic people. If you do not practice any of these inaccurate methods, then this chapter is not about you. But I trust that the sincere scholars are totally aware of the powerful political methods of manipulation in their academic environment which lead to inaccuracies in what people believe and what people are taught. I am hoping that you will take my side in this argument. More than that, I am hoping that you will come forward with evidence of the kinds of corrupting things that are whispered in academic circles, the social manipulations, that I am not privileged to hear.

When I say "corruption" in regard to academia, I am referring to two things — inaccuracy and incompleteness. There are two components of knowledge — the scope of the knowledge and its accuracy. When either of these is reduced by social pressures being applied, I call that "corruption."

The social group, with its social pressures, extends across all of academia, and along with it the opinions, attitudes, and beliefs, which I call "corruption," which have no basis in legitimate scholarly work, also extend across all of academia. The fact that there is only one such social group, or at least a dominant social group covering all of academia, is the basis for my assertion that this group has "absolute power."

Harvard and Yale compete in athletics, and they compete in trying to achieve academic excellence, in attracting the best professors and the brightest students. But they don't offer competing belief structures. For example, when I was at Harvard, people with strong religious beliefs were ridiculed unmercifully. This was shortly after William F. Buckley had written *God and Man at Yale*, complaining about this same kind of pressure and prejudice.

Where there is no evidence and no scholarship supporting this anti-religious stance, this is simply anti-religious prejudice. People with very little or no knowledge of spiritual reality are passing judgment upon it.

This social attitude interferes with the much-advertised "freedom of inquiry" and steers academic people away from exploring the spiritual. Somehow they all pick up the same signals, if not by words, then by a look or a snicker, that certain subjects and certain beliefs are legitimate in academia, and certain other subjects and beliefs are not. There may be isolated places where academic people are moving ahead with an exploration of the spiritual dimensions, just as there might be places where people are still studying the mind with the mental senses. But if it were brought to the attention of the conformists in the social group that such studies were being made, the people performing these studies would be subject to ridicule, or worse. Just as the chemicals from a spray can can affect the ozone layer at the South Pole, so the threat of ridicule can affect the whole academic atmosphere. The social group may not extend across all of academia, but its influence does.

Just the fact that prejudices exist, prejudices that have no basis in any legitimate academic study, and that these prejudices are not being seriously challenged [I don't see any evidence] from within academia itself, is evidence of the absolute power of this social group and its social pressures.

On the subject of aliens, I assume there is a government cover-up. It would certainly help to solve the mystery if academic people were working on it. Why the academic community is biased against it, I don't know.

Harvard psychiatrist John Mack had to take a phenomenological stance in working with people who had experienced alien abductions. In other words, he was able to say, "Yes, they have truly experienced this," without having to claim that aliens were real — walking a very fine line, indeed. And yet the Harvard Establishment still had him investigated — an indignity which a tenured professor was never supposed to suffer.

I was reading a piece on UFOs on the Internet and came across the expression "scientific ridicule." Of course "scientific ridicule" is an oxymoron. Ridicule is not part of the scientific method. But ridicule by scientists is so common in our culture that "scientific ridicule" is generally understood without any need for an explanation.

As for parapsychology, I was asking The Rhine Research Center whether they could apply scientific dating methods to establish the age of my "Gerald Ford Carter" document, and their Director, Sally Rhine Feather, said the following in her reply to me:

> No, we do not seek to verify or get proof of the veracity or the paranormal quality of any of our reports, as was once the custom back in the old psychical research days. The early psychical researchers went to enormous effort to obtain highly documented cases, and books are filled with excellent cases that could stand for as much scientific proof as case material could ever be. And you know what? No one in the scientific world seemed to pay much attention. (Not that they pay so much attention to scientific research results [in parapsychology] either, I hasten to add).
> (from an email of September 20, 2001)

If scientific people aren't paying much attention to research results, then what are they paying attention to? What is their source of information that supercedes research results? And if some other source of information is more important, are they doing science?

If scientific people ignore something, they disqualify themselves from holding a scientific opinion on it. Ignoring things also leads to ignorance, which is the opposite of what academia is all about. And yet with their enormous status, they are able to get away with it. This is just status-snobbery.

Along with science there is "scientism," the belief that there is no reality beyond the physical. Scientism has been reinforced over the years as people have made thousands and millions of scientific observations and have never seen any spiritual reality in the universe. But please note that these observations were made with the physical senses, and one isn't likely to be able to observe the spiritual reality with the physical senses. So to conclude that the spiritual doesn't exist, on the basis of physical observations, is simply bad logic. Note also that I am not criticizing scientists for not having "faith," which is not one of the values of science, but for having bad logic, where good logic is one of the values of science. As Stephen Jay Gould has indicated with his "Non-Overlapping Magisteria," it should be possible to be a fine scientist and also a devout churchgoer at the same time.

90% of Americans believe in a spiritual reality. 90% of scientists do NOT believe in a spiritual reality. One would expect that the percentage of scientists believing in a spiritual reality would be the same as the general population, unless there were an extreme bias operating, to have swung it to the opposite extreme. Some scientists say that this is because scientists are knowledgeable, and the general population is ignorant and superstitious. But it hasn't been determined by the scientific method that there is no reality beyond the physical, although they may think it has. It is the social pressure of people all believing in the same logical error that creates this bias, and prevents people from spotting the logical error. Here is more evidence to show that the influence of this social group, with its common opinions, attitudes and beliefs, not based on scholarship, extends across all of academia.

In the computer field where I have worked, companies come and go. Somebody comes up with a better product and puts other companies out of business. If any product is limited in scope or functionality or performance, somebody will soon come along with a better product and drive it out of the marketplace. What was superior five years ago becomes today's "clunker."

Why is this not true of academia? Why are there not alternative institutions that correct the errors of the academic Establishment? I guess one answer is that the Establishment gets it right most of the time, enough to overlook minor prejudices.

But I think the main reason is that academia is judged on its reputation, not on its product. Harvard is thought to be a very good university, probably the best in the country. Because of this, it attracts the best and the brightest, and currently accepts only about 10% of them. So right away Harvard has performed a selection process that guarantees that only superior people will come out of Harvard, whether they learn anything there or not.

When I applied for my first job, I was selected out of 75 applicants as one of the ones to be interviewed, because the name "Harvard" was on my resume. The rest was up to me, of course. But I think people leaned more favorably towards me through the interview process, and through the job itself, because they knew I had been to Harvard.

So it all has to do with reputation. And reputation feeds on itself, attracting better people, and thus enhancing reputation.

There are alternative universities, but they don't present a serious challenge to the established universities. I saw one ranking in which the alternative university was dead last out of 200 universities. In another ranking, no alternative universities were named in a list of 124 universities. In respect to the competition, then, the Establishment maintains as close to absolute power as might be expected in the real world.

Businesses in the 1950s and 1960s recognized that people with college degrees did better at higher-level positions requiring intelligence than people without college degrees. College degrees quickly became a requirement for those higher-level positions. And then it didn't take long for people to figure out that a college graduate was likely to earn more than a million dollars more than a high-school graduate in his/her lifetime. Therefore one could easily justify paying $100,000 or more for a college education on economic terms alone.

And college tuitions have risen in accord with their economic value. It cost my father $1800 a year to put me through Harvard, room, board, and tuition, in the years 1952 to 1956. The cost of that same education for the academic year 2002-3 was more than $39,000. That's more than 21 times as much. In the same time period a gallon of gas has risen about 10 times, and the Consumer Price Index has risen about 7 times.

So the cost of a Harvard education has risen 3 times faster than the cost of living, and people are willing to pay it because of the increased amount of money they can earn once they have the degree.

And what are you buying with this money? You are buying status — the status of having the degree, and not really for any knowledge you may have gained in the process. Businesses don't quiz you on European history, etc. The most they ever do is verify that you have the degree.

So, then, if people are willing to spend all this money just to buy status, this is one more indication of the power of academia. And of course the money then buys more power for academia.

Most professions require advanced degrees — doctor, lawyer, scientist, teacher, professor, and so on. Here people have no choice but to go through academia, and as far as I know the information they receive is accurate. But they can't help but be exposed to the social bias of academia, especially in the fields of medicine and psychology, where the mental and spiritual dimensions are so important.

Only the gifted few can rise to the highest ranks in society without going through academia — those few entertainers and artists whose talents are so great that they can earn a living by them, and the rare individuals like Bill Gates, Steve Jobs, and Ted Turner. The rest of us must submit to the power and judgment and bias of academia.

So I think I have been fair here in calling this "The Tyranny of Academia." I have defined "corruption" as anything that detracts from the scope or accuracy of knowledge. I have shown that there is corruption because there are certain widely-held beliefs in academia which are not supported by academic studies but are supported by social manipulation. I have shown the power of the social group academia by showing that it has allowed the corruption to exist, and the absolute power because this corruption goes unchecked and unchallenged. I have shown the tyranny by showing that most of us must submit to the absolute power of academia to get a high-paying job and a high level of status in society.

And that influence doesn't end when we graduate from college. The status of academia and its influence are with us all our lives.

For example, I thought it was inappropriate for Congress to ask scientists to testify on the subject of whether abortion could be considered the taking of a human life. I mean, what does a scientist know about the essential quality of human life, the occupying of a physical body by a human soul? And yet the scientists, with their social status of those-who-know-all-the-answers, were the ones called in to testify.

Eklal Kueshana teaches that no two souls can occupy the same body. Therefore the soul can't enter the body until the time of birth. Therefore a fetus doesn't become "human" until the time of birth. It's as simple as that. But Eklal Kueshana has no status within the culture. In fact, within academia Eklal Kueshana is thought not even to exist.

I was telling a friend of mine who lived in Boston about *The Ultimate Frontier*, and she went looking for it at her favorite bookstore. When she didn't see it anywhere, she asked the clerk about it, and the clerk pulled it out from UNDER THE COUNTER. My theory is that because the bookstore was near Harvard and MIT and other colleges in the Boston area, they kept the book out of sight so as not to lose business from the academic people, who buy most of the books.

I just want to list some of the inaccuracies and gaps in our cultural knowledge that have been created by academic social pressures:

First of all, there is the assertion that Freud did "bad science." This is the red herring to draw people's attention away from the great discoveries that Freud made.

I was reading a piece by a brain scientist denouncing Freud, and he started off by saying, "Of course I am not too familiar with Freud's works." Of course the social laws of his social group prevented him from being too familiar with Freud, or admitting it.

Describing Carl Jung as a "mystic" is of course inaccurate and misleading. Carl Jung was doing science with mental observations, as Freud was. Perhaps his observation that the spiritual could also be observed in dreams was too radical for his times, especially since scientists were trying to break away from the authority and judgments of religion.

If you don't know what to make of it, don't pretend you have a word for it. This is a cause of inaccuracy.

In general, pretending to know what you don't know always creates inaccuracies. I think the academic community is particularly vulnerable to this kind of error, being the ultimate source of knowledge in our culture.

Edgar Cayce has been very much maligned in academic circles. I will not repeat what has been whispered about him because it is defamatory. I think the academic people need to come forward and say out loud what they have been whispering, with documentary evidence if they have it.

As far as I know, there have been only the two serious academic investigations of Edgar Cayce that I have already mentioned. Hugo Munsterberg of Harvard felt that the phenomenon warranted further investigation. William Moseley Brown of Washington and Lee was convinced of the genuineness and the accuracy of the readings. If academic detractors have evidence to the contrary, let them present it.

The assertion that Ayn Rand was "right wing" is an inaccuracy. Ayn Rand, as she described herself, was a "radical capitalist," not a "reactionary capitalist," which is what we call "right wing." Ayn Rand was moving past socialism to a future which rewards people who make major contributions to society. Ayn Rand in *Atlas Shrugged* showed how "Socialism doesn't work" about 30 years before Gorbachev actually said it. Ayn Rand, like Carl Jung, was so far ahead of the culture that she was out of phase with it. Here is another case of academia trying to fit a social innovator into the cultural stereotypes of the past.

The gaps — the major gap is where psychologists are not studying the mind. There may be small pockets where the mind is being observed with the mental senses, but generally "evidence" is seen as the evidence of the physical senses. Also I believe that the basis of the criticisms of Freud and Jung is that many of their discoveries were made with the mental senses and therefore not considered to be based on "evidence."

In psychology the spiritual component is also ignored. Forgiveness (forbearance) is a spiritual quality that is essential to resolving psychological problems. How that is explained away in terms of Darwinian theory, I don't know. Psychological growth moves towards behavior which has been thought of as "morality," a spiritual quality. Psychological development is spiritual development. Psychology is really "the study of the soul," as its Greek roots tell us.

Transpersonal psychology may be getting more into the spiritual aspects of psychology. When I looked up "transpersonal psychology" on the Internet, I found only names of alternative universities. At least it's a start.

In science, a special rule has been made that excludes "anecdotal evidence." This is useful because it allows scientists to reject reports of spontaneous experiences like UFOs and psychic revelations, while at the same time accepting reports of spontaneous experiences with "legitimate" subjects like gorillas and hurricanes. Actually, all reports are "anecdotal." It is just a question of who is telling the story and how they are telling it. The word "anecdotal" just seems to exclude the "undesirables." This compromises both the accuracy and the scope of the scientific record.

The place where I notice the gaps the most is in the field of philosophy, because philosophy is what I claim to be doing. "How shall I live?" is my defining question. Philosophy, to me, as it was originally with the ancient Greeks, is all mental effort bearing on the question of how one lives one's life. It is central to all learning, and includes all knowledge.

The development of the mind, with logic and mathematics, and the development of the ability to communicate, is all part of philosophy. The identification of bad logic and manipulative methods and mind pollution is all part of philosophy. Psychotherapy — the elimination of distortions caused by emotional problems — is part of philosophy. In the Dewey Decimal System, psychology is categorized as part of philosophy. Questions of religion and theology and spiritual existence are part of philosophy.

The development of higher senses — psychic abilities — and questions of how and when to use them all are part of philosophy. Anything bearing on the general question of how to live life is part of philosophy.

And what is "philosophy" in American universities today? It is some academic debate about what philosophers of the past have said. I don't know what it is, really, because I understand very little of what contemporary philosophers are saying. What I do know is that anything outside of this intellectual debate is called "poetry." This whole book would be called "poetry."

I think the young people of today are asking, "What does philosophy have to do with anything?" The answer, if you are talking about the academic version, is "Nothing." The answer, if you are talking about my definition, is "Everything." People need this general background on the living of life, and it is missing from our culture.

"Philosophy" comes from the Greek, meaning "love of wisdom." There is this attitude in academia that knowledge should be sought for the pure joy of obtaining knowledge, and not for any practical end. It is considered somehow tainted if there is some practical goal in mind.

So, where I set out to solve cultural problems, like the threat of nuclear annihilation, I am not considered to be doing "philosophy" because I have a practical goal in mind. This narrows the territory covered by "philosophy" even further.

But aha! "The love of wisdom." If you really are in the pursuit of wisdom, then psychotherapy and dream analysis is where you will find it. You will discover, as I did, that the power of the subconscious mind makes the conscious mind look puny. So if philosophy is truly "the love of wisdom," it must include psychotherapy and dream analysis.

One general thought that irks me is the idea that all thinking takes place in universities — because it excludes me, of course. There is a difference between scholarly ability and creative ability, and the two don't usually go together. In the computer field I observed that, on the one hand, there were consultants who had the greatest knowledge of the computer field, and on the other hand, creative people like myself who could design and write the best software systems, and that these were two very distinct and separate skills.

With *Re-Educating Myself*, I was hoping that scholars would read and evaluate what I had to say, from the point of view of their superior knowledge, to see whether it represented a significant contribution to the culture. Instead, what I got from many was a careless dismissal, with the comment that what I was saying had been said before, as sort of a snobbish display of their superior knowledge.

Actually if they had bothered to look up what had been said before, they would have seen that it wasn't the exactly the same, in most cases. Some of the simplest statements are exactly the same, but the context is not. For example, I have since learned that Aristotle said that the way to happiness was to develop your potential as a human being. But then in the very next paragraph he claimed to know exactly what the human potential was. Contrast that with what I said. Because I arrived at these ideas independently, they are not usually the same as what was said before, and if they do happen to be the same, they reinforce what was said before, very much like scientific replication.

I am counting on the sincere scholars to recognize that scholarship, or the ability to learn, preserve, and teach the knowledge of the past, is a whole different kind of ability from the creative thinking that is creating the knowledge of the future. And I am counting on their ability to evaluate, with a more careful appraisal than before, whether I have anything to add to the culture. I guess if people like Kahlil Gibran, Ayn Rand, Edgar Cayce, and Richard Kieninger aka Eklal Kueshana are being ignored and dismissed, who am I to complain?

It is because of these biases and gaps in the teachings of academia that I don't think of academia as representing "knowledge," but only as one of the "camps."

JOHN B. WATSON, MANIPULATOR

I got the idea that John B. Watson might be a manipulator when I read the following in a psychology textbook:

> Watson argued that introspection was, if anything, the province of theology.
> (Alloy et al, 1999, page 123)

This led me to check out Watson's major works. His 1913 paper, "Psychology as the behaviorist views it," I thought was very reasonable. It certainly makes sense to learn what we can about human behavior that can be observed with the physical senses, and I think a great deal has been learned from this approach.

His 1919 book, *Psychology from the Standpoint of a Behaviorist*, is very technical. I don't see much to complain about, except for a reference to "the Freudian mystics" on page 396, and on page 1, where he is trying to make all of psychology into behaviorism:

> Psychology a Science of Behavior. — Psychology is that division of natural science which takes human activity and conduct as its subject matter. ...
> (Watson, 1919, page 1)

But in the book *Behaviorism* (1924, 1925) he starts becoming very free with his logic and his theories, and in my view very manipulative with his audience. Here is where he makes the connection between psychology and religion:

> ... Indeed we should point out at once that behaviorism has not as yet by any means replaced the older psychology — called *introspective psychology* — of James, Wundt, Kulpe, Titchener, Angell, Judd, and McDougall. Possibly the easiest way to bring out the contrast between the old psychology and the new is to say that all schools of psychology except that of behaviorism claim that *"consciousness" is the subject matter of psychology*. Behaviorism, on the contrary, holds that the subject matter of human psychology is the *behavior or activities of the human being*. Behaviorism claims that "consciousness" is neither a definable nor a usable concept; that it is merely another word for the "soul" of more ancient times. The old psychology is thus dominated by a kind of subtle religious philosophy.
> (Watson, 1925, page 3)

254

So here, with a hop, skip, and jump, he goes from "consciousness" to "soul" to "religious." That is his complete argument. Thus he misrepresents the introspective psychology in a destructive way: Using the word "religious" to describe a branch of science is simply a smear-tactic. And this inaccuracy has survived to be reported in a psychology textbook 75 years later.

Then, in a section called "The Religious Background of Current Introspective Psychology," he goes on to ridicule religion, saying how certain lazy individuals were able to exploit people's fears and become medicine-men, and thus not have to work. He concludes his satire on religion with the following:

> ... It was the boast of Wundt's students, in 1879, when the first psychological laboratory was established, that psychology had at last become a science without a soul. For fifty years we have kept this pseudo-science, exactly as Wundt laid it down. All that Wundt and his students really accomplished was to substitute for the word "soul" the word "consciousness."
>
> (Watson, 1925, page 5)

Watson quickly flips here from "science" to "pseudo-science" (the smear-word) without taking the trouble to explain how the transformation was made. He then repeats the assertion that "consciousness" is "soul," in the face of Wundt's students, and perhaps exploiting the doubts of his own students. So who are you going to believe? Who is giving the grade in this course?

Contrast the "pseudo-science" with what recent textbooks say about Wundt:

> Wilhelm Wundt, the founder of experimental psychology ...
> (Lazerson, 1975, page 337)

> In short, with Wundt, psychology had evolved from the *philosophy* of mental processes to the *science* of mental processes.
> (Bernstein et al, 1997, page 7)

Many of the early psychology books in my great-grandfather's library did go on excessively about the "soul," but to slide this attribute over to people like Wundt, Kulpe ("systematic experimental introspection"), Titchener, and McDougall is a misrepresentation.

Watson then starts attacking William James, something he does throughout this book.

Note that Watson's field is behaviorism, but he is talking here about introspectionism, the competition, to make them look bad. If he was using valid arguments, that would be one thing. But he is just making assertions to discredit the opposition. That's what I call "mental warfare." And I can't see that he needs to discredit the opposition in order to teach behaviorism. His rationale was perfectly spelled out in his 1913 paper — let's just see what we can learn by studying human behavior. If the study of human behavior was so superior, then it would have proved itself, without any need for trashing the opposition.

Then we get to the untenable assertions I have already discussed in Chapter 3 — that there is no such thing as the "mental," that thinking is subvocal talking, that "creativity" is simply manipulating words, that Freudian psycho-analysis is "Voodooism," and so forth. And some of these assertions have stuck in the minds of some academic people.

On page 200, he brings in the name of "Mrs. Eddy" to make a point, knowing, I'm sure, that Mary Baker Eddy is somebody his students have already been conditioned to reject.

After pages and pages of what I see as a propaganda campaign against the "mental" and "consciousness" and "introspection," Watson makes the following statement:

> ... The unscientific nature of Freud's conception is surely apparent to you ere this. If it is not I'll have to give you up.
> (Watson, 1925, page 242)

That's why I call him a "manipulator."

Actually if you recognize that there are "mental senses" and that observations made with the mental senses are "evidence," then Freud's discoveries were highly scientific. I recognized this intuitively when I was first exposed to Freud at age 20. But Watson is not opening up the question to discussion here. He is telling his

young students that if they don't believe the propaganda he has been
feeding them, they will be subjected to the supreme ridicule of "I'll
have to give you up" — one of the manipulative expressions that
adults used to use with young children.

He goes on to predict:

> ... I venture to predict that 20 years from now an analyst using Freudian
> concepts and Freudian terminology will be placed upon the same plane as a
> phrenologist. ...
>   (Watson, 1925, page 243)

Of course 35 years from then, I was enjoying good results, life-
changing results, with a psychiatrist using Freudian concepts and
Freudian terminology — updated of course, as the 1960 automobile
was an improvement over the 1925 automobile. And Freudian
psychology is still alive and well and respected, despite all the
bashing. Karmic justice is served here, as Watson falls victim to his
own propaganda.

There are probably many like him who take advantage of their
position of power to manipulate innocent young undergraduates, but
they aren't all so foolish as to put their manipulations in print.

REFLECTIONS OF ACADEMIA

Harvard biologist Edward O. Wilson has won two Pulitzer Prizes. Classmates of mine have spoken very highly of him. He was the honored speaker at our 50th reunion. But when he crosses the line from biology into my territory, he doesn't do so well, in my opinion.

In his book *Consilience* (1999), to the best of my understanding, he is saying that if we all thought like biologists, we would have "consilience," or agreement in the world. To that end, he dismisses or puts down other ways of thinking. I may be oversimplifying it, but that's the way that I see it.

What makes *Consilience* interesting to me is that it seems to be reflecting some of the opinions, attitudes, and beliefs of the social group academia at the time. It also displays some of the unscientific methods.

Let's start off with some social manipulation:

> I mean no disrespect when I say that prescientific people, regardless of their innate genius, could never guess the nature of physical reality beyond the tiny sphere attainable by unaided common sense. Nothing else ever worked, no exercise from myth, revelation, art, trance, or any other conceivable means; and notwithstanding the emotional satisfaction it gives, mysticism, the strongest prescientific probe into the unknown, has yielded zero.
> (Wilson, 1998, page 46)

First of all, when he says, "I mean no disrespect," it means that he does mean disrespect and is making an effort to disguise it. He then proceeds with his put-down of the "prescientific," whatever that means.

As a scientist, he should know the logical implications of saying that anything has yielded "zero." This is just an authoritarian pronouncement, taking advantage of his enormous status as a scientist.

Cats catch mice, not because they are quicker, but because they understand their patterns. What does that have to do with anything? I learned it from a dream.

Also Joseph interpreted the Pharaoh's dream, and Daniel interpreted King Nebuchadnezzar's dream, to learn something about physical reality. I suppose he can dismiss all that because it is legend. And he can say that the Edgar Cayce readings are "useless," and thereby have yielded "zero."

And he can say that my dream analysis is based on discoveries by Freud and Jung, and therefore is "scientific." But that would then work against him if he tries to say that their discoveries were not "scientific."

And I suppose that the terms "prescientific" and "mysticism" could be defined in such a way as to make the statement come out true — almost. But logic will win out in the end, because the prescientific has yielded at least one thing — science.

Edward O. Wilson, with his enormous credentials as a scientist, describes five "diagnostic features of science that distinguish it from pseudoscience":

1. repeatability (replicability)
2. economy (elegance)
3. mensuration (measurability)
4. heuristics ("stimulates further discovery ... and the new knowledge provides an additional test of the original principles ...")
5. consilience (consistency with explanations of other phenomena)

And then he goes on to say:

> Astronomy, biomedicine, and physiological psychology possess all these criteria. Astrology, ufology, creation science, and Christian Science, sadly, possess none. ...
> (Wilson, 1998, page 54)

With the one word "sadly" he sweeps away all these things that he calls "pseudosciences" — before we have even had a chance to think about what he is saying. "Sadly" is the kind of word that publishers use when they reject your manuscript. It implies that somebody has the absolute authority to make a judgment, and that that judgment has already been made, and that now the only thing left to do is to tell you the sad news.

In the face of Wilson's enormous scientific credentials, I question his authoritarian pronouncement right from the beginning. Science is accurate observation and valid logic applied to phenomena of the real world to create knowledge. I don't see the need to pile on it all these intellectualizations, some of which I see as essential to science (replicability) and some not.

And then I question his "sadly" in regard to Christian Science, which has:

1. Repeatability: Mary Baker Eddy called it "science" because people sent her testimonials of miraculous cures, thousands of them.

2. Economy: The theory is simple enough: You can use prayer to combat disease. Also certain mental attitudes, like not believing in disease, are effective.

3. Mensuration: You live or you die. You get well, or you don't. You do better than the doctors expected, or you don't.

4. Heuristics: People have devised experiments to test these theories and expand our knowledge in this area (Pennebaker, IONS).

5. Consilience: The Catholic Church also has thousands of records of miraculous cures. Many of Edgar Cayce's cases were cases where medical science had failed. Also the theory is consistent with the Edgar Cayce readings.

(Much of this stuff that so-called "science" is rejecting is becoming a consistent body of knowledge in itself.)

Scientists reject Christian Science, but still they accept something they call "the placebo effect." Logically, you can't do both. You have to admit that Christian Science is at least the placebo effect. And then I would ask, "Why should there be a placebo effect? What causes it?"

Where Christian Science is incomplete as science is that they don't have a logically complete picture: How often did Christian Science fail to overcome disease, and how often were there spontaneous "miraculous" cures, without Christian Science? Certainly there are things that are called "scientific" that do not have a logically complete picture, either. And certainly it is not accurate to say that Christian Science has "none" of the attributes of science that Wilson describes.

Wilson lumps in Christian Science with other unrelated subjects in his blanket dismissal. Each subject deserves its own individual treatment. Creation science is not science. Astrology doesn't even call itself "science," although I think that scientific experiments could be devised to show that there is at least something to astrology (beyond chance guessing). Ufology needs to be investigated by responsible people, in the face of an apparent government cover-up. But all these things do share one thing in common, to continue with Wilson's statement:

> ... And it should not go unnoticed that the true natural sciences lock together in theory and evidence to form the ineradicable technical base of modern civilization. The pseudosciences satisfy personal psychological needs, for reasons I will explain later, but lack the ideas or the means to contribute to the technical base.
>
> (Wilson, 1998, page 54)

All of these things he calls "pseudosciences" are threats to what he calls "the ineradicable technical base of modern civilization." They all indicate that there are more dimensions to reality than what we now know as physical reality. The technical base we now have is incomplete, and needs to be opened up to include other phenomena, if our knowledge is to expand — to keep us from eradicating it and us. He is arguing his point not with a valid scientific argument, but by suggesting that people who are trying to extend our knowledge further have "personal psychological needs."

Actually, the "personal psychological needs" work the other way. There is a certain satisfaction and security in thinking that you have most of the answers, especially when you are being paid to do just that. Within this comfortable security, there is a resistance to see or admit that whole dimensions of the universe have barely been explored. This knowledge-inertia keeps belief systems in place.

On page 74, there is a quick smear of Swedenborg: "I suspect that he would have enjoyed a stiff dose of *ayahuasca*."

Wilson then proceeds to contribute to the Freud-bashing. He sets the tone by comparing dream symbols to "characters in a bad Victorian novel," thus giving people the social signal that Freud is being ridiculed. After a reasonably accurate, although colored, description of Freudian psychology, he then proceeds with his authoritarian pronouncements:

> Freud's conception of the unconscious, by focusing attention on hidden irrational processes of the brain, was a fundamental contribution to culture. It became a wellspring of ideas flowing from psychology into the humanities. But it is mostly wrong. Freud's fatal error was his abiding reluctance to test his own theories — to stand them up against competing explanations — then revise them to accommodate controverting facts. ... In dreams Freud was faced with a far more complex and intractable set of elements than genes, and — to put it as kindly as possible — he guessed wrong.
> (Wilson, 1998, page 75)

"But it is mostly wrong." Again, does he have enough status to pull off this demolition of Freud, or is he going to lose his own credibility as a result? And the punch line, "to put it as kindly as possible," is really very unkind, as an attempt to gain the sympathy of the reader as he bashes Freud one more time.

If he wants some credibility, he needs to make a list of Freud's errors, show how they outweigh Freud's discoveries, and explain how any errors are "fatal." Without any details, he loses this argument by default.

Actually, Freud was mostly right, although he did make a number of errors. None of these errors were fatal, and they were corrected by Carl Jung and others, including myself. Procedural errors have been noted by physical scientists, but physical scientists, including Edward O. Wilson, are simply not qualified to operate in the area of the mental. Freud's theories have been thoroughly tested by me and millions of other people in psychotherapy, using the mental senses.

Freudian psychology has now gone well beyond Freud. People who are trying to discredit psychoanalysis by bashing Freud are missing their target by at least 70 years.

The culture accepted Freud completely until 1973. Freud was "in;" then Freud was "out." I think part of the reason for the Freud-bashing is an emotional one, to compensate for having accepted him too completely in the past.

When Wilson tries to describe dreams, he is largely uninformed, reflecting the opinions, attitudes, and beliefs of physical scientists of his time, based on physical images of the brain at work:

> In brief, dreaming is a kind of insanity, a rush of visions, largely unconnected to reality, emotion-charged and symbol-drenched, arbitrary in content, and potentially infinite in variety. Dreaming is very likely a side effect of the reorganization and editing of information in the memory banks of the brain. It is not, as Freud envisioned, the result of savage emotions and hidden memories that slip past the brain's censor.
> (Wilson, 1998, page 75)

Again, here is the authoritarian pronouncement.

I am trying to find an appropriate metaphor to explain why the brain-scanning equipment is not able to experience a dream as a person does, with the mental senses. Let's say you are completely deaf, and you are trying to experience a violin concerto by physically monitoring the vibrations of the violin. Yes, this brain-scanning equipment is truly awesome, but that's about as close as it is going to get to understanding dreams. There is just no connection between the physical monitoring of brain waves and proving whether Freud or Jung were wrong.

> Dreaming is triggered when acetylcholine nerve cells in the brain stem begin to fire wildly ...
> (Wilson, 1998, page 76)

What causes these cells to begin to fire wildly?

> ... In dreams we are insane. We wander across our limitless dreamscapes as madmen.
> (Wilson, 1998, page 77)

This has propaganda value, to portray our dream states as insanity. But I know differently. I have experienced a meaningful and purposeful education from my dreams, as valuable as my 4 years at Harvard. I have experienced "the self-steering process," guiding me towards the truth. So I know that Wilson doesn't know what he is talking about here. Again, he is just picking up on ideas that are floating around academia.

> The brain and its satellite glands have now been probed to the point where no particular site remains that can reasonably be supposed to harbor a nonphysical mind.
> (Wilson, 1998, page 99)

Is a nonphysical mind supposed to exist in a physical place? This is the same argument as probing the physical universe and finding no God. Other dimensions need to be explored.

On the subject of evolution, Wilson says:

> ... Perhaps God did create all organisms, including human beings, in finished form, in one stroke, and maybe it all happened several thousand years ago. ...
> (Wilson, 1998, page 129)

Like most people who believe in evolution by purely physical means, he is picking on the Fundamentalists. It is easy for them to pick on the Fundamentalists, who aren't generally as intelligent or well educated, and are tied to a rigid belief in a text that was written thousands of years ago. The chronology of the Creation of course has been totally disproved scientifically.

It is also easy to pretend that the only opposition to the idea of physical evolution is coming from the Fundamentalists, and that it is necessary only to show that the world wasn't created in 6 days in 4004 BC. Later on I'll be presenting the view of evolution by Eklal Kueshana, which fits the evidence better than Darwin's theory does.

In all these things — dismissing Christian Science, UFOs, astrology, and the spiritual, and bashing Freud, and seeing dreams as meaningless nonsense, and accepting the view of evolution by purely physical means — Edward O. Wilson is reflecting views of the social group academia that were fashionable at the time.

FRESHMAN ORIENTATION

I was surprised to find a highly biased propaganda piece against parapsychology in the textbook for the beginning psychology course at Dartmouth College in the fall of 1998 (Bernstein et al, 1997), illustrating how social signals are given to young and impressionable college freshmen to insinuate that parapsychology is somehow disreputable. I'll just quote a few choice bits here. I have capitalized certain words to point out the bias that is being applied.

> ... Throughout history, however, various people have CLAIMED *extrasensory perception*, the ability to perceive stimuli from the past, present, or future through a mechanism beyond vision, hearing, touch, taste, and smell. ALLEGED forms of extrasensory perception (ESP) have included *clairvoyance* ... , *telepathy* ... , and *psychokinesis* ... . CLAIMS for ESP are widely BELIEVED (Alcock, 1995; Lett, 1992). Research on them is called *parapsychology* ... .
> (Bernstein et al, 1997, pages 131-132)

The words that I have capitalized convey the desired bias — that this is just somebody's belief system and not to be taken seriously.

The references above to Alcock and Lett are to *Skeptical Inquirer*, which I like to call "Skeptical Enquirer" because of the high level of inaccuracy of its methods and its content. I am not including these people in "academia," not wanting to pollute academia by including them in with reputable academic people, but I see here that the people of academia don't mind polluting themselves.

> Many APPARENT parapsychological phenomena are weak and difficult to replicate. Under close scrutiny by OUTSIDE OBSERVERS, reported ESP phenomena often FAIL to occur (Swets & Druckman, 1990).
> (Bernstein et al, 1997, page 132)

Again, I have capitalized words to show the bias being conveyed. It is true that parapsychological phenomena are weak and parapsychological tests often fail when administered by people who are biased against it. I have capitalized "outside observers" because

265

this carries with it the bias that there are "inside observers" who are biased and "outside observers" who are unbiased. This insinuation is not accurate.

Actually there are people who believe in parapsychology and people who don't. Parapsychological abilities are so delicate, so sensitive, that an experimenter who is biased against parapsychology can actually block the perceptions through his/her mind-jamming abilities or just creating a general aura of negativity. It is like asking the subject to sing a tune while another tune is being played loudly in the room, or having a wine-tasting session in a kitchen where sauerkraut is being cooked.

I have actually seen results of a parapsychological experiment where the subjects scored significantly LESS than chance, and the experimenter concluded that since the results were "negative," parapsychology was disproved.

If you have ever studied mathematical statistics, you know that that conclusion is wrong. The result is significant, therefore there was a parapsychological force operating to cause the person to score less than chance — most likely a negative bias on the part of the experimenter and/or the subject. Either or both were using their parapsychological abilities to make the results come out to support their bias.

So let us not assume that these "outside observers" are either unbiased or exert a neutral effect on the experiment. Some people, because of their strong negative bias, are simply not qualified to perform experiments in psychology. All it takes is a little smile at the beginning: "Today, we are going to test your psychic powers," (smile).

What the authors fail to mention here, in order to convey their bias, is that the *Journal of Parapsychology* has been reporting successful experiments in parapsychology since 1937, and the British *Journal of the Society for Psychical Research* has been reporting successful results for much longer than that. To counter the claim that parapsychological tests "often" fail, there is this vast body of research to show that experiments in parapsychology have more often been successful.

The expression "extra-sensory perception" is a contradiction in terms. There must be a sense, even though it may not be recognized or named, in order to perceive. Because "ESP" is a contradiction in terms, researchers in parapsychology since the 1970s have used the word "psi" to represent those paranormal psychic abilities.

It is interesting that the authors here (1997) don't use the word "psi" anywhere. Maybe they aren't aware of it. But they refer to "ESP" over and over again. I don't know their intentions, of course, in doing this, but I do know that the effect of using this expression which is a contradiction in terms is to convey the message at some subconscious level, "Perception without a sense is impossible; therefore ESP is impossible."

The text continues:

> In one set of experiments, subjects were asked to predict which of four randomly illuminated lights would appear next (Schmidt, 1969). After several thousand trials, a few subjects correctly predicted the illumination up to 26.3 percent of the time, a performance that — statistically speaking — is significantly better than the 25 percent to be expected by chance alone (Rao & Palmer, 1987).
>
> (Bernstein et al, 1997, page 132)

They seem to have picked the least impressive result of a parapsychological experiment they could find. Mathematically, after several thousand trials, the result may be significant, but intuitively, by Weber's Law (which they have just been discussing), a person perceives that 26.3 percent and 25 percent are essentially the same.

They didn't mention Hubert Pearce, who scored 39.6% in 300 trials, where he would have scored 20% by chance. In 1850 trials he scored only 30% (maybe he got bored), but still the odds against doing this by chance were 22 billion to one (Broughton, 1991, page 69).

Continuing with the text:

> Many psychologists have also challenged the use of apparent changes in random number - machine output as a measure of psychokinesis. They note that randomness is not an all-or-none concept. If you flip a coin seven times and it comes up heads each time, is the pattern really nonrandom? Does it mean you have psychokinetic ability? A sequence of seven heads in a row is

unlikely (it will occur on average only once in 128 tries), but it certainly can happen. Indeed, a seven-heads sequence is just as likely as any of the 127 other possible seven-flip sequences. In other words, it is far more difficult than one might think to determine that something really is "nonrandom" (Hansel, 1980). Thus, a very plausible interpretation of apparently nonrandom events in ESP experiments is that they are random after all.
   (Bernstein et al, 1997, page 132)

   This is just wonderful mathematical mind-jive. There are accepted standards of non-randomness in psychology. If there is less than one chance in 20 that the outcome of an experiment could have occurred by chance, the results are considered "significant." If you are anxious that the one chance in 20 might actually have occurred by chance, you can do the experiment again. If you get the one chance in 20 again, then the probability that the results for both experiments combined are by chance is one in 400, and so on. Generally accepted confidence limits for psychological experiments are two standard-deviations (one chance in 20) and four standard-deviations (one chance in 10,000) of arriving at the outcome by chance. What the authors don't seem to realize is that their mathematical mind-jive, if accepted, would invalidate a great many experiments in psychology as well as parapsychology.
   Computers can't generate random numbers (at least not when they are working properly). They generate "pseudorandom" numbers, by multiplying two 10-digit numbers and taking the middle 10 digits, or some such scheme. These pseudorandom numbers are never exactly random. But the difference should never be statistically significant. If questions can be raised, then experimenters should be running their computers in a neutral "control" situation as a comparison. But I don't think that is what they are talking about here.

   A photograph of a woman in a bizarre position calls our attention to the box in the wide margin of the textbook. The caption reads:

AN ESP EXPERIMENT   This woman is attempting to use clairvoyance to "see" objects in another room while hearing only white noise and wearing goggles that provide unpatterned visual stimulation. She is unlikely to succeed.
   (Bernstein et al, 1997, page 132)

The woman is made to look foolish, and thus parapsychology is made to look foolish. This is the unscientific method of ridicule.

The evidence (ganzfeld procedure) indicates that she IS likely to succeed, despite the authoritarian pronouncement here.

The caption continues:

... Since 1964 James Randi, an expert magician and ESP skeptic, has carried a $10,000 check that he will give to anyone who can perform clairvoyance, telepathy, or any other feat of ESP under scientific conditions (Randi, 1987). After investigating hundreds of claims, he still has his money.
(Bernstein et al, 1997, page 132)

I am wondering how many of these cases were decided by an independent arbitrator. I have suggested to The Rhine Research Center that they consult with a good law firm to collect the $10,000 from Randi. Also they might collect a few more dollars for the defamation inherent in his book title, *Flim Flam!*

Finally, some apparently remarkable results of ESP experiments can be attributed to fraud. A few researchers have tampered with their equipment and measurements, thus destroying their credibility and raising suspicions about all parapsychological research.
(Bernstein et al, 1997, page 132)

This is a nice propaganda move. Now that our brains are befuddled by the mathematical mind-jive and insinuations of "flim flam," the authors are trying to slip this accusation of "fraud" past our critical faculties for the killer blow. Note that they can say the word "fraud" out loud, since it is aimed in nobody in particular, but also note that it applies to nobody in particular, unless they are actually identified. It is just a broad-brush smear, as in racial prejudice or class prejudice, to taint the reputations of the whole class of people it is aimed at.

Accusations of "fraud" are not part of the scientific method and are not necessary in science. The key to science is replication. If a finding is fraudulent, it will simply not be replicated by reputable investigators, and therefore not accepted as scientifically demonstrated. It is as simple as that.

There are instances of fraud in every branch of science, so it can be said by the same faulty reasoning "thus destroying their credibility and raising suspicions" about all scientific research. Again, the smear-tactics aimed at parapsychology can be applied to other branches of science as well. The propaganda backfires.

Here they conclude:

> As a science, psychology depends for evidence on clear, reliable, and replicated observations. Skeptical scientists place the burden of proof for the existence of ESP on parapsychologists, who must be able to show robust, replicable ESP effects that do not depend on interpretations of nonrandomness and that occur under tightly controlled conditions. ...
> (Bernstein et al, 1997, page 132)

Given the tactics they used, we would expect that the authors would arrive at these conclusions, or actually that they had begun with these conclusions. To counter these insinuations, I offer the following quotes, for the freshman student to decide which viewpoint sounds more accurate:

> Since the publication of the first ganzfeld-psi experimentation in 1974 there have been over 108 ganzfeld studies encompassing some 2,549 sessions reported in at least forty publications by researchers around the world. Have they all demonstrated psi? Certainly not — hardly any experiments involving human psychology are successful every time. Nevertheless the ganzfeld procedure has seen sufficient successful independent replication that it has come to be viewed as one of parapsychology's best techniques for examining psi under controlled laboratory conditions. Those who have examined the ganzfeld database consider it, as a whole, to be some of the best evidence for a replicable psi effect in parapsychology to date (Utts, 1991). *
> (Rhine Research Center, 2001, page 12)
>
> * Utts, J. (1996). An Assessment of the Evidence for Psychic Functioning. *Journal of Scientific Exploration*, Vol. 10, 1, p. 3-30.

The following is a statement by Margaret Mead, speaking in favor of the application of the Parapsychological Association (PA) in

1969 for affiliation with the American Association for the
Advancement of Science (AAAS):

> For the last ten years, we have been arguing about what constitutes science
> and scientific method and what societies use it. We even changed the By-Laws
> about it. The PA uses statistics and blinds, placebos, double blinds and other
> standard devices. The whole history of scientific advance is full of scientists
> investigating phenomena that the establishment did not believe were there. I
> submit we vote in favor of this Association's work.
> (quoted in Broughton, 1991, page 74)
>
> (Quoted in E. Douglas Dean, "20th Anniversary of the PA and the AAAS,
> Part I: 1963-1969." *ASPR Newsletter*, Winter 1990, pages 7-8.)

Richard Broughton goes on to say, "Following her statement, the
membership voted five-to-one in favor of granting that affiliation."
Parapsychology had official status as a "science" in 1969. Then, in
1979, Broughton says, there was a campaign to "drive the pseudos
out of the workplace," which failed. I would say that what was
corrupting the workplace were smear-tactics, posing as "science."

> The major strategy of parapsychology is to declare that by adhering to the
> strictest canons of scientific methodology, it is possible to (a) demonstrate the
> existence or nonexistence of psi, and (b) gain knowledge concerning psi (if it
> exists). Because of this adherence to scientific methodology, parapsychologists
> claim that mainstream scientific recognition and legitimacy are rightfully
> theirs. ... an overall review of parapsychological literature (which numbers in
> the thousands of articles) indicates that psi does indeed exist and even reveals
> various patterns that seem to be related to its occurrence (Palmer, 1978;
> Wolman, 1977).
> Numerous experiments could be cited as evidence that the existence of psi
> has been proven. For the purpose of illustration, Beloff (1980) has listed seven
> experiments that can be considered as highly evidential in support of the
> existence of psi.

Palmer, John. "Extrasensory Perception: Research Findings." Pp. 59-243 in
Advances in Parapsychological Research, 2: Extrasensory Perception, Stanley
Krippner, ed. New York: Plenum, 1978.

Wolman, B.B., ed. *Handbook of Parapsychology*. New York: Van Nostrand
Reinhold, 1977.

Beloff, John, "Seven Evidential Experiments." *Zetetic Scholar*, 6 (1980), 91-94.

(McClenon, 1984, pages 82-83 and References)

I leave the references above for the freshman student who wants to pursue this subject further. It was interesting to me to note that the seven experiments listed by Beloff did not all take place at The Rhine Research Center (formerly FRNM), but were performed at 6 different laboratories in 5 different countries — to answer any insinuations that parapsychological experiments have not been replicated. It should also be noted that, while I have tried to make a case for the evidence of the mental senses, parapsychological research has been conducted by the strictest rules of established physical science, using the evidence of the physical senses only.

Dartmouth College Library has every issue of the *Journal of Parapsychology* going back to Volume #1 in 1937. Anybody can read it and refute the claims of this textbook, except that everybody knows, once the social signals have been sent, that they aren't supposed to read it.

SCIENTISM AND EVOLUTIONISM

When I was twelve years old, in the eighth grade, I was first introduced to science. Science was a wonderful thing for me. It gave me a way to break free of the moral judgments of religion. Science didn't judge whether a thing was good or evil, but only whether it was true or false. Science didn't ask me to believe on faith what authorities told me were the Commandments of an invisible God, but only to believe in the evidence of my senses. I could perform experiments and decide for myself what was true and false. And most important, I no longer had to be afraid of spooks in the night, because "Scientists know there are no such things."

This last sentence is "scientism." Scientism, as I have already said, is the belief that there is no reality beyond the physical. Scientism is not science, although it has arisen out of science and a major logical error on the part of persons of science, which is worth repeating: Because only physical phenomena have been observed with the physical senses, it is concluded that only physical reality exists. It is sort of like saying, "Because we do not see the music with our eyes, music does not exist."

An essential part of this belief in a purely physical reality is to be able to explain how life originated, without having to postulate Creation by some invisible higher spiritual being. Darwin's theory of the origin of species, as enhanced by T.H. Huxley and others to include the origins of life itself, fit that need perfectly.

Darwin's theory is based on the observed phenomenon of "adaptation." "Adaptation" means that species modify themselves to adapt to their environment, through a process of random mutation and natural selection. Minor mutations take place in nature all the time. It is easy to show, mathematically, that if a given mutation has a greater chance of survival, such that it will produce 10% more offspring than the norm for the species, that after 64 generations its offspring will outnumber those of the norm by 446 to 1, and after 128 generations, more than 199,000 to 1.

The process of adaptation has been proved many times. But did adaptation ever go so far as to create a new species? New species

273

have appeared relatively suddenly in geological time, and the process of adaptation, as observed, is too slow to account for this. Any high-school student can learn this, as I did, by going to the public library and looking up "Evolution" and related subjects in the *Encyclopedia Britannica.*

Because adaptation is too slow to account for the sudden appearance of new species, biologists have slid off onto the theory of "punctuated equilibria," which postulates that there must have been some dramatic change in the environment to force the species to adapt very rapidly and become a new species.

The problem with the theory of punctuated equilibria is that then we need to find evidence of a sudden and severe change in the environment — global cataclysms or whatever. And we need to find that evidence for every single species that has originated. It would also help to find that the original species did NOT survive. Else why should there be this sudden urgency to evolve into a new species?

There are just too many factors involved with this theory of punctuated equilibria, too many conditions that have to be satisfied in order to prove it. Add to this the fact that scientists have never created a new species in the laboratory, despite applying severe environmental pressures, although they have demonstrated adaptation many times, and it appears that Darwin's theory of the origin of species has been disproved.

There are many ways biologists slide off this conclusion, and they are all invalid. Let's just start with mental bullying. T.H. Huxley ridiculed people who had less of an education than he had. In answering the critics of his essay "On the Physical Basis of Life," he said:

> ... My unlucky "Lay Sermon" has been attacked by microscopists, ignorant alike of Biology and Philosophy; by philosophers, not very learned in either Biology or Microscopy; ...
> (Huxley, 1871, page vii)

More than a hundred years later, Richard Dawkins continues along the same lines:

Darwinism, unlike "Einsteinism," seems to be regarded as fair game for critics with any degree of ignorance.
(Dawkins, 1986, page xi)

"Einsteinism," of course, is accepted because it has been proved for all the world to see, at Alamogordo, Hiroshima, Nagasaki, and a thousand other places. You don't have to know the meaning of "$E = mc^2$" to know that it is the power that ended World War II, and the power that has since threatened to annihilate us.

Evolution, on the other hand, is far from proved, and after 8 hours reading about "Evolution" and related subjects in the *Encyclopedia Britannica*, I was able to see that the evidence was actually against it. So yes, the weak points in the evolution argument can be easily pointed out, accurately, by "critics with any degree of ignorance," like me.

Another invalid argument is definition-switching: Evolution has been proved, beyond any doubt. Evolution has been disproved. Both of these statements are true. How can this be? Because these are two different definitions of "evolution." I am going to use the expressions "evolution-1" and "evolution-2" so that we can tell the difference.

"Evolution-1" is the fact of evolution. Life on earth has evolved, in millions and billions of years, from simple organisms to the complex species we see today. Species like human beings share certain common attributes with other species, like frogs, to show that they must have evolved from the same common ancestor. All this has been proved, with "mountains of evidence."

"Evolution-2" is the Theory of Evolution, as proposed by Darwin, that new species come into existence as a result of random mutation and natural selection. The process of random mutation and natural selection is called "adaptation." Adaptation has been proved, but the process of adaptation is too slow to account for the appearance of new species, which happens relatively quickly in geological time. So Darwin's original theory of "the origin of species" has really been disproved, although the biologists won't admit it. Instead they have slid off onto the new theory of "punctuated equilibria," which, as I have pointed out, raises more questions than it answers.

I should also add "evolution-3," the theory that life evolved from non-life by a purely physical process. At this point in time this is all just pure speculation of how it "might have happened."

People then switch these definitions to argue in favor of evolution. They point to the "mountains of evidence" supporting evolution-1 to claim that evolution-2 is an undisputed fact. One critic actually compared me to the Holocaust-Revisionists because I questioned evolution-2.

Stephen Jay Gould seemed to be well aware of the definition-switching when he said, in his criticism of William Jennings Bryan: "First, he made the common mistake of confusing the fact of evolution with the Darwinian explanation of its mechanism." (Gould, 1999, page 154) But he doesn't say that any of the scientific elite make that mistake. Maybe they don't. Maybe it is only lesser minds that get confused.

Then there is the implied premise in Darwin's theory, which, if it is stated, is not stated often enough, that new species evolved WITHOUT ANY DIVINE INTERVENTION. Here is where biologists are stretched beyond the limits of biology by the Theory of Evolution. Because their observations are limited to those of the physical senses, they are not qualified to say anything about the spiritual. They are not qualified to say that evolution DIDN'T happen by spiritual intervention. They resolve this question by sliding over from science into scientism, and asserting that the spiritual does not exist. This, of course, is not a valid argument. There is always room in the universe for the spiritual, unless you know the whole universe, absolutely, in all its dimensions.

Eklal Kueshana has offered the explanation that angels created new species by genetic engineering when the environment was ready to support those new species.

My friend asked me, "Have you ever seen an angel?"

And I told him about my death experience, how I shot up into the presence of the Light and the figure of Christ. It certainly was very convincing that there were very real spiritual beings "up there," as I experienced it. And New Age bookstores have whole shelves of books on the subject of angels. Some of those people must have seen angels. It is not logical, not valid, not scientific to simply dismiss the idea of angels.

Stephen Jay Gould has dismissed Eklal Kueshana's explanation under the category of "Some personal versions of creation" (Gould, 1999, page 126). I have already explained how the word "personal" is used by authoritarian types as a put-down, to mean "not important," or "none of the rest of us care." *The Ultimate Frontier* by Eklal Kueshana had sold 200,000 copies by the time I became aware of it, in 1971. That's 199,999 more than "personal." Of course I don't know whether anybody actually knew what to make of it, but the theory is certainly out there, and published, and publicized, and far from "personal." In fact it reflects badly on Stephen Jay Gould as a scholar that he is not aware of it.

Another way of dismissing Eklal Kueshana's theory is to lump it in with "Creationism," so that you can pretend you are arguing with Fundamentalists. But if this theory is not dismissed, or ignored, or put down, or misrepresented, it can be seen that it fits the experimental results much better than Darwin's theory.

All it is doing, really, is replacing the idea of "random mutation" with "genetic engineering." Well, actually, it is postulating angels, and a whole other dimension or dimensions in the universe. I guess that's just too much for some people to swallow — even more preposterous than "little green men."

But if there were such things as angels, operating on a whole higher level of existence than human beings, and if these angels had the ability to get into the substance of species and alter their genes, to know, first of all, precisely what alterations were necessary to create the desired species, then, yes, this process would take place faster and more predictably and allow new species to evolve in the time frame that has been observed.

I realize that the theory of Eklal Kueshana is as radical in our day as Darwin's was in his day. And who would be qualified to test it? Biologists aren't qualified to test it. You would have to be able to read the Akashic Record, or something like that, to know whether angelic intervention occurred.

And you would also have to be able to read the Akashic Record to be able to say with certainty that angelic intervention DIDN'T occur. The Theory of Evolution, either way, is beyond the scope of biology. So for now, I guess we'll just have to go back to "faith." It all depends on what you believe in.

The Theory of Evolution has been a part of our culture for a long time, since Darwin first published it in 1858. It has become ingrained in our culture. People all the time are explaining things in terms of "evolution," things often very remote from the biological process of adaptation. For many people, as it was for me at one time, the Theory of Evolution was the key to a belief system that postulated no God, no higher beings, and only a physical universe that operated according to physical processes understandable by physical science. You can't just say to these people that the Theory of Evolution has been disproved. That leads to what Leon Festinger called "cognitive dissonance." They then have to rationalize things to make their belief system whole again. And some of the strongest believers are the same people who have disproved the Theory of Evolution. They can't announce it to the world until they are ready to announce it to themselves.

Despite the fact that they themselves have accumulated the evidence to disprove evolution-2, biologists continue to believe in both evolution-2 and evolution-3 as explanations for the existence of life. They continue to hold to this fixed belief in spite of evidence to the contrary. That makes it more like a religion.

The Creationists are right in saying that the biologists' belief in evolution is like a religion. But the creationists are wrong in claiming that their own beliefs are "scientific." What would be more accurate would be to say that the beliefs in evolution-2 and evolution-3 aren't scientific, either.

I think the unfortunate thing is that scientists, by the social pressures of their social laws, are locked into scientism, so that we don't have responsible investigations of the spiritual dimensions by academic people, so that we have to rely on people who have done drugs to move forward with these explorations.

I see scientism as a Grand Experiment, a necessary stage for the culture to go through. When authoritarian religion is asking people to believe on "faith" in an invisible God who appeared to people thousands of years ago and allegedly laid down laws by which people are judged in the present, it is only natural to break free of that "authority" and say that we are only going to believe on the basis of evidence. And it is quite natural that the only evidence acceptable at the time was the evidence of the physical senses, and therefore natural that a purely physical universe would be postulated.

But I said "postulated." This is a cultural experiment. Nothing is carved in stone. As we accept that there are means of perception other than the physical senses, and as the evidence of these other senses accumulates to show us that this is more than just a physical universe, it would be reasonable to reject the physical hypothesis and accept a hypothesis that is at least designed to accommodate spiritual phenomena, if such things exist.

Now physical science, because of its success, has gained enormous status, and because of its status has become the authoritarian system that religion once was, telling us what to believe and passing judgment on all beliefs. But the ultimate judge of all this is you. Just as the accuracy of science was seen by individual human beings who then gave science status, now the inaccuracy of scientism needs to be seen by individual human beings, who will then remove the status of scientism, which is blocking cultural change, and allow us to move on to some new hypothesis.

12. THE TRASHING OF THE
AMERICAN MIND

"I'm wasted, man."

That's what friends of mine in Provincetown were saying when they returned from Haight-Ashbury in the winter of 1967. LSD was a recreational drug, taken solely for pleasure, orgiastic and multi-orgasmic pleasure, leaving body and mind totally drained. I had no idea it was going to become a powerful philosophical and political force.

I mean, when people get totally drunk, they feel wonderful and think they can sing better, but people more in touch with reality can tell them, "No, you weren't singing better; you were singing worse. And no, you weren't so wonderful, because you couldn't walk, and we had to carry you home." But when people have been totally under the influence of LSD, they make that the standard by which to judge what is "reality." The altered perception is the "reality," the higher truth. The normal perception is "uptight" — outdated and limited.

And so, when the person on LSD jumps out of a third-story window, thinking she can fly, the person who has done drugs can say, "In her mind, she really did fly, and she is still flying."

But in her mind, with her enhanced perception, I'm sure she saw her smashed body down there and realized that she had screwed up this time and would just have to incarnate all over again.

LSD quickly became the way to find the spiritual, and some people, as they experienced the spiritual, or thought they did, on some very high level, began to feel very superior, or at least gave that impression.

One guy I knew was telling me that on his most recent LSD trip he was on the next level to God. Then shortly after that, he left his wife who was 8 months pregnant and a baby who cried for the first 2 years of his life. Again, this is the same level of accuracy as the woman who thought she could fly. LSD has been described as a "hallucinogen," but for many people who took it, the drug state was seen as a higher level of truth than the normal state. What I observed was not how superior these people were, but how they were able to put down the rest of us.

In this chapter I am going to discuss the philosophical effects of this altered perception and how these effects have introduced inaccuracies into our culture — as opposed to the claims that the altered perception and "expanded consciousness" represent a whole new level of thinking and awareness. This is going to be quite different from my article of the same title in *Outlander* #2 in 1995. That was more emotional, because I was still suffering from the wounds I had received from the Drug Revolution. This is going to be more analytical, but my conclusions are still the same: The Drug Revolution was basically destructive — for individuals, for the culture, and in its long-term effects.

I think that a good place to start is with this criticism of my 1995 article:

> What I see you doing is mostly putting down a long list of people, movements and subjects. Including a number of the movements I find to be part of the most positive directions of change on the planet.
> (Flemming Funch, 1995)

Well, not really "putting down," but criticizing and pointing out inaccuracies — there is a difference. I am criticizing this very popular belief system, even though I know it will make me unpopular, because I care about people, and I think that many have been misled by the hype and the promises into making the Drug Revolution the great hope for the future.

Yes, people were blasted out into spiritual space. It was the greatest spiritual awakening since the days of Christ. People dropped their suburban values, the pursuit of money, and saw that love was the important thing. But after the jump-start, there wasn't much more to say. They were on their own to develop further. They talked about "the beautiful people," the spiritual leaders, who were on drugs. But the spiritual leaders quickly realized that they would do better in their explorations of the spiritual without the distorting influence of drugs. The people who opened me up to the spiritual — Jeane Dixon, Carl Jung, and Edgar Cayce — never did drugs.

But all that was a long time ago. It is history. When the 30th anniversary of Woodstock was being celebrated in 1999, people of younger generations had no interest in it. Most of them hadn't even been born in 1969. But their whole culture has been shaped and changed by the Drug Revolution, as the people who did drugs assumed important positions in the culture — as educators, as publishers, as writers of books and songs that have influenced the culture.

It isn't really obvious how much of our culture has been shaped by the Drug Revolution. The New Age people don't talk about drugs; they talk about "the spiritual." The postmodern people don't talk about drugs; they talk about "Multiple Realities."

I didn't see the connection until I received an advertising package from a New Age magazine in 1994 and happened to notice the demographics of their readers:

— Baby boomers — average age 48
— Upscale annual household income of $45,400 average

The average age of the U.S. population in 1994 was about 36. So these aren't young people. And most likely they aren't old people, either. Most likely they represent a cluster at around age 48. A person age 48 in 1994 would have been born in 1946, and would have been 20 or 21 years old at the time of Haight-Ashbury, in the winter of 1966-67. The only thing that I can see that would have created a cluster of people about that same age all sharing the same values and beliefs would have been the Drug Revolution. Yes, there was also the Vietnam War, but I can't make a connection between the Vietnam War and a New Age magazine, but I can with the Drug Revolution.

In *The Aquarian Conspiracy*, published in 1980, after we have been fed all the hype about how this conspiracy of enlightened people is taking over the world, the following statement is printed in an appendix, where we are not likely to notice it:

> Many respondents chose not to answer the questions relating to former or present use of major psychedelic drugs. Thirty-nine percent of all respondents acknowledged that psychedelic experiences had been important in their own transformative process; 28 percent said they still used psychedelics on occasion; 16 percent said psychedelic experiences continued to be important to them.
>
> (Ferguson, 1980, page 419)

How many is "many?" This doesn't tell us what percentage of respondents didn't answer the questions relating to drug use, so we can't do any math here. But the fact that the word "many" is the first word in the paragraph implies to me that it was a significant percentage. Starting with the 39% who acknowledged that psychedelic drugs were an important part of their transformative experience, add to that $x\%$ who did drugs and didn't think it was important to their transformation, and $y\%$ who chose not to respond, and $z\%$ who lied (nobody is under oath here), and I would say that $39 + x + y + z$ would add up to pretty near 100% who did drugs. And a great many were still doing drugs as of the time of this survey (late seventies), reinforcing the drug experience.

But the really conclusive evidence of the influence of psychedelic drugs on New Age or postmodern thinking is in the ideas themselves. Let's just look at the psychedelic experience. I don't know this first-hand. This is just what I have read in books.

"We are all part of one interconnected whole." Fritjof Capra repeats this assertion over and over again in *The Tao of Physics*. But he never explains exactly what this "whole" is, or how we are all connected. Yes, the universe is probably all made up of the same basic substance, but that substance manifests itself in discrete objects and beings. That's the way I see it.

But if you have done drugs, you know exactly what he is talking about, because you have experienced that oneness with the universe. There is no need to explain it or define it, because you have experienced it, just as people in the normal state have experienced grass and trees and flowers. It would be difficult to define or explain grass and trees and flowers in words, and really there is no need to, if people have experienced them. The interconnectedness of all beings works the same way. People who have experienced it know exactly what is meant.

Astronaut Edgar Mitchell, looking back at Earth from space, experienced this same perception of the interconnectedness of all beings. Because of this perception, he founded the Institute of Noetic Sciences (IONS), to study such phenomena. I doubt very much that Edgar Mitchell was on drugs. So this is a phenomenon that can occur naturally — an altered state of perception.

Similarly, in the book *Beyond Ego* (Walsh and Vaughan, Editors, 1980), I was waiting for them to define what they meant by "ego." Was it the ego-compensation that we see in persons of low self-esteem? Or was it the real ego, the sense of self, the "I" that exists in the world and interfaces with it? I never found any definition of "ego." They didn't have to define it, because in the drug experience you lose that sense of self, the real ego, and become one with the universe. This book was written by and for people who have had that experience, whether on drugs or not.

"I am the chair." In becoming one with all the objects in the universe, of course I become one with all the objects in the room. In order to be able to discern that there is a thing called the "chair" that I am at one with, I must be able to recognize at the same time that the chair is a distinct entity apart from myself, that "I am NOT the chair." So, at the same time, "I am not the chair," and yet "I am the chair." Logic is turned off.

Logic is also apparently turned off under hypnosis. People are able to believe contradictory things. This suggests that suggestibility is more powerful than logic. Under LSD, one's suggestibility is heightened, according to Sidney Cohen MD in *The Beyond Within*. As suggestibility becomes more powerful, logic just seems to become discounted.

I live in a universe of discrete objects and beings. I use my logic to differentiate between these objects and beings and to perceive the relationship between them, to accumulate what I call "knowledge." I believe that my purpose here on earth is to learn the earth environment, to accumulate this "knowledge," and to improve my ability to differentiate, until I master the earth environment.

Eastern philosophy would dismiss all that, and call it "The Ten Thousand Things." Eastern religions, as Capra points out in *The Tao of Physics*, go along with the drug experience of seeing the unity and interconnectedness of all those things which I see as discrete objects and beings.

To see the universe as a unity of all things works against my philosophy, which values the ability to differentiate. To turn off logic works against my philosophy, which needs logic to differentiate and to know anything. To dismiss "The Ten Thousand Things" is simply a put-down. My function in these earth-incarnations, as I see it, is to master "The Ten Thousand Things." When I have done that, I'll consider some other philosophy. Besides, my philosophy works, and I see no reason to change it as long as it works.

So I am happy to stay within my "bag of skin." Also I am more secure. One problem with interconnectedness is the possibility of interference by other entities. I am constantly saying the Protective Prayer to keep my mental environment free of such interference, especially as I write this book, and it is amazing how many little things have come up to delay the writing of this book. It may feel wonderful to dissolve your "bag of skin," but I think that the people who do this and advocate this are generally naive about the possibility of interference by Black Mentalists.

The drug experience thus becomes the basis for a philosophy of life, which ties in with Eastern philosophy and Eastern religions. And while I personally reject this philosophy, I accept, as part of my knowledge of "The Ten Thousand Things," that this experience and this viewpoint exist. And I am always on the lookout to see how this represents a greater awareness.

"You create your reality." Again, this statement has always puzzled me. They never define what they mean. Do they mean, as George Berkeley claimed, that when you perceive reality you are actually creating it? and that the universe is created by our collective "perception" of it? Or do they mean, in a psychological sense, that you create how people relate to you by the way you approach them — friendly or hostile, weak or strong? Do you create the ball, or only the spin you put on the ball?

They aren't talking about any of the above. Again, they are relating to the drug experience. In the drug experience, you are able to create your "reality," simply by the power of suggesting it to yourself. It is well known that the suggestions, positive or negative, of the people around you, are very important in determining whether you have a good trip or a bad trip. So the suggestions you make to yourself, the auto-suggestions, are even more important.

LSD has been described as a "hallucinogen." What you are creating is not "reality," but something like a hallucination. Dreams are also something like hallucinations.

I always wondered about the fascination with "lucid dreaming"— knowing you are dreaming and creating a dream experience for yourself. The value of dreams for me has always been that they were created from some source beyond my consciousness, and therefore I could learn something from them. It seemed to me that the fascination with lucid dreaming was just to be able to say, "I am so superior. I am aware that I am dreaming when I am dreaming."

But I think that the fascination with lucid dreaming also ties in with the drug experience. You create your dream-reality the same way you create your "reality" in waking life with psychedelic drugs.

Understanding the drug experience helps to understand the culture it has produced, that has taken the drug experience as its model.

"Reality," to me, as it used to mean before the drug experience changed its meaning, is the collection of everything that exists, in all its dimensions. There is one and only one reality. I am part of that reality, in my bag of skin, and I interface with the rest of it, altering it to some degree as I interface with it. The reality is independent of my perception of it, as I learn when I stub my toe (unless I created the obstacle in order to stub my toe).

"My reality" means something else. It can mean my perspective on reality, or my perception of reality, or my distortions and inaccuracies as I perceive reality. It can mean the reality I have created in my drug experience, my hallucination, my dream, my movie. It can mean the very real effect I have on reality through my thoughts and actions. It can mean my "environment," which is everything and everybody that I interact with, to the degree that I interact with them. There is no definition in my 1996 dictionary that would fit the expression "my reality." The word "reality" here can mean a great many things, and so means nothing. The word "reality" has been trashed.

The expressions "my truth" and "your truth" work the same way as "my reality" and "your reality." The word "truth" used to mean the quality of accuracy in one's representation of the reality. Now it just means anybody's perception of the reality, whether it is accurate or not: "All statements are equally true." (Leonard and Laut, 1983, page 12). So the word "truth," like "reality," has also been trashed. Actually it was corrupted a long time ago, when people who were lying claimed to be telling "the truth." But now it just doesn't mean anything.

If you remove the words "reality" and "truth" from the vocabulary, it becomes hard to communicate anything intellectually, hence "the trashing of the American mind." The intellectuals call this "postmodern" thinking, as if it was more advanced than the "modern." But I say it is a step all the way back to chaos. Think "post-apocalyptical."

The drug-oriented people are not bothered by this, since with no logic there is no "truth," as it has been defined in the past, and "reality" to them is just a lucid dream that they have created. But with no logic and no absolute reality to explore, there can be no science and no knowledge. "Knowledge" is really knowledge of "The Ten Thousand Things," and with the unity of all things, everything is like a boundless undifferentiated ocean. So what is there to know?

But the drug-oriented people do manage to find food and to find their way home at night, and they did manage, according to the demographics, to have an average annual household income of $45,400 in 1994. So they do function in my reality with my truth and a certain amount of logic and differentiation. There is just a certain amount of hypocrisy between what they are saying and what they are doing.

The people who experienced psychedelic drugs moved on, many of them, to meditation, and some of them to sensory deprivation, as in Avatar, to gain insights into the spiritual. In both meditation and sensory deprivation, people are making an effort to remove themselves from the earthly environment they incarnated into. Time spent removing oneself from the earthly environment is time lost from the learning experience of one's time on earth, in my opinion. Half an hour or an hour a day to gain spiritual insights may be a good trade-off. Five hours a day of meditation may be a waste of one's precious time incarnated into a human body.

Yes, the knowledge of the spiritual is important, but so is the knowledge of the physical and the mental that physical science and psychology have accumulated. As my dream of the spiritual teacher pointed out, there are equally valid and binding laws on both sides, and the problem for the mind is to reconcile them.

With the rejection of reality, truth, and logic, it follows naturally that people would reject science. Here is a statement on science from Harry Palmer in *Creativism*, the defining work on Avatar:

> Current scientific methodology, whereby one believes he is determining his beliefs by a carefully controlled examination of reality, presents an amusing picture to someone who has grasped the principles of Creativism. The study of any science is the study of the reflection created by the beliefs of the collective conscious. The only way something can be discovered is by first believing that it exists.
> (Palmer, 1990, page 29)

With the one word "amusing" he puts down science. This is his whole and complete argument to dismiss science. As for first believing that something exists before it can be discovered, I disprove this argument every time I stub my toe.

There is really no need for Avatar to dismiss science or to have anything to say about science. Science and Avatar can work independently, and discoveries from both sides can be valuable.

With LSD, all your psychological problems are revealed in one LSD trip. I would think that this would be overwhelming to a person with even mild psychological problems, as was illustrated to me in the dream where I was half crazy. Actually the people who do best on LSD are the people who have no psychological problems to speak of, and they become the leaders and the spokespersons of the social group, and we hear very little about those others who made themselves crazy.

So it is not surprising that the people who did drugs felt that psychotherapy was a thing of the past, a part of the old "uptight" culture that they were rejecting. Either they didn't need it, or they did it all in one LSD trip, or they had been made crazy and had no voice and were discounted by the others. Here is a statement by Alan Watts, from *The Book*:

> I am not thinking of Freud's barbarous Id or Unconscious as the actual reality behind the facade of personality. Freud, as we shall see, was under the influence of a nineteenth-century fashion called "reductionism," a curious need to put down human culture and intelligence by calling it a fluky by-product of blind and irrational forces. They worked very hard, then, to prove that grapes can grow on thornbushes.
> (Watts, 1966, page 11)

If this statement was created in put-down school, I would give it an 'A+.' It masterfully combines smear-words, truth, falsehoods, and nonsense to say really nothing comprehensible. But it certainly sends a very clear social message rejecting Freud.

During the Drug Revolution, people picked up the slogan "Psychiatrists are tools of the Establishment," which was driven into people's heads by hypnotic implant, and repeated over and over whenever the subject of psychotherapy came up.

Actually I first heard the slogan from an academic person in 1960. A great many people would like to do away with psychotherapy, as I'll be discussing in the next chapter.

All the New Age books that I have read have made "reality" and "truth" into something personal, and have sent out social signals that logic and science and psychotherapy were things of the past, to be shunned. That pretty much blocks any mental effort working towards knowledge, and completes "the trashing of the American mind."

THE HIPPIES

In Provincetown they were trying to pass laws against the hippies. This created a debate over how to define a "hippie." Nobody could define a "hippie," and so no laws against hippies per se were passed.

I would define a "hippie" as "anybody who has done drugs and believes in it." Psychedelic drugs altered people's minds in a way that was fairly uniform, leading to a common belief structure. And where the drugs didn't do it, the normative pressures of the social group forced people into common values, beliefs, and attitudes. I couldn't decide whether the word "Hippie" should be capitalized. I suppose if you think of the Hippies as a religion or a political party, the word should be capitalized. And they were both.

LSD is a power trip. I want to give Paul Tasha credit for that idea — it wasn't my own. Of course he is aware that LSD was also many other things to people, but I think that this one insight is a key to understanding what the Drug Revolution was all about.

First of all, there were the confrontations, at Kent State, at the Democratic National Convention in 1968, and at various demonstrations across the country. Exactly why they were demonstrating wasn't always clear to me, but the statement they were making was very clear: "We can exert a force."

From Gandhi and the Civil Rights Movement they picked up methods of passive resistance, like sitting in, or lying in, so that law-enforcement officials would be forced to physically carry you away. They learned from the Civil-Rights Movement that if you were arrested, the event was more likely to be reported in the media, thereby giving free publicity to your cause. Then the people who were arrested became martyred heroes, like the Chicago Eight. And of course the supreme martyrs were the students who were killed at Kent State.

Publicity and public opinion were their main source of power, and they were masters of hype. And what were they selling? It is interesting that they weren't promoting their own product or lifestyle so much as they were putting down the opposition. This is more evidence that this was a power trip:

> Psychedelic drugs cause panic and temporary insanity in people who have not taken them.
> (Timothy Leary and Richard Alpert, quoted in Grinspoon and Bakalar, 1997, page xiii, also page 66)

> Everyone clucks, fumes, grinds their teeth over the bad taste, the bad morals, the insolence, the vulgarity, the childishness, the lunacy, the cruelty, the irresponsibility, the fraudulence. ...
> (Tom Wolfe, *The Electric Kool-Aid Acid Test*, quoted in Grinspoon and Bakalar, 1997, page 70)

> We [he and Alpert] had moved beyond the game of psychology, the game of trying to help people, and beyond the game of conventional love relationships. ... the parochial social insanities.
> (Timothy Leary, quoted in Grinspoon and Bakalar, 1997, page 65)

From the Drug Revolution to transpersonal psychology, there is this continued effort to ridicule, put down, and generally make destructive remarks about the ordinary state of conscious awareness:

> ... we all convince one another that the waking condition is a healthy and proper one, for no other reason than that we are all its common victims.
> (Quoted from C.D. King, *The States of Human Consciousness*, in Walsh and Vaughan, 1980, page 41)

> We are all prisoners of our minds.
> (Ram Dass, quoted in Walsh and Vaughan, 1980, page 54)

> ... psychosis is attachment to any one reality.
> ... this conditioned tyranny of the mind.
> (Walsh and Vaughan, 1980, page 55)

> ... our usual state of consciousness is one in which we are, quite literally, hypnotized.
> ... ego appears to come into existence as soon as awareness identifies with thought, to represent the constellation of thoughts with which we tend to identify, and to be fundamentally an illusion produced by limited awareness.
> ... traditional Western psychologies are ego psychologies and hence are studies of illusion.
> (Walsh and Vaughan, 1980, page 58)

They aren't talking here about people with psychological problems, who might be trapped in a prison that their mind has created. They are just sweeping away all "straight" thinking, perception, and feelings of love with the same destructive statements.

I want to counter that barrage with a statement that I feel is very accurate:

> From the other side, a psychiatrist, Daniel X. Freedman, wrote that the psychedelic prophets were victims of a delusional autonomy and bland sense of superiority, protected themselves by using the ego defense known as denial, and had a need to proselytize in order to allay their own doubts: ...
> (Grinspoon and Bakalar, 1997, page 69, quoting Freedman, Daniel X., 1968, "On the use and abuse of LSD," *Archives of General Psychiatry* 18: 330-347, page 338)

And to counter this statement, I have one last quote, the trump card over everything:

> ... Students surveyed at a high school in California in 1967, when asked whom they would trust as the narrator of an anti-LSD film, answered "no one."
> (Grinspoon and Bakalar, 1997, page 75, citing Braden, William, 1970, "LSD and the press," in B. Aaronson and H. Osmond, eds., *Psychedelics: The Uses and Implications of Hallucinogenic Drugs*, page 413)

So this really is very much like a war. People's opinions on the subject depend very much upon which side they are on.

The hippies developed the art of mental warfare to new levels:

A hassles B, and then turns to B and says, "You wouldn't hassle me, would you?"

And then there was the constant assertion that they were doing "peace," when what they were really doing was war:

The Flower Child says to the Arresting Officer, "But we love you, Officer," and projects a picture of loving innocence to the world. This is not a genuine statement of love, but really a vicious attack, an attempt to undermine the Officer's dedication to duty by playing to the most basic human values and Christian ethics of the

Officer and the public at large, at a mental level beneath their conscious comprehension, which has been dazzled by the picture of loving innocence. When the Officer carries out the arrest, which is his job, it is made to appear as a crime against humanity and Christian values, as in "How could you arrest us when we love you?" And then the Flower Child is seen as justified in screaming "Fascist Pig!" at the Officer, and the whole world is in sympathy, maybe. Because when the "love" instantly turns to hate, it is clear that the loving innocence was just a lie, and part of the attempt to manipulate, along with the "hate."

More subtle even than the verbal methods were the telepathic methods the hippies used to communicate their disgust, their contempt, and their total rejection of another human being if you weren't one of them.

I am surprised that volumes haven't been written (or maybe I am just not aware of them) on the methods of mental combat that were developed by the hippies. This is their greatest real achievement (as opposed to all the fantasy stuff they thought they were accomplishing, like spiritual advancement).

The mental warfare was also used to create rigid conformity among their ranks — more rigid than their parents in suburbia. You had to wear the uniform, and you had to share the opinions, attitudes, and beliefs. Any deviation from this was grounds for revulsion and expulsion. I remember in 1971, when I was going to visit The Stelle Group, I got my hair cut, because I knew they were very conventional in appearance and dress. And I was absolutely railed at in Provincetown. "Rail" is a word I don't usually use, so I had to look it up. According to my Merriam-Webster dictionary, it means "to revile or scold in harsh, insolent, or abusive language." Yes, that's exactly how I was treated.

I was already on probation anyway, because I was going around Provincetown saying, "Marijuana is poison." The interesting thing about that is that nobody ever asked me WHY I thought that way. They just replied with the adversarial statement, "Well, you smoke cigarettes." This is just one more indication that this was a power trip, and warfare, and not an enlightened exploration of alternative states of consciousness.

One last clue to the power trip is the put-down. A person who is truly superior does not put people down. We all want companionship on our level, and I suspect that a truly superior person would try to raise people up to his/her level. A first-grade teacher is clearly superior to her students, but she doesn't put them down. She patiently and lovingly instructs them so that some day they might reach her level. The put-down is evidence that these people aren't really superior and are just using mental warfare to compensate for it.

Provincetown was named in the *East Village Other* as the only "safe" place in Massachusetts for the hippies. And they came into Provincetown in 1970 like the Okies, cars piled high with their belongings. They were attracted to Provincetown because of its tolerance, but then they were the ones who were intolerant, trying to impose their standards on everyone. They tried to take over Town Meeting, and the townspeople turned out in record numbers to prevent them. The police got everything they wanted — that didn't usually happen.

But the hippies took over the social scene. Everywhere I went I had to breathe marijuana smoke. Even standing on third base in a softball game, I could smell the marijuana smoke coming from the stands. But that wasn't the worst part: I wasn't one of them. I had my own philosophy. I didn't need theirs. I was socially undesirable. It was a time of great sexual freedom, but what I remember most about the hippie women was seeing their long hair as they turned their backs on me. The young woman who enjoyed my company and enjoyed having sex with me didn't want to be seen with me in public. That was a reversal for someone coming from the privileged class.

The hippies finally drove me out of Provincetown in 1973, by making my mental environment so unpleasant that I couldn't do anything enjoyable or creative. At that point, I wrote the following intuitive statement, trying to sum up my feelings about the hippies. I credit the late Eddie Euler for calling them "the zombies." I'm sure there was plenty going on in their heads, but outwardly they were (many of them) expressionless, like zombies:

THE ZOMBIES

The zombies came,
The living dead,
Controlled by the powers of Darkness.
They came with slogans that passed for wisdom,
Hypnotic suggestions given by the Masters of Deception.
"Fight for peace."
"You might as well be insane — everyone else is."
"You might as well be dead — see the horrible things the living have done."
If a zombie touched your soul, you became one.

"You wouldn't hassle me, would you?"
Not unless you hassle me first.
Hard children of a hard society,
Drugged.
Warning: Loss of Identity Plus Loss of Defenses Can Lead to Loss of Soul.
"How can you turn against your children?"
This is not my child. I do not see my child's soul here.
This was her body, yes, but the soul is a stranger.

The zombies came,
First only a few, and then by the hundreds in motor caravans,
Armies of the living dead serving the dead living.
Like the locusts, they lived off the land,
Taking over the places where people gather,
For they had nothing to do but gather.
The bars thrived.
They ridiculed our human ways and threatened us with scorn.
"Uptight."
The power of the human brain, relieved of the constraints of soul ...

"We are superior people."
The people in brown shirts and boots tried to take over the government.
We have seen this before.
"A whole generation can't be wrong."
We have seen this before.
"If you haven't experienced drugs, what do you know?"
"Mr. Leary, we have known about drugs in our country for hundreds of years.
    Now please leave."

"Throw away your defenses."
So that you can destroy me or control me?

I defend what is mine, what I have built in a thousand incarnations.
"Throw away the ego, and be one with God."
The egoless state is the mindless state.
"Throw away the mind, and discover your true spiritual being."
I need my mind to differentiate between Light and Darkness.

Do I dare speak my mind, to oppose the powers of darkness?
Blackness surrounds me; I can't see.
For Thine is the Power.

(Provincetown 1973)

I sent this off to a couple of magazines, but I had little hope that anyone would ever publish it, because by this time the Hippies (religion or political party) totally dominated the popular culture. Nobody would have dared publish anything to offend them, for fear of total mental assassination.

It took me years to be able to say what I am saying now, because of that same fear. Even now, I respect their power to make me appear ridiculous, vicious, and insane, because that's what they do, and that's what they have been refining for years — the power trip.

You can't criticize religion because it is sacred. You can't criticize academia because they buy most of the books, and no publisher would want to offend them by publishing your criticism. And you can't criticize the hippies, because they are masters of mental warfare, and they can annihilate you with a single word.

THE LSD LEGACY

In 1966, a 16-year-old girl was telling me that marijuana was absolutely harmless. She had this on the highest authority from her gurus at Columbia University.

I didn't believe that. I needed to hear it from some more reputable authority. So the next time I was in New York, I went to the best bookstore I knew, looking for books on drugs. They had plenty of books on heroin and drug addiction, but nothing on marijuana, and only one on LSD, which I bought, *The Beyond Within* by Sidney Cohen MD. I loaned it to my young friend, and it disappeared, never to be seen again. The book was also missing from the Dartmouth College Library when I looked for it in 2002. I have a theory that the hippies got rid of books that were unfavorable to their cause.

Sidney Cohen MD observed people under the effects of LSD and found that the effects of LSD were very similar to schizophrenia. This was before LSD became a political issue, so these findings are not likely to be biased. Psychiatrists were experimenting with LSD, for its possible uses in psychotherapy, long before it ever became a popular drug (Grinspoon and Bakalar, 1997, pages xiii and 192).

But Sidney Cohen's research findings were totally drowned out by the hype of the Drug Revolution: The LSD state was not "hallucination;" it was an "alternative reality." The LSD state was not like "schizophrenia;" it was a higher level of sanity than the normal state. I credit the power trip and the power tactics of the Hippies for being able to totally defeat the Establishment at mental warfare and totally dominate the culture with their message. Yes, warfare does often decide what we think and believe, but that doesn't make those beliefs accurate.

I also blame the Establishment for being totally unprepared for the Drug Revolution, even years after it happened. First of all, there was only the one book available to me, at least 2 years after Timothy Leary first said, "Turn on, tune in, drop out, get well." The gurus of the new drug age were then free to tell young girls anything they wanted to. And then, even after the use of marijuana was well established, scientists couldn't tell you the mental effects of marijuana, because they had disqualified themselves from studying the mental when they limited their studies to the physical, starting with John B. Watson in 1913.

So physical scientists could study people on marijuana and report that there were no adverse physical effects. But what about the mental effects? Obviously marijuana has its mental effects. That's why people take it. Are there adverse mental effects, like making you crazy?

One story tells that the word "assassin" comes from the word "hashish," because after prolonged use of hashish these people became uncontrollably violent, and vicious criminals. The other story says no, hashish was only the reward they were given after they had done their dirty deeds. Which story is true? Have scientific studies ever been done on the long-term use of marijuana and hashish? My experience with "the dregs of the drug movement," as I called them, was that people did become hostile and angry and vicious after long-term use of drugs. And when I no longer saw people giving me the "evil eye," I decided it was safe to move back to Provincetown.

Psychedelic drugs do something to us mentally, and science has still disqualified themselves from studying the mental, so I might as well take a shot at it.

Psychedelic drugs dissolve our defenses. All our psychological problems are revealed to us. We can have multiple orgasms because we are no longer "uptight." Spirit entities can come sailing in.

There is a reason for defenses. The mind protects us from things we aren't consciously ready to handle. If you are exposed to these things suddenly and uncontrollably, there is an emotional overload. The mind takes other measures to deal with it, like making you crazy.

Even for those who are psychologically ready to handle it, the experience is overwhelming. People simply don't know what to make of it. Their rational faculties just aren't capable of assimilating this experience into any consistent worldview. Yes, I sincerely believe that psychedelic drugs, by breaking down the defenses, are opening people up to perceptions of reality they will have when they are much more spiritually advanced. But that doesn't make them more spiritually advanced. They will get there sooner or later, when they are able to assimilate the experience. Meanwhile they just come up with wild interpretations of what it all means.

When a child, with a child's mind, is faced with an advanced problem in the-living-of-life that the child isn't able to handle, this creates a traumatic experience. Human psychology then forces the person to keep recreating the experience and keep coming back to the problem until he/she is able to resolve it.

I think the drug experience is the equivalent of a traumatic experience, even though it may be pleasurable. Just the fact that a person doesn't know what to make of it makes it a "hang-up." One is doomed to become hung up on the drug experience until one is able to fit it into a consistent world view. Right now I see mostly inconsistencies and paradoxes.

(The reality is consistent with itself. What is, is. Therefore a representation of the reality must also be consistent in order to be accurate. A paradox is an inaccuracy in thinking, a mental error. Some people seem to think that paradoxes exist in the reality itself, and that it is a sign of their intelligence that they recognize them.)

So people took drugs and gave themselves hallucinations and made themselves something-like-schizophrenic, and yet through it all were able to have a clear view of a higher spiritual reality. This in itself is apparently inconsistent and a paradox. In order to reconcile it, they have tried to throw away the whole belief system they had before — reality, truth, logic, science, ego, and psychotherapy. That's about where we are now.

The Drug Revolution has not only created this confusion in the minds of many of the best and the brightest of a whole generation, but it has also driven it home via peer-group pressures and heightened suggestibility, so that people defend the confusion with all their mental resources.

Dead people were coming into my dreams, just from the effects of smoking marijuana. I would assume that this would be even more likely to happen under LSD. But the only mention of this I could find in the literature was this one sentence:

Psychedelic drugs produce not only these disarrangements of space, time, and human identity but also intensely realistic encounters with disembodied entities: astral bodies, spirits of the dead, angelic guides, deities, inhabitants of other universes, and so forth. ...
(Grinspoon and Bakalar, 1997, page 148)

There then follows a description of a trip by John Lilly, where he meets two spirit guides:

Slowly but surely, the two guides began to come toward me from a vast distance. ... Their thinking, their feeling, their knowledge was pouring into me. ... They stopped just as it was becoming almost intolerable to have them any closer. As they stopped, they communicated, in effect, "We will not approach any closer as this seems to be your limit for closeness with us at this time. ... You can come and permanently be in this state. However, it is advisable that you achieve this through your own efforts while still in the body so that you can exist both here and in the body simultaneously. Your trips out here are evasions of your trip on your planet when looked at in one way. ..."
(John Lilly, quoted in Grinspoon and Bakalar, 1997, page 149)

The interesting thing about this, to me, is that the last two sentences agree with my thoughts, as derived from Edgar Cayce and Eklal Kueshana: You can reach this state naturally by working on it "while still in the body," and your time on earth is the important thing, and these trips are just "evasions" from that.

The two guides seem to be higher beings and not lower beings, because they didn't intrude too closely into Lilly's environment, and because they seemed to be giving good advice.

I can't find any specific mention of Evil entities interfering with people or possessing them as a result of LSD trips, so maybe it never happened. But, as I indicated in "The Zombies," loss of defenses plus loss of ego can leave a person in a particularly vulnerable state. Also the heightened suggestibility of the LSD trip would make a person ultra-receptive to telepathic suggestion. It seems very unlikely to me that interference by Black Mentalists DIDN'T happen often and seriously on LSD trips.

One reason this may not have been reported in the literature was because of the power trip — unfavorable information was suppressed, put down, squashed — "Paranoid." Another reason would have been that the people thus afflicted could have become insane and not able to express themselves. They might talk about "Martians sending radio messages to the brain," which might be closer to the truth than anybody suspects, but still would just be interpreted as "wacko."

Anyway, the experience of spiritual reality and the desire for spiritual knowledge would lead people logically to want to be in contact with spirit entities, and it seems to be more than coincidence that this happened right after the Drug Revolution. At the very least, the Drug Revolution made people more receptive to this kind of information or misinformation, especially since the spirit entities seemed to be echoing the philosophy of the hippies.

The Seth books were enormously popular during the seventies and the eighties, and I think the main reason for their success was because they echoed beliefs that had already been established by the drug culture.

Here is the spirit entity Seth, from *The Nature of Personal Reality*:

> Experience is the product of the mind, the spirit, conscious thoughts and feelings, and unconscious thoughts and feelings. These together form the reality that you know. You are hardly at the mercy of a reality, therefore, that exists apart from yourself, or is thrust upon you.
> (Roberts, 1978. page xviii)

The people who have done drugs would have no problem with that. But most of us, from the age of two, have believed that the reality is independent of our perception of it, and that we didn't create the universe we live in. So if this is a great new revelation from a superior being, asking us to believe something totally backwards from the way we learned it, then I would expect a clear and patient explanation, to help me overcome the accumulated habit of years of thinking just the opposite. Instead what I get is this (next sentence):

> You are so intimately connected with the physical events composing your life experience that often you cannot distinguish between the seemingly material

occurrences and the thoughts, expectations and desires that gave them birth.
(ibid.)

He is just trying to create self-doubt in the mind of the reader, with "often you cannot distinguish," which reads like a hypnotic suggestion, and "the seemingly material occurrences," which reinforces the doubt. He is just trying to undermine the reader's thought process. He makes no attempt to build a great new thought process. He then continues with a statement that might be construed to represent a psychological truth:

> If there are strongly negative characteristics present in your most intimate thoughts, if these actually form bars between you and a more full life, still you often look through the bars, not seeing them. Until they are recognized they are impediments. Even obstacles have a reason for being. If they are your own, then it is up to you to recognize them and discover the circumstances behind their existence.
> (ibid.)

This looks like the accepted psychological truth that one's perception of the reality is distorted by one's mental "bars," and that one's life is limited by one's mental bars. That's still a long way from creating the reality — about as far as bending a spoon mentally would be from creating the universe.

Interspersed with the psychological truth, though, note that the negative hypnotic suggestions continue, with "strongly negative characteristics present in your most intimate thoughts" (this is YOU he is talking about), and "you ... not seeing [the bars]." Finally it just deteriorates into pure negativity:

> Your conscious thoughts can be great clues in uncovering such obstructions. You are not nearly as familiar with your own thoughts as you may imagine. They can escape from you like water through your fingers, carrying with them vital nutrients that spread across the landscape of your psyche — and all too often carrying sludge and mud that clog up the channels of experience and creativity.
> (ibid.)

If he can get you to believe on his authority, because he is a superior being and can see things that us mortals can't see, if he can get you in the con game of thinking you can get "something for nothing (i.e. a superior view of things), or if he can get you via his hypnotic suggestions — if he can get control of your mind in any way, then he can make you crazy, or at least confused. And that seems to me to be what he is trying to do. Nowhere in this book is there the clear and patient explanation that one would expect of a truly superior being trying to teach us that the reality is truly just the opposite of the way we perceive it.

Of course these spirit entities present themselves as highly evolved benevolent beings, and the evil that they do is deliberately engineered to be at a level of subtlety that is not perceived by the average person. For example, a friend of mine once did automatic writing, and as she was reading the beautiful silvery words that were written, I stopped her when she read "Help people."

I said, "Wait a minute! That's a put-down of the whole human race." Because it implies that all people need help — not just people who are actively asking for help, but all people. At the very least it is encouraging you to interfere where you are not wanted. We argued about it. She thought it was just an innocent and benevolent statement. Most people argue about it. It was engineered so that they shouldn't be aware of the negativity they are reading.

A Course in Miracles is another product of spirit guides, showing the same characteristics — the negativity in the guise of helping humanity, the attempt to undermine one's rational thinking and replace it by confusion (or insanity), and the use of hypnotic suggestion at a subliminal level, or disguised within a context which can also be construed to be helpful. Of course the first idea that is implanted in our heads is that we are going to learn to do miracles here.

I tried *A Course in Miracles* — at least the first lesson:

LESSON 1: Nothing I see in this room [on this street, from this window, in this place] means anything. ...
(Foundation for Inner Peace, 1992, "Workbook for Students," page 3)

You are supposed to do one exercise each day. So I thought about this one for a while, and it didn't mean anything. So I decided, *"This lesson does not mean anything."* From there, the whole thing opened up: This is an attempt to negate something.

> LESSON 3: I do not understand anything I see in this room [on this street, from this window, in this place]. ...

Again, this is the negation of something. This time it is understanding. As I read the sentences that follow, trying to make sense out of what is being said, I don't understand any of them: *I don't understand this lesson.*

I guess they are trying to break me away from my normal mental process. And the lesson they are teaching seems to be confusion. And then the hypnotic suggestions start working their way in:

> LESSON 5: I am never upset for the reason I think. ...

This continues the negative, destructive train:
a. I am upset.
b. I don't ever know why I am upset.
c. Therefore I know nothing about myself, etc.

The suggestion "I am upset" is followed by "I am angry," "I am afraid," "I am worried," "I am depressed," ostensibly to work you out of these moods, but actually to tell you you have these moods, and then:

> *There are no small upsets. They are all equally disturbing to my peace of mind.*

This is the further negative statement that all upsets are great. It goes on to cover up the suggestion (hypnotic intrusion/invasion) with the more philosophical statement in the second sentence. The word "equally" smoothes things over, and conceals the barb thrown in the first. And while it is smoothing things over, and you are sopping up the syrup, it is sneaking across a lie. Because obviously there are greater and lesser disturbances to the mind.

LESSON 10: My thoughts do not mean anything. ...

LESSON 11: My meaningless thoughts are showing me a meaningless world. ...

LESSON 12: I am upset because I see a meaningless world. ...

LESSON 13: A meaningless world engenders fear. ...

The hypnotic suggestions continue. The effect is to undermine one's thinking by hypnotic suggestion, or command. The whole book is written in command language, in an impersonal mode — no author is named. If there are people who could be captivated by this, I would say that *A Course in Miracles* is potentially the most destructive book I have ever seen. And who needs it, when you can deal precisely with your own personal problems through psychotherapy and dream analysis.

The practice of "mindfuck" and its results are also important legacies of the Drug Revolution. Psychedelic drugs increased people's suggestibility and made it easier to implant suggestions in people's minds. Then people discovered that they could implant suggestions in people's heads whether they were on drugs or not. Many slogans of the times were implanted in people's heads by hypnotic suggestion, and became part of the culture.

"Go with the flow."
Where does the flow go?

"You can't trust anybody over 30" was one of the slogans of the Drug Revolution. They apologized for it when they came to lecture at a college in the 1980s, because of course they were well over 30 by then. This slogan is basically self-destructive, but they didn't recognize that when they were using it. Because it was potentially self-destructive, and because they weren't aware of that at the time, I would look for the influence of Black Mentalists in creating this slogan and possibly others.

When I was in school and college (up to 1956), the only "substances" we used were tobacco and alcohol. We had heard of drugs, but they were something used only by jazz musicians and fringe people, mostly in large cities.

The Drug Revolution, of course, with LSD, spread the use of drugs to the children of the upper middle class in suburbia, and to mainstream America. Drugs have become a multi-billion-dollar, or maybe even a multi-trillion-dollar, illegal industry. And just as Prohibition stimulated the growth of organized crime in America, now drugs support huge networks of organized crime. People with expensive drug habits are forced to sell drugs in order to maintain their habits, and so they are motivated to find new users. As the untapped market gets younger and younger, now every school child is threatened by the temptations of drugs. Where once we had only heard of marijuana, now almost half of high-school seniors have used it, and 10% or more have used LSD. I credit the Drug Revolution for creating this huge illegal industry and this huge threat to our children.

There are many little inaccuracies that have entered our mental environment as a result of the Drug Revolution. One of them is the attempt to use the Heisenberg Uncertainty Principle to prove that "You create the reality." All the Heisenberg Uncertainty Principle is saying, as I understand it, is that the observation of a phenomenon interferes with the phenomenon itself, and as the object gets smaller, attempts to measure it introduce a greater amount of inaccuracy. For example, if you stick a thermometer in a bucket of water, it doesn't change the temperature of the water that much, but if you stick it in a thimbleful of water, it will change the temperature significantly. Even greater inaccuracies are potentially introduced in trying to measure sub-atomic particles. At sub-atomic levels, there may even be differences introduced by the intentions of the experimenter. This would be psychokinesis. But again, spoon-bending is not the same as creating the universe. And people many times rattle off the words "Heisenberg Uncertainty Principle" just to create uncertainty.

Another source of confusion is the expression "linear thinking." I have never seen it defined anywhere. I think it is just used to put down logical thinking.

Along with this is the put-down of "the Cartesian-Newtonian worldview," because it has been replaced by more recent discoveries in physics, starting with Einstein. Yes, Einstein theorized, and others demonstrated, that Newtonian physics is not precisely accurate. But I think that for most applications, except for atomic physics and astronomy, Newtonian mechanics still works just fine.

If you take the speed that the average spot on earth is moving relative to the sun, which is about 34,000 MPH, and divide that by the speed of light, which is 669,600,000 MPH, and square the result, you get a number which is too small to show on my calculator. That's the maximum correction that needs to be made for Einsteinian physics over Newtonian physics for any application on earth except for atomic physics and astronomy.

In many other little ways, the Drug Revolution which became the Counterculture which became the New Age has introduced inaccuracies into our mental environment.

The "alternative" culture blocked other solutions to world problems, like my own, partly because of the power trip, and partly because they were seen as the publishing "market" for anything avant-garde. The first publisher to read my manuscript said that it should be "more intuitive." I had no idea what she meant, because my thinking is very intuitive. It took me years to figure out that she meant, "Write something that the hippies would want to read." I couldn't possibly write anything that the hippies would want to read.

Baba Ram Dass renounced both drugs and meditation, and yet millions of people have read his books. Why? Because most of them share the same drug experience. Books catering to that market were instantly published, because they would sell, because millions of people shared that same bias. Books or information unfavorable to that bias were generally unpublishable, maybe for fear of offending such a large number of people. (M. Scott Peck had enormous success with *The Road Less Traveled*, because he called psychotherapy "spiritual.") The publishing industry, because of its marketing standards — the desire to maximize profits at the expense of other values — became a partner in the trashing of the American mind.

One day I was finding a great deal of rapport and mutual attraction with a woman I was working with in an office. She was telling me that she was involved in a relationship with the local yoga guru, and hadn't I heard of him? Then suddenly he showed up, apparently having known by telepathy of our particular rapport. And as he stood there, just staring, it was apparent that he was mentally blocking my ability to concentrate on my computer work. So I figured I had to acknowledge him in some way. I asked him where in my 5 manuals to find the particular instruction I was looking for. He named the correct manual, without apparently any prior knowledge of the system. I thanked him, and he left. After he left, neither the woman nor I had the presence of mind to comment on his visitation, or even continue our conversation any further.

It was an impressive display of mental powers, but did this represent spiritual development? I don't think so, any more than if he had been able to beat me up physically. A psychologically mature person does not have this need to control or possess another human being. And psychological maturity is an essential ingredient in spiritual development, not just from my point of view, but also from the point of view of Edgar Cayce and Eklal Kueshana and many others, I'm sure.

For years I have been trying to explain to people who are focused on the spiritual that psychological development is also important and should not be neglected. Just as I would like to see religions get together and pool their resources, I would also like to see philosophies get together. Psychotherapy is an important part of spiritual growth, and spiritual growth is an important part of psychotherapy.

I see LSD, even though it has created major problems, as a Grand Experiment, just as scientism and evolutionism were part of a Grand Experiment. It was necessary to do these experiments, for the growth of the culture. Can we learn from these Grand Experiments and move on, or will they create cultural forces that cripple us and block our progress?

13. FREUDAVOIDANCE

I see three stages in the mental development of the human species. The first stage I call "innocence." People started out in a primitive state, living pretty much like animals, doing whatever they were naturally inclined to do. They would kill and steal and rape, if they were powerful enough to do these things, and think nothing of it.

Then they reached a stage where they wanted to think of themselves as "civilized" — not animals, not savages, not barbarians. They put on clothes to hide their animal bodies, and wore fine perfumes to cover up the stink, and adopted fine manners to hide their animal desires. They refrained from killing and raping at will, or at least they knew it was "wrong." But somewhere down underneath, that animal with the animal drives was still there.

Some of them became Christians, trying to obey "moral" laws that allegedly came from God. All the natural human inclinations from the stage of "innocence" became "The Seven Deadly Sins" — greed, sloth, lust, gluttony, envy, pride, anger. It wasn't enough to refrain from natural sexual activity; even the desire was sin. A person couldn't even think it. The thoughts were repressed into the subconscious.

"Be ye Christ-like" was the commandment. But it was impossible to be Christ-like. The best people could do was pretend to be Christ-like, while deep down inside all that lust and hate and desire was lurking. This second stage I call "hypocrisy."

And then Freud came along and exposed the hypocrisy. He showed that the buried impulses don't stay buried, but work their way to the surface in "Freudian slips" and disturbing dreams and inappropriate behavior. Freud demonstrated that morality doesn't work.

People's illusions were shattered. They weren't really "civilized" after all. They had just become hypocrites. They wanted to maintain their high opinion of themselves. Their defensive mechanisms resisted having their illusions shattered. The collective defense-mechanisms of millions of people became a huge backlash against Freud which gathered momentum throughout the twentieth century. "Freudavoidance," I call it.

Somebody on the Internet told me that Freud was "brilliantly refuted" in 1961, but didn't tell me by whom, or in what book. I assumed he meant *The Myth of Mental Illness*, by Thomas Szasz, which was published in 1961.

Right away the smear-word "myth" signals what kind of book this is going to be, and Szasz confirms this right away by linking psychiatry to alchemy twice and astrology 4 times in the first 2 pages. "By page 6," I wrote in my notes, "I am so deep into the twisting and warping of words that I have to stop."

On page 5, he says, "The psychoanalytic theory of behavior is, therefore, a species of historicism." He then defines "historicism" as "Historical ... events are viewed as fully determined by their antecedents ..." He then goes on to say, "This unsupported — and, I submit, false — theory of personal conduct has become widely accepted in our present day." I am sparing you diversions into Popper, Plato, Nietzsche, and Marx. He is processing psychoanalytic theory through the abstraction of "historicism," which he defines in such a way as to make psychoanalytic theory false.

I leave it to the student of mind pollution to study this book. I plowed through most of it. It is certainly brilliant. I'll give him credit for that. But it does not refute Freud. It is convoluted and confusing.

There are many instances of the kind of devious logic that appears on page 5. The word that popped into my head to describe this book is "obfuscation." It does the opposite of shedding light upon the subject — it sheds darkness upon it.

The scholars who wrote the textbooks seem to have found a clear and coherent message in what Szasz was saying. Here is one example:

> In *The Myth of Mental Illness*, Thomas Szasz suggests that most mental disorders involve *problems in living*, problems that in the final analysis are solvable only by the person who has them. They cannot be cured in the way that a medical doctor cures a disease.
> (Lazerson, 1975, page 543)

This is what I believe, but did Szasz say that? Most of what I saw in this book was just an attempt to discredit the thing that I call "psychotherapy."

He goes on, in *The Myth of Psychotherapy*, to discredit psychotherapy even more:

> ... ostensibly scientific activity — rationalized ... pontificate ... pure rhetoric ... ostensibly scientific languages ... anti-individualistic, and hence threats to human freedom [page 19] ... Freud and the psychoanalysts and psychohistorians he spawned as base rhetoricians. ... Hitler's ... big lies [page 21] ... The basic ingredients of psychotherapy are religion, rhetoric, and repression [page 25] ...
> (Szasz, 1988)

I am not really taking these statements out of context. They are the context. Those of us who have successfully completed psychotherapy know that he is misrepresenting the process in a derogatory way. It doesn't seem that he knows what he is talking about. As a practicing psychiatrist, has he been through therapy himself? Here is his statement on that aspect of psychotherapy:

> ... All this decency and wisdom have been cast aside in modern psychiatry and psychoanalysis, which are animated by the despicable totalitarian principle that if something is bad it ought to be forbidden and if something is good it ought to be compulsory. How else can we account for the flourishing of coercive psychiatry, the famous compulsory training analyses of psychoanalysts, and

the massive medical, psychiatric, psychological, and legal apologetics written
on behalf of such compulsory soul-curing?
   (Szasz, 1988, page 37)

I wouldn't go to a therapist if I didn't think that that person had
been through psychotherapy and succeeded at it, any more than I
would accept as my guide to climb the Matterhorn somebody who
had not successfully climbed it. As for the despicable compulsory
training, how did he get his M.D. degree except through compulsory
training? I am wondering what motivated this strong propaganda
piece? What is his personal experience with psychotherapy? He
doesn't say. He talks about Luther.

Another propagandist against psychotherapy is Frederick Crews.
He raises the question of whether "only the analyzed can judge"
(Crews, 1995, page 8). Like Szasz, he gives no indication that he has
experienced psychotherapy. In fact, he comes right out and says,
"... My qualifications for making pronouncements about
psychoanalysis and psychotherapy without benefit of analytic
training or even of a personal analysis ..." (Crews, 1995, page 6). He
seems to have studied the works of philosophers and other
intellectuals on psychotherapy.

Crews is very, very intelligent. I am not intelligent enough to
argue with Crews. He knows a great deal, yes, but, like Szasz, he
doesn't seem to know very much about psychotherapy and the way it
works. So is he really saying anything about psychotherapy?

People like Szasz and Crews are taking advantage of the huge
demand for literature supporting people's defenses against
psychotherapy:

   ... And there is such a ready audience for publications that speak ill of
   psychotherapy that potential debunkers can be published when they have no
   data at all to substantiate their claims. ...
      (Smith et al, 1980, page 47)

Thomas Szasz makes one good point, though, which answers the
argument "Psychiatrists are tools of the Establishment." Psychiatrists
are working for whoever pays them. If the Establishment pays them,

they are working for the Establishment. If the client pays them, they are working for the client (Szasz, 1974, pages 48-69).

I think the people best qualified to write about psychotherapy are the people who have experienced it, and have been successful at it, or those who have steered others successfully through the process. That's how it works in other fields, whether it be mountain climbing or mathematics or music. Those who haven't done it, or have failed at it, just aren't qualified to write about it. And that's how it should work in psychotherapy, except for people's defenses, which are a social force that needs to be dealt with.

The defensive people can (and do) say that those of us who have successfully completed psychotherapy are a "cult," and that we have all been brainwashed into the same belief structure. But if you study the specifics of brainwashing and psychotherapy, you will see that they are quite different processes. For example, my psychiatrist never made me stand for hours on ice with my bare feet frozen to the ice, reflecting on my "crimes."

I think that the best evidence that we are not a "cult" is the product. I am evidence. This book is evidence. It is a unique collection of ideas, not like those of my psychiatrist or other people in the field. Yes, individual ideas are mostly the same, but the collection is unique. If we were a "cult," all our beliefs would be the same. I disagreed with my psychiatrist about my precognitive dream, of him meeting me at Grand Central Station. I disagreed with him about taking my girlfriend out to the movies and opening the car door for her. I was allowed to keep these beliefs, and was not forced into submission. I discovered my own will in psychotherapy, as opposed to what other people, including the psychiatrist, wanted me to do or expected me to do. Actually the brainwashing was done by the culture, and psychotherapy helped me to undo it.

Also there are differences of opinion among psychotherapists on the existence of a spiritual reality. My psychiatrist did not believe in the spiritual, but Jungian and transpersonal therapists do (in different ways). I agreed with my psychiatrist at the time, but the continuing psychotherapeutic process enabled me to grow beyond his belief structure. Does that sound like brainwashing or a "cult?"

Another defensive argument is "Of course the psychotherapists are promoting psychotherapy. Look at all the money they are making from it."

I am also evidence to refute that. I am a satisfied customer. I am not making any money from psychotherapy.

I think that more satisfied customers like myself need to come forward and testify to the benefits of psychotherapy. The problem with that is that there still may be some social stigma against having been to a psychotherapist. In my day, you could be denied a security clearance if you had ever been in psychotherapy. So there are risks involved in declaring yourself.

Another defense against psychotherapy is that it costs so much. I think that a single person making $40,000 a year should be able to afford it. And nobody should be married and supporting children until they have at least been checked out by a psychotherapist — unless they want to pass along "the sins of the fathers" to succeeding generations.

Some people avoid psychotherapy by doing "alternative" therapies. Let your State decide who is really doing psychotherapy and go only to somebody licensed by your State. Also group therapy isn't as good as individual therapy because it subjects you to the social pressures of the group. It is hard to develop your individual real self in that kind of environment.

"Half the therapists are crazy themselves." There is some degree of truth in this. I think the profession needs to clean up its act and make the successful completion of psychotherapy a requirement for anybody practicing psychotherapy. Meanwhile, the prospective client needs to be cautious: Don't just pick a name out of the Yellow Pages. Get recommendations, preferably from satisfied clients. We need feedback systems, like the one in eBay, for all professions.

And now finally we get to the third level of human mental development, which I call "genuineness." We just have to get out from under hypocrisy and become real people. We can do that with psychotherapy.

PART V

CONCLUSIONS

14. WRAPPING IT UP

There are just a few more things that I would like to say.

First of all, there is just one more major "camp" that I haven't mentioned. They are the "television people," people for whom television shows are the most interesting things in their lives and a major portion of their life's experience. They talk about TV shows. They read magazines about TV shows and personalities, like the newly remodeled *TV Guide*. They don't have a great influence on the culture, except that there are a great many of these people, and they vote, so they are a source of power for the manipulators.

Television, of course, exerts a major influence on the culture. I am not talking about advertising, which of course is a constant attempt to manipulate. I am talking about what passes for "news," or factual reporting. We saw Rodney King, motorist, being clubbed by police officers, and we saw this over and over again. We were never shown what led up to the clubbing. But when that evidence was shown in a courtroom, the police officers were excused. This led to major riots, because television had only shown one side of the story. How about a retraction from every TV station and network in the country, telling us the events that led up to the clubbing?

Another major influence in the culture is the insurance industry. They preach "safety" and fear "in the public interest," but really it serves to increase their profits. They also create mind pollution with bad logic.

For example, there is the seat-belt argument, "You can learn a lot from a dummy." This of course is insulting and manipulative, but mainly it presents a much-distorted picture of reality. The dummy knows that every time it goes for a ride in a car, it is going to crash. But for the rest of us, we will be in a major accident once in 50 years, on the average. So there is a trade-off: Is it worth the nuisance and discomfort of wearing a seat belt for 50 years, for the one time when it may or may not save our lives?

Medical people disagree with me. They only see the injured people. They don't have to ride with them in the car for 50 years.

It should be up to the individual to decide, but in most states now, the decision has already been made for us by the law: Buckle up.

I want to introduce the word "univalence," which means being dedicated to one value and ignoring all others. The insurance companies are dedicated to their profit motive. The medical people are dedicated to making you live as long as possible. They are ignoring other values and the possibility of trade-offs among competing values in the living of life, such as, for example, that getting pleasure out of life may involve taking some risks.

So, what do I have for conclusions? I really don't have conclusions; I only have beginnings. This is really only an elementary course in mind pollution. Maybe I can defeat Joe McCarthy's tactics of 55 years ago, but new and improved methods of mind pollution are being developed every day, and there is a social need to keep up with them.

And I think where mind pollution is most effective is not in the obvious lies and manipulations of politics and advertising, but in the social pressures of the people closest to you. If you happen to be a member of one of the "camps" I have mentioned (and if you are still with me here), ask how much of what you have been persuaded to believe is based on social pressures, and how much on valid argument. And if you are independent of all those "camps," I hope this will help you to be aware of their biases, and stay independent.

For the culture at large, I would like to see what would happen if a majority of people developed psychologically to the psychological age of puberty and beyond. I would like to see the academic community drop their prejudices and accept the writings of Mary Baker Eddy, Edgar Cayce, Carl Jung, Ayn Rand, and Richard Kieninger / Eklal Kueshana as working hypotheses, in the name of "free inquiry." I would like to see all religions get together and pool their insights into the spiritual. I would like to see the people who have done drugs recognize that this is hallucination as well as revelation, and make an effort to know the difference.

Once significant numbers of people are aware of the mind pollution in even our most respected institutions, then the culture may be able to move ahead towards mental and spiritual development.

REFERENCES

----- *The Holy Bible*, Containing the Old and New Testaments, Translated out of the Original Tongues and with the former Translations diligently compared and revised, by His Majesty's special command, Authorized King James Version. New York: Oxford University Press.

----- *The Holy Bible*, From Ancient Eastern Manuscripts, Containing the Old and New Testaments Translated from the Peshitta, The Authorized Bible of the Church of the East, translated by George M. Lamsa. Philadelphia: A.J. Holman Company.

Alloy, Lauren B., Jacobson, Neil S., Acocella, Joan (1999). *Abnormal Psychology: Current Perspectives*. McGraw-Hill College.

Alpert, R., Cohen, S., Schiller, L. (1966). *LSD*. New York: The New American Library, Inc.

Anderson, Walter Truett, Ed. (1995). *The Truth about the Truth: De-Confusing and Re-Constructing the Postmodern World*. New York: Jeremy P. Tarcher / Putnam.

Ardrey, Robert (1961). *African Genesis*. New York: Dell Publishing Co., Inc.

Barr, H.L., Langs, R.J., Holt, R.R., Goldberger, L., Klein, G.S., Research Center for Mental Health, New York University (1972). *LSD: Personality and Experience*. New York: John Wiley & Sons, Inc.

Berelson, Bernard, and Steiner, Gary A. (1964). *Human Behavior: An Inventory of Scientific Findings*. New York: Harcourt, Brace & World, Inc.

Bernstein, D.A., Clarke-Stewart, A., Roy, E.J., Wickens, C.D. (1997). *Psychology*, Fourth Edition. Boston: Houghton Mifflin Company.

Blass, Rachel B. (2002). *The Meaning of the Dream in Psychoanalysis*. Albany: State University of New York Press.

Bogart, Greg (2004). Therapeutic Dreamwork: A Case Study with Mythic Dimensions, Part 1. *Dream Network*, Vol 23 No 1: 38-43.

Boring, Edwin G. (1950). *A History of Experimental Psychology*. New York: Appleton-Century-Crofts, Inc.

——— (1953). A History of Introspection. *Psychological Bulletin*, 50: 169-186.

Bowler, Peter J. (1989). *Evolution: The History of an Idea*. Berkeley: University of California Press.

Bro, Harmon H. (1968). *Edgar Cayce on Dreams*, under the editorship of Hugh Lynn Cayce. New York: Paperback Library.

Broughton, Richard S. (1991). *Parapsychology: The Controversial Science*. New York: Ballantine Books.

Browne, Sylvia (2000). *Life on the Other Side: A Psychic's Tour of the Afterlife*. New York: New American Library, a division of Penguin Putnam, Inc.

Buckley, William F., Jr. (1951). *God and Man at Yale: The Superstitions of "Academic Freedom"*. Chicago: Henry Regnery Company.

Bunnin, Brad, & Beren, Peter (1983). *Author Law & Strategies: A Legal Guide for the Working Writer*. Berkeley: Nolo Press.

Cairns-Smith, A.G. (1985). *Seven clues to the origin of life: a scientific detective story*. Cambridge University Press.

Capra, Fritjof (2000 [1975]). *The Tao of Physics: An Exploration of the Parallels Between Modern Physics and Eastern Mysticism*, Fourth Edition, Updated. Boston: Shambhala.

Cayce, Edgar Evans, & Cayce, Hugh Lynn (1971). *The Outer Limits of Edgar Cayce's Power*. New York: Harper & Row, Publishers.

Cayce, Hugh Lynn (1964). *Venture Inward*. New York: Paperback Library.

Cerminara, Gina (1950). *Many Mansions*. New York: William Morrow and Company Inc.

Christie, Richard, and Geis, Florence L. (1970). *Studies in Machiavellianism*. New York and London: Academic Press.

Cohen, Sidney MD (1967 [1966]). *The Beyond Within: The LSD Story*. Atheneum.

Committee for the Scientific Investigation of Claims of the Paranormal (CSICOP), Inc. (1996). *The Outer Edge: Classic Investigations of the Paranormal*. Edited by Joe Nickell, Barry Karr and Tom Genoni. Amherst, NY: CSICOP.

Consumer Reports (1995). Mental Health: Does Therapy Work? *Consumer Reports*, Nov 1995: 734-739.

Crawford, Tad, and Murray, Kay (2002). Defamation Dangers, *PMA Newsletter*, June 2002.

Crews, Frederick (1975). *Out of My System: Psychoanalysis, Ideology, and Critical Method*. New York: Oxford University Press.

—————, et al. (1995). *The Memory Wars: Freud's Legacy in Dispute*. The New York Review of Books.

Csikszentmihalyi, Mihaly (1990). *Flow: The Psychology of Optimal Experience*. New York: Harper & Row.

Dawkins, Richard (1987). *The Blind Watchmaker: Why the evidence of evolution reveals a universe without design*. New York: W.W. Norton & Company.

Descartes, Rene (1977 [1637]). *Discourse on Method.* Indianapolis: The Bobbs-Merrill Company, Inc.

Eadie, Betty J. (1992). *Embraced by the Light.* New York: Bantam Books.

Eldredge, Niles (1985). *Time Frames: The Rethinking of Darwinian Evolution and the Theory of Punctuated Equilibria.* Simon and Schuster.

Eliot, T.S. (1922). The Waste Land. In *The Waste Land and Other Poems* (1962). New York: Harcourt Brace Jovanovich.

Elkins, David N., Ph.D. (1998). *Beyond Religion: A Personal Program For Building A Spiritual Life Outside The Walls Of Traditional Religion.* Wheaton, IL: Theosophical Publishing House.

Encyclopaedia Britannica (2002). Evolution, The Theory of, in *The New Encyclopaedia Britannica*, Volume 18, MACROPAEDIA, Knowledge in Depth. Encyclopaedia Britannica, Inc.

Fawcett, P.H. (1953). *Lost Trails, Lost Cities* (published in England under the title *Exploration Fawcett*). New York: Funk & Wagnalls.

Feather, Dr. Sally Rhine and Schmicker, Michael (2005). *The Gift: ESP, the Extraordinary Experiences of Ordinary People.* New York: St. Martin's Press.

Ferguson, Marilyn (1980). *The Aquarian Conspiracy: Personal and Social Transformation in the 1980s.* Los Angeles: J.P. Tarcher, Inc.

Friedman, B.H. (2006). *Tripping: A Memoir.* Provincetown: Provincetown Arts Press.

Feuerstein, Georg (1992). *Sacred Sexuality: Living the Vision of the Erotic Spirit.* Los Angeles: Jeremy P. Tarcher, Inc.

Foundation for Inner Peace (1992 [1975]). *A Course in Miracles.* Glen Ellen, CA: The Foundation for Inner Peace.

Franken, Al (2003). *Lies (And the Lying Liars Who Tell Them): A Fair and Balanced Look at the Right.* New York: Dutton, a member of Penguin Group (USA) Inc.

Franzoi, Stephen L. (1996). *Social Psychology*. Dubuque, Iowa: Brown & Benchmark Publishers, A Times Mirror Company.

Gaarder, Jostein (1994 [1991]). *Sophie's World*. Translated by Paulette Moller. New York: Farrar, Straus & Giroux, Inc.

Garfield, Sol L. and Bergin, Allen E. (1986). *Handbook of Psychotherapy and Behavior Change*. John Wiley & Sons.

Gebelein, Bob (1985). *Re-Educating Myself: An Introduction to a New Civilization*. Provincetown: Omdega Press.

Gibran, Kahlil (1923). *The Prophet*. New York: Alfred A. Knopf.

Goldberg, Bernard (2002). *Bias: A CBS Insider Exposes How the Media Distort the News*. Washington: Regnery Publishing, Inc., An Eagle Publishing Company.

Goleman, Daniel (1995). *Emotional Intelligence*. New York: Bantam Books.

Gould, Stephen Jay (1999). *Rocks of Ages: Science and Religion in the Fullness of Life*. New York: The Library of Contemporary Thought, The Ballantine Publishing Group.

Grinspoon, Lester, and Bakalar, James B. (1997 [1979]). *Psychedelic Drugs Reconsidered*. New York: The Lindesmith Center.

Gruenberger, Fred J. (1964). A Measure for Crackpots. *Science*, 50: 1413-1415.

Harman, Willis, Ph.D. (1988). *Global Mind Change: The New Age Revolution in the Way We Think*. New York: Warner Books, Inc.

Hastings, Arthur (1991). *With the Tongues of Men and Angels: A Study of Channeling*. Fort Worth: Holt, Rinehart and Winston, Inc.

Hawken, Paul (1975). *The Magic of Findhorn*. New York: Harper & Row.

Hayakawa, S.I. (1949). *Language in Thought and Action*. New York: Harcourt, Brace.

Herman, Edward S., and Chomsky, Noam (1988). *Manufacturing Consent: The Political Economy of the Mass Media*. New

York: Pantheon Books.

Huxley, Thomas Henry (1871). *Lay Sermons, Addresses, and Reviews*. New York: Appleton.

————, (1894). *Science and Christian Tradition*. New York: D. Appleton and Company.

————, (1997 [1861-1894]). *The Major Prose of Thomas Henry Huxley*, ed. Alan P. Barr. University of Georgia Press.

Jung, C.G. (1959). *The Basic Writings of C.G. Jung*. Edited by Violet S. de Laszlo. New York: The Modern Library. From *The Collected Works of C.G. Jung*. Bollingen Foundation.

————, (1983). *The Essential Jung*, selected and introduced by Anthony Storr. Princeton, NJ: Princeton University Press.

Kant, Immanuel (1866 [1781]). *Critique of Pure Reason*. Translated by J.M.D. Meiklejohn. London: Bell & Daldy.

Karagulla, Shafica, M.D. (1967). *Breakthrough To Creativity: Your Higher Sense Perception*. Los Angeles: DeVorss & Co., Inc.

Kieninger, Richard (1971). *Observations*. Stelle, IL: The Stelle Group.

————, (1974a). *Observations II*. Stelle, IL: The Stelle Group.

————, (1974b). *Observations III*. Stelle, IL: The Stelle Group.

————, (1978). Ten Qualities of Mind, in *On Becoming an Initiate*, lecture series. Stelle, IL: The Stelle Group.

————, (1979). *Observations IV*. Stelle, IL: The Stelle Group.

————, (1986). *Spiritual Seekers' Guidebook: And Hidden Threats to Mental & Spiritual Freedom*. Quinlan, TX: The Stelle Group.

Kueshana, Eklal (1963). *The Ultimate Frontier*. Stelle, IL: The Stelle Group.

————, (1982 [1963]).). *The Ultimate Frontier*. Fifth printing, indexed. Stelle, IL: The Stelle Group.

Langley, Noel (1965). *The Hidden History of Reincarnation*. Virginia Beach: A.R.E. Press.

————, (1967). *Edgar Cayce on Reincarnation*, under the editorship of Hugh Lynn Cayce. New York: Paperback

Library, Inc.

Lazerson, Arlyne, Publisher/Editor (1975). *Psychology Today: An Introduction*, Third Edition. New York: CRM / Random House.

Leonard, Jim, and Laut, Phil (1983). *Rebirthing: The Science of Enjoying All of Your Life*. Hollywood: Trinity Publications.

Luborsky, L., Chandler, M., Auerbach, A.H., Cohen, J., Bachrach, H.M. (1971). Factors influencing the outcome of psychotherapy: A review of quantitative research. *Psychological Bulletin*, 75: 145-185.

Malraux, Andre (1934). *Man's Fate (La Condition Humaine)*, translated by Haakon M. Chevalier. New York: The Modern Library, Random House.

McClenon, James (1984). *Deviant Science: The Case of Parapsychology*. Philadelphia: University of Pennsylvania Press.

Merriam-Webster, Incorporated (1996). *Merriam-Webster's Collegiate® Dictionary*. Springfield, MA: Merriam-Webster, Incorporated.

Montgomery, Ruth (1965). *A Gift of Prophecy: The Phenomenal Jeane Dixon*. New York: Morrow.

O'Reilly, Bill (2001). *The No Spin Zone: Confrontations with the Powerful and Famous in America*. New York: Broadway Books, a division of Random House, Inc.

Ostrander, Sheila, and Schroeder, Lynn (1970). *Psychic Discoveries behind the Iron Curtain*. Englewood Cliffs, NJ: Prentice-Hall, Inc.

Ouspensky, P.D. (1949). *In Search of the Miraculous: Fragments of an Unknown Teaching*. Harcourt, Inc.

Oxford University Press (1964[1933]). *The Shorter Oxford English Dictionary on Historical Principles*. Prepared by William Little. Revised and edited by C.T. Onions. Oxford: At the Clarendon Press.

Palmer, Harry (1990 [1987]). *Creativism: The Art of Living*

Deliberately. Longwood, Florida: Star's Edge International.

Peck, M. Scott, M.D. (1978). *The Road Less Traveled: A New Psychology of Love, Traditional Values and Spiritual Growth.* New York: Simon & Schuster Inc.

Popper, Sir Karl (1959 [1934]). *The Logic of Scientific Discovery.* Harper & Row.

————, (1985 [1934]). *Popper Selections*, ed. David Miller. Princeton University Press.

Press, Bill (2001). *Spin This! All the Ways We Don't Tell the Truth.* New York: Pocket Books, a division of Simon & Schuster, Inc.

Psychology Today (2000). Are Freud's Dreams Coming True? *Psychology Today*, January/February 2000.

Rand, Ayn (1957). *Atlas Shrugged.* New York: Random House, Inc.

Rennie, John (2002). 15 Answers to Creationist Nonsense, *Scientific American*, July 2002.

Rhine Research Center (2001). *Parapsychology and the Rhine Research Center.* Durham, NC: The Parapsychology Press.

Richardson, J.E. (1928). *The Great Psychological Crime: The Destructive Principle of Nature In Individual Life.* The Great School of Natural Science.

Roberts, Jane (1978 [1974]). *The Nature of Personal Reality: A Seth Book.* New York: Bantam Books.

Robinson, Daniel N. (1997). *The Great Ideas of Philosophy.* Lecture series, audio tapes. Springfield, VA: The Teaching Company.

Russell, Bertrand (1959). *Wisdom of the West: a historical survey of Western Philosophy in its social and political setting.* Editor Paul Foulkes. London: Rathbone Books Limited.

Sargant, William (1997 [1957]). *Battle for the Mind: A Physiology of Conversion and Brain-Washing.* Cambridge, MA: ISHK.

Schultz, Duane P. (1969). *A History of Modern Psychology.* New York: Academic Press, Inc.

Scorpio (Grant Lewi) (1935). *Scorpio's Horoscope Book: Heaven Knows What.* New York: Doubleday, Doran & Company,

Inc.

Shapiro, Lawrence E. (1997). *How to Raise a Child with a High EQ: A Parents' Guide to Emotional Intelligence*. New York: HarperCollins Publishers.

Simpson, George Gaylord (1983). *Fossils and the History of Life*. New York: Scientific American Library.

Smith, David Livingstone (2003). *Psychoanalysis in Focus*. London: SAGE Publications.

Smith, M.L., Glass, G.V., Miller, T.I. (1980). *The Benefits of Psychotherapy*. Baltimore: Johns Hopkins University Press.

Stevenson, Ian (1966). *Twenty Cases Suggestive of Reincarnation*. New York: American Society for Psychical Research.

Sugrue, Thomas (1967 [1942]). *There Is a River: The Story of Edgar Cayce*. New York: Henry Holt & Co., Inc. (Dell Edition, 1967).

Szasz, Thomas (1961). *The Myth of Mental Illness*. New York: Hoeber Medical Division, Harper & Row, Publishers, Inc.

————, (1974). *The Myth of Mental Illness: Foundations of a Theory of Personal Conduct* (Revised Edition). New York: Harper & Row, Publishers.

————, (1988 [1978]). *The Myth of Psychotherapy: Mental Healing as Religion, Rhetoric, and Repression*. Syracuse University Press.

————, (1990 [1976]). *Anti-Freud: Karl Kraus's Criticism of Psychoanalysis and Psychiatry*. Syracuse University Press.

Thoreau, Henry David (1854). *Walden*. In *Walden and Other Writings of Henry David Thoreau* (1937). New York: The Modern Library, Random House.

Toynbee, Arnold J. (1957 [1946]). *A Study of History*. Abridgement by D.C. Somervell. New York and London: Oxford University Press. New York: Dell Publishing.

Trevelyan, George (1984). *A Vision of the Aquarian Age: The Emerging Spiritual World View*. Walpole, New Hampshire: Stillpoint Publishing.

van Erkelens, Herbert (2002). Wolfgang Pauli, the Feminine and the Perils of the Modern World. *Harvest: Journal for Jungian Studies*, Volume 48, No 2: 142-148. (From an interview with Marie-Louise von Franz by Hein Stufkens and Philip Engelen, IKON-television, Kusnacht, November 1990, and published in the *Yearbook of the Dutch Interdisciplinary Society for Analytical Psychology*, Vol. 13 (1997) 67-75.)

Walsh, Roger N., M.D., Ph.D., and Vaughan, Frances, Ph.D., Eds. (1980). *Beyond Ego: Transpersonal Dimensions in Psychology*. Los Angeles: Jeremy P. Tarcher, Inc.

Watson, John B. (1913). Psychology as the behaviorist views it. *Psychological Review*. 20: 158-177.

————, (1919). *Psychology from the Standpoint of a Behaviorist*. Philadelphia: J.B. Lippincott Company.

————, (1925 [1924]). *Behaviorism*. New York: W.W. Norton & Company, Inc.

Watts, Alan (1966). *The Book; on the taboo against knowing who you are*. New York: Pantheon Books.

Wilber, Ken (1998). *The Marriage of Sense and Soul*. New York: Random House.

Wilson, Edward O. (1998). *Consilience: The Unity of Knowledge*. New York: Alfred A. Knopf.

Winn, Denise (1983). *The Manipulated Mind: Brainwashing, Conditioning and Indoctrination*. London: The Octagon Press.

Wright, Austin Tappan (1942). *Islandia*. Rinehart & Company, Inc.

Zohar, Danah (1983). *Through the Time Barrier: A Study in Precognition and Modern Physics*. London: Paladin Books.

INDEX

def = defined
(many) = many references, not all
  listed

mentalism (see also "Black Mentalists")
mercy 107
merit 31, 211, 215, 216
Merriam-Webster 23, 152, 181, 295
military 214
mind (many)
  suppressed 238
  universal 122
mind-dump 70
mindfuck 125, 159, 307
mind-jamming 126, 266, 310
mind pollution 3, def 4, 150, 162, 190, 197, 203, 210, 228, 239, 251, 312, 320, 321
mind's eye 19, 20, 43, 116
mind scrambling 126
mind trip 14
miraculous cures 260
mirage 120
misconstruing (see "construing")
misinformation 126, 303
misrepresentation (see also "representation") 137, 140-142, 144, 147, 150-152, 156, 157, 162, 166, 168-171, 179-181, 277, 313
  preemptive (see under "preemptive")
mistakes 182
Mitchell, Edgar 285
Mohammed 97, 175, 231
money 54, 152, 211, 212
monogamy 236, 237
moose principle 75
moral laws (see "laws - moral")
moral stain 151
morality 68, 113, 178, 226, 237, 251, 273, 311, 312
Moses 97, 175, 227, 231
motivation 14, 18, 107, 109, 197, 229
movie stars 212
Mozart 161
Munsterberg, Hugo 132, 250
mutation 273, 275, 277
mysticism 23, 24, 36, 118, 189, 249, 259
The Myth of Mental Illness 312, 313
"The Myth of the Self-Made Individual" 138, 139

Nagasaki 275
name-calling 36, 211
National Guard 158, 159
natural laws (see "laws - natural")

natural selection 273, 275
The Nature of Personal Reality 303
Navy 60, 99
Navy Officer Candidate School (OCS) 59
Nazis 53, 69, 164, 206
King Nebuchadnezzar 259
negativity 266, 304-306
New Age 5, 14, 146, 276, 283, 284, 291, 309
  demographics 283, 289
new civilization def 56, 57-59, 78, 79, 82, 94, 95, 138, 142, 144, 146, 147, 166, 180, 184
new beliefs 56
new goals 56
new ideals 56
new standard of living 56
new values 56
new way of life 56
new way of thinking 54, 56
New York 64
  Mayor of 189
Newton, Isaac 71
Newtonian physics 309
Nietzsche 56
nightmares 60
nobles 214
Non-Overlapping Magisteria (NOMA) 230, 246
nonsense 290
nonviolent methods 164
normal (see "psychologically normal")
"look normal" 182, 183
normative pressures def 5, 152, 154, 292
norms 5, 6
nuclear annihilation 53, 252, 275
doing a number on 159

obedience 96, 235
obfuscation 313
objective 17, 44-46, 218
objectivity 44-46
observation 15, 18
old civilization 56, 180-182
oneness with the universe 285
operating in the environment 200, 201
opinions, attitudes, and beliefs 242, 243, 246, 258, 263, 292, 295
optical illusions 119
organizations 211, 212, 215
organized crime 207, 308
orgasms 237

multiple 300
origin of species 273-275
original experience 22, 80, 131
original sin 234
Ouija Board 97, 167, 170
out-of-body-travel 167
Outlander 282
outside observers 265, 266
overkill 53
overlay 20
overpopulation 238
The Shorter Oxford English Dictionary 151
the ozone layer 244

packaging and labeling 189
pain 109, 116
Palmer, Harry 289
Palmer, John 271
paradoxes def 301
paranoia 180, 198, 302
Parapsychological Association (PA) 270
parapsychology 117, 129, 131, 243, 245, 265-272
  documentation 245
  replication 270-272
Parapsychology, Journal of 266, 272
parents 205, 206, 210, 218, 225, 229
passive resistance 292
patience 96
patriotism 152
Pauli, Wolfgang 24
peaceful coexistence 228
Pearce, Hubert 267
pecking (see "social pecking")
pecking order 31, 33, 34, 211, 213, 215, 216
peer group 154, 155, 210
peer-group pressures 7, 155, 213, 242, 301
peer review 242
Pennebaker, J.W. 260
People's Word 226
perception 14, 18, 115-121, 146
  inner 26
  internal 29, 33, 47
  reality independent of 119
  and sensation 115
permission to think 209
personal psychology (see "psychology - personal")
the word "personal" 168, 169, 171, 277
The Pharaoh 259
philosophy def 106, 193, 251, 252